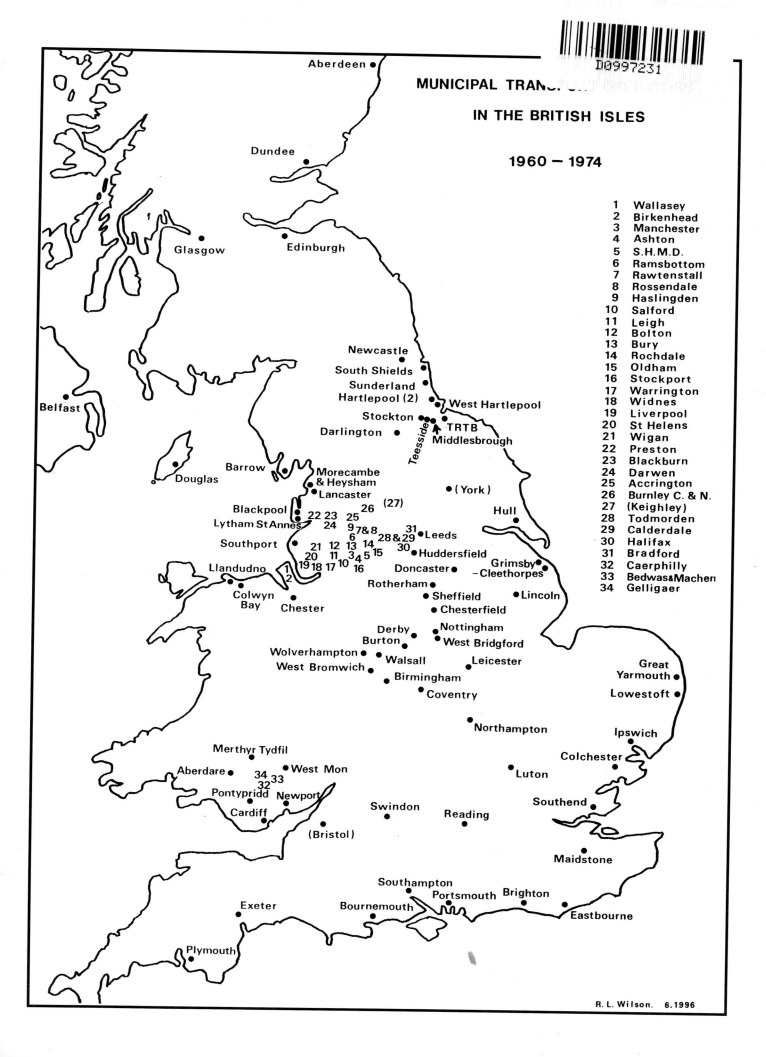

MUNICIPAL TRANSPORT

IN THE BRITISH ISLES

1960 — 1974

Aberdeen

Dundee

Glasgow   Edinburgh

Belfast

Douglas

Newcastle
South Shields
Sunderland
Hartlepool (2)   West Hartlepool
Stockton
Darlington   TRTB
Teesside   Middlesbrough

Barrow
Morecambe
& Heysham
Lancaster   (York)

Blackpool   26   (27)   Hull
Lytham St Annes   22 23   25
24   9   7&8   31
6   28&29   Leeds
Southport   21 12 13 14   30
20 11   3 4 5 15   Huddersfield
19 18 17 10 16   Grimsby
Llandudno   1   Doncaster   –Cleethorpes
2
Colwyn   Rotherham   Lincoln
Bay   Chester   Sheffield
Chesterfield

Derby   Nottingham
Burton   West Bridgford
Wolverhampton   Walsall   Leicester   Great
West Bromwich   Yarmouth
Birmingham   Lowestoft
Coventry   Ipswich

Northampton   Colchester

Merthyr Tydfil
Aberdare   34 33   West Mon   Luton
32   Southend
Pontypridd   Newport
Cardiff   Swindon   Reading
(Bristol)   Maidstone

Southampton
Portsmouth   Brighton
Exeter   Bournemouth   Eastbourne

Plymouth

1	Wallasey
2	Birkenhead
3	Manchester
4	Ashton
5	S.H.M.D.
6	Ramsbottom
7	Rawtenstall
8	Rossendale
9	Haslingden
10	Salford
11	Leigh
12	Bolton
13	Bury
14	Rochdale
15	Oldham
16	Stockport
17	Warrington
18	Widnes
19	Liverpool
20	St Helens
21	Wigan
22	Preston
23	Blackburn
24	Darwen
25	Accrington
26	Burnley C. & N.
27	(Keighley)
28	Todmorden
29	Calderdale
30	Halifax
31	Bradford
32	Caerphilly
33	Bedwas&Machen
34	Gelligaer

R. L. Wilson. 6.1996

MUNICIPAL BUSES
IN COLOUR 1959-1974

MUNICIPAL BUSES
IN COLOUR 1959-1974

REG WILSON

ngtons for **EFFICIENT REMOVALS**
FURNITURE STORED Phone **28121**

FOR HOUSEHOLD LINENS AND
BEDDING, **VOKINS** ARE BEST

R.P.WEBB
FOR GRASS CUTTING
& MOWER REPAIRS
32233
PERSONAL SERVICE

HTON
PORATION

IAN ALLAN
Publishing

First published 1997

ISBN 0 7110 2544 4

All rights reserved. No part of this book may be reproduced or transmitted in any form or by any means, electronic or mechanical, including photocopying, recording or by any information storage and retrieval system, without permission from the Publisher in writing.

© Reg Wilson 1997

Published by Ian Allan Publishing

an imprint of Ian Allan Ltd, Terminal House, Station Approach, Shepperton, Surrey TW17 8AS.
Printed by Ian Allan Printing Ltd at its works at Coombelands in Runnymede, England.

Code: 9710/C

Dedication and Acknowledgements

This book is dedicated to my wife Marjorie and our daughter Alvina and son Christopher, without whose patience many of the photographs would never have been taken.

Help from the following people is gratefully acknowledged:
Jack N. Barlow for checking the texts and for advice; Geoffrey G. Fearnley for providing the photograph of the seal used by Hartlepool Borough pre-1967, and C. H. Hull for taking it; Robert Kell for providing the Tees-side RTB logo, West Hartlepool coat of arms, and Hartlepool County Borough post-1967 bus photos; Roy Marshall/Photobus for providing the West Bridgford logo photograph; Stagecoach Transit Management for permitting me to photograph Stockton insignia; Chris Hall, Allan Purvis, Tony Mernock and David Slater for information.

Picture Credits

All photographs were taken by Reg Wilson except where otherwise credited.

Contents

Front cover:
A local government building known as the Council House provides an appropriate background on 28 May 1971 for Derby Corporation No 156 (BCH 156B), a Daimler CVG6 with Roe H37/28R body which was new in 1964. By 1971 green-liveried buses were outnumbered by those bearing the replacement blue and grey. Four of the 10 buses in the 1964 batch still carried the latter when shipped to Canada in 1979 to be used on tourist services in British Columbia. No 156 still survives in Derby Industrial Museum

Rear cover, top:
Manchester's Daimler CVG6s gave long service, some over 20 years. One such was No 4459 (NNB 269), depicted here on 6 December 1969, five weeks after SELNEC PTE became its owner. It has an MCW H32/28R body, was new in April 1954 and withdrawn August 1974.

The red roof signifies 8ft width. Prewar, roofs were cream. Grey was adopted as an air raid precaution and retained later for 7ft 6in vehicles until the last were withdrawn in the 1960s (see photograph in main section).

Rear cover, bottom:
Aberdeen ran a fleet of half a dozen coaches in the 1960s. No 11 (CRG 811), photographed on 14 August 1962, is one of two stylish Daimler CVD6s with Alexander C35F bodies bought in 1947.

Half title page:
More cream brightened the postwar livery of Morecambe & Heysham Corporation — compare with No 25 featured on page 74. AECS were bought from 1932 until 1960

and No 69 (LTF 254) is one of a batch of six Regent IIIs delivered in 1950. The Park Royal H33/26R body, being of four bay construction, has suggestions of London RT.

It is depicted running on the promenade near Bare on 3 October 1964. Light bulbs festooned in the background are part of Morecambe's annual illuminations.

Title page:
When this scene was captured on 31 May 1972, transition from red and cream to blue and white livery by Brighton Corporation was well advanced. Featured is No 32 (LUF 132F), a Leyland Titan PD3/4 carrying a Metro-Cammell H39/30F body, one of a batch of three delivered in 1968. It was later converted to open-top.

Above:
Displaying the later style of fleetname beneath Exeter's crest is No 79 (479 CFJ), a Massey-bodied Leyland Titan PD2A/30, new in 1961. The date is 25 August 1963 and also in the view is an AEC Regent of Devon General, the company which took over the Exeter undertaking, including No 79, in 1970.

Foreword

Municipalisation

Between the late 1940s and late 1980s we in Great Britain experienced the part-nationalisation of public road transport and its privatisation. It could be said, however, that the first of these major movements in ownership was Municipalisation. This occurred a century ago, when local authorities bought or de-leased local companies operating trams and/or buses, usually horse-drawn. The incentive was not central government decree but a desire to control burgeoning enterprise and divert profits to rate (local tax) relief. Once a few towns embarked successfully on this course, many others followed, driven also by local pride.

The process had begun in 1861, a year after a street railway was established in Birkenhead; Birmingham Corporation

Below:
Although in preservation by the date of this photograph (5 August 1979), and strictly outside the timescale of the book, Stalybridge Hyde Mossley & Dunkinfield No 76 (VTU 76) shows to good effect the 1950s dark green livery. One of a batch of six new in 1956, its Daimler CVG6 chassis carries a Northern Counties H35/25CD body. This centre entrance configuration was used on only seven double and five single-decked SMHD buses, all bought between 1953 and 1956.

obtained powers (not used immediately) under an Improvement Act to lay a tramway in its streets, to be leased to others. In 1870 a Tramways Act was passed by Parliament to facilitate and regulate the building of tramways throughout the country. Many municipalities took advantage of that but it was still not legal for them to operate the lines themselves without special powers. Leasing to a company was usually arranged, with a limit such as 21 years, after which the council could buy the assets at a negotiated or adjudicated price.

In 1883 Huddersfield became the United Kingdom's first municipal (steam) tram operator, almost by accident. The Corporation had in 1880 obtained powers to build lines and these were offered on lease but unsuccessfully. An application made to the Board of Trade for a licence to run the system itself was granted, with the proviso that should a private company subsequently offer fair terms, the Corporation must accept. No such offer was received.

Electric motive power had been demonstrated in Germany by Siemens in 1879 and in 1881 he ran short services both there and at Crystal Palace in England. Operationally these trials were successful but feeding electric current to the vehicle via the running rail was held to be unsafe. Similar trials were held in St Petersburg around that time. In 1883 Magnus Volk opened a narrow gauge line in Brighton, at first using running rail conduction, but soon changing to a third rail. This line still exists, having been 'municipalised' by Brighton Corporation in 1940.

A Corporation-owned but company-operated electrical conduit line on the promenade at Blackpool opened in 1885 and in 1892 the council took over its oper-

ation. The year 1891, however, had seen the opening of the first British tramway to use overhead conductor wire and trolley-poles – a company-owned line between Roundhay and Oakwood, purchased by Leeds Corporation in 1894.

Overhead wires, although considered by many to be unsightly, were a technical advance which eliminated some previous difficulties and prompted a country-wide surge of municipalisation around the turn of the century. The imminent end of many company leases assisted this trend, as most private companies were unable or unwilling to invest large sums in electrification. By 1905 dozens of cities and towns had municipally-operated tramways of which they were justly proud and which, in some cases briefly, generated profits to benefit citizens generally.

In 1903, Eastbourne Corporation, never a tramway operator, bought Milnes-Daimler buses to serve one route, thus becoming the first UK municipal bus undertaking.

Trolleybuses made their debut in Britain not much later when, in 1911, services were started by the cities of Bradford and Leeds. The former authority was the last operator of these quiet vehicles when its system closed in 1972. Between those years over 40 trolleybus undertakings had come and gone. Most were municipal, some tiny, one or two ran hundreds of vehicles.

Appendix 1, showing fleet sizes in 1961, gives Birmingham as owning over 1,700 buses, while Hartlepool had four. Such variety made for great interest. The total number of buses, trams and trolleybuses operated by local government then was nearly 20,000. If lined up they would have occupied 120 miles of road. The same passenger capacity carried in cars, each holding two people, would stretch over 1,600 miles. Efficiency and Progress?

Introduction

The main purpose of this book is to present in one volume a pictorial record of the main liveries and insignia used by all the municipal public transport departments which operated in Great Britain and Northern Ireland between 1959 and 1974. The collection therefore also depicts a good cross-section of the types of vehicle which served the country during that period.

A secondary purpose is to chronicle concisely the history of each undertaking between about 1860 and 1996, tracing its antecedents, with dates for the introduction of tram, bus and trolleybus ownership, detailing abandonments, and describing successors, both semi-municipal and privately owned.

The choice of 1959 as a starting date for photographs is dictated by the author's earliest colour work, and the cut-off year 1974 (1975 in Scotland) marks the local government reorganisation that brought many municipal name changes.

Apart from preserved vehicles (which, with two extraordinary exceptions, have been excluded) the scenes depicted have gone for ever. Many readers will remember them with pleasure. Others, younger, will regret the passing of such colour and interest before their time.

Starting at an earlier date would have included only two in addition to over 100 municipalities covered; Grimsby Corporation's dark brown and cream and Cleethorpes UDC/Corporation's blue and grey would be recorded in addition to their Joint Committee, but no others since 1934.

Although most operators are represented by buses, where appropriate I have used tram or trolleybus photographs to add variety and increase appeal. The vehicles depicted represent a good cross-section of manufacturers.

A fascinating aspect of local authority liveries was, and still is in the case of the few survivors, civic insignia and fleet titles. The former are referred to as armorial bearings, coats of arms and crests (or perhaps as emblems, seals, badges or logos). No attempt has been made to describe the devices illustrated nor delve into their heraldic origins, though some features are self-explanatory – a bee denotes industry, a

shuttle or bobbin textiles, a ship or an anchor maritime associations, etc. Mottoes, often in Latin, typically underline the arms and can sometimes be understood without resort to a Latin grammar. Supporters (of shields), real or mythological, add a medieval touch to mundane vehicles.

Common usage in heraldic terminology has been adopted in this book and it should be noted that a purist may sometimes disagree. For instance, 'crest' has a narrower meaning.

Fleet titles in the early 1900s often took the form of large, serifed gilt capital letters on the rocker boxes of trams, eg 'Leicester Corporation Tramways'. In the 1930s lettering was smaller and often sanserif. By the 1950s many fleets carried even smaller transfers and the preferred forms were such as: 'Maidstone Corporation', 'Salford City Transport', 'Newcastle Transport', etc or simply 'Stockport'. The civic pride of many was satisfied by a crest, with the title shown as part of the 1in-high legal ownership lettering.

The last of the old school was Wallasey County Borough which, until the 1960s, proclaimed 'Wallasey Corporation Motors' on its buses in large gilt serifed transfers. This looked distinctly quaint on half-cabs

Below left:
Waiting at a stand in a main street of its home town on 1 September 1962 is Aberdare UDCTD No 73 (GTG 865), a H30/26R ECW-bodied Bristol K6A built in 1947. It is in fact a sibling of No 74 pictured on page 13, but wears the later, brighter livery.

Right:
Glasgow bought one of the earliest Leyland Atlantean PRD1/1 in 1958, numbering it LA1, but took no less than four years to place orders for the Mark II version, also PDR1/1. Those had Alexander H44/34F bodies and LA44 (SGD 622) depicted is one of that 1962 batch. It is seen in Sauchiehall Street (as was) on 1 June 1963 wearing a livery containing less cream than hitherto. Albion Atlantean badges were carried, front and rear, although the buses were built in Leyland.

but bizarre on the modern rear-engined Leyland Atlanteans pioneered by the town in 1958.

The Local Government Act of 1972 authorised municipal changes effective from April 1974, which caused the word 'Corporation' to become obsolete as part of a transport undertaking's title.

During the century or more since municipal public transport started in the British Isles, many more civic undertakings have existed than are represented in these pages. Many long-vanished ones were tramways, supplanted for one reason or another by company-owned buses. Appendix 2 lists them. Monochrome photographs of them all exist in archives but until electronic 'colourification' of them becomes commonplace – it is already possible – we rely on artwork to evoke their liveries.

Although colour film was available before 1939, materials were expensive and the 'speed' so slow that photographing a moving vehicle was difficult. The 1950s brought easily-found and faster Kodachrome 25 and other makes. Transport photographers quickly adopted the medium, especially for recording liveries. Some film dyes have proved time-resistant. Others, no longer sold, turned pink or some weird hue after 20 or more years. A few of the author's earliest slides suffered that fate but fortunately he was recommended to trust slightly more expensive Kodak or Agfa products before going too far on a project which even then was intended as a livery archive.

All the photographs in this book are reproduced from transparencies, mostly Kodachrome, and some reds suffer the lightening of shade which was (and to a far lesser extent still is) characteristic of that brand. All are 35mm and, where quality of image permits, the slides selected are the oldest, depicting the most venerable and interesting vehicles. Later slides may have finer grain but depict buses not long vanished from our streets.

It has been tempting to include preserved vehicles in the photographic selection, as they may be pristine and occasionally carry a livery obsolete before 1959, but enthusiasts can photograph those for themselves. The principle of depicting vehicles in original service has, therefore, been adhered to except for a Bradford tram (municipally owned) and an Exeter bus, both of which were already preserved when photographed 30 years ago. One or two of the coats of arms were photographed on restored vehicles.

To gain an appreciation of the municipal scene a quarter of a century ago, it is helpful to be able to compare fleet sizes. Appendix 1 details numbers of buses, coaches, trams and trolleybuses in stock in 1961, a year when peak passenger loadings were recent history but fleets were yet to shrink. Two size rankings are shown: one for municipalities alone, the other in relation to company fleets as well.

Appendix 5 shows the local registration marks assigned to new municipal PSVs. (Trams were, and still are, exempt from the regulations provided an identity [fleet number] is displayed. Trolleybuses were likewise exempt until 1921, for the same reason – that being restricted in movement by power supply, a fleet number was seen as legally sufficient.) Registrations, once of minor interest to students of public transport, always contributed a flavour to photographs and as the allocation of two-letter marks changed somewhat on 1 October 1974, a reference to the original situation may be useful. Since 1986, enthusiasts have found that registration mark identification is of great assistance in tracing the source of second-hand vehicles, many of which were new before 1974. Before deregulation it was unusual for a municipality to buy used buses. Now it is commonplace throughout the industry and a knowledge of registration marks can sometimes solve a mystery.

The photographs used in this book have, with a few exceptions which are acknowledged, been taken by the author, many on holiday trips. The British Isles contain much varied and beautiful scenery and it was possible to arrange family motoring tours to pass through Aberdeen or Plymouth, Lowestoft or Llandudno. Fortunately, home has always been in the northwest of England, within two hours' travelling time of a great many municipal operators. Most picture locations nearer home were reached using public transport.

Difficulties in securing worthwhile photographs have increased in recent years. Traffic congestion makes moving 'shots' less certain, bus stations often have (perfectly reasonable) access restrictions, buses are generally less well-tended and more prone to being plastered with unsightly advertising.

By no means the least of problems for the itinerant photographer in unfamiliar distant towns is parking. Thirty years ago double yellow lines were almost unknown. One could see a potential picture, draw in to the nearest kerb and a couple of minutes later have it 'in the bag' and be away. Happy days. Now one searches for 10 minutes for somewhere legal to park, pays a pound and walks back a quarter of a mile, only to find that the quarry is miles away.

It has become fashionable in some quarters to denigrate three-quarter-front views of PCVs as too formal, lacking in imagination, short on potentially historic background, but I make no apology for using that format. It is the only way to illustrate a livery properly and also record the main structural details of a vehicle in one photograph.

It is hoped that readers will enjoy the portrayals.

Explanatory Notes

Colour Descriptions

Colour names used to describe liveries are drawn from the author's observations supplemented by published information and have been kept simple, employing for instance 'red' to cover many shades from dark to light. There are several reasons for this. Firstly, although modern paint manufacturers identify their colours with British Standard numbers, it is not practicable to quote them, even if known, in a book such as this. Secondly, colour names used by manufacturers are often fanciful and may vary from those quoted by the user.

Additionally, weathering and fading have a significant effect on perceived colour, and slight colour deficiency (especially in males) is more common than supposed. Not all 'colour blindness' involves those affected seeing only shades of grey.

Therefore, at the risk of readers being displeased, I have sometimes used 'cream' as an omnibus term (no pun intended) covering off-white, broken white, light cream, cream, dark cream, light primrose, ivory, very light yellow and others such as buttermilk.

Readers may have noticed that livery descriptions in other publications are sometimes contradictory in the use of cream/white, maroon/crimson/red. Hence the simplification.

Fleet Details

It is not practicable in a book of this size to include more than passing reference to fleet profiles between 1959 and 1974. Many fleets of that period are, however, covered in detail by PSV Circle publications.

Insignia

Some operators have, over the years, employed more than one version of their municipal insignia and therefore a photograph date is usually given to assist armorial students. Several changes occurred after 1974 to reflect enlarged territories but the illustrations, although a few were photographed later, relate to the period covered.

Municipal Management

Ownership of municipal transport undertakings was typically vested in a council consisting of elected councillors and aldermen and alderwomen (alder = elder). The latter were co-opted in recognition of long elected service combined with special knowledge or sagacity. The position was abolished in 1974.

The chief official of a council was chosen annually and titled, in urban districts, Chairman. Boroughs had Mayors

and cities of any size (which were usually county boroughs) Lord Mayors.

The undertaking would be overseen by a Transport Committee drawn from the council. This operated like a company's Board of Directors. A chairman chosen from among the committee was responsible for progressing policies decided by the full council. In large cities a long-standing chairman could wield a good deal of power to influence those policies.

Committee members were not remunerated of course, as they were very much part-time. Responsible to them was a professional management team, usually consisting of a General Manager supported by Chief Engineer, Traffic Manager, etc. It was this type of dual-control organisation which, in its heyday, gave local communities good transport, operating surpluses to assist local 'rates' (taxes), while sustaining municipal pride with smart vehicles and crews.

Where there was an inadequate revenue surplus, municipal undertakings employed funds from the (government) Public Works Loan Board to pay for vehicles and infrastructure. Consequently, transport managers had little financial power, applications for loans, payment of interest, and repayment of capital being handled by the municipal treasurer.

That system contrasted with company undertakings financially based on permanent shareholdings, capital never paid back, but sustained by interest payments.

Operators' Titles

The titles heading the subject pages are those notified to *Passenger Transport* by the operators in the 1960s and may not always reflect names in common usage.

Use of Dates

The individual municipal transport histories on the following pages are necessarily concise. Dates are usually given as the year, even where the day and month are available. This saves space and is all the average reader requires to appreciate the time-scale. I trust that those with, or who have a need for, precise knowledge will understand.

Three dates in particular are frequently referred to in the text. Such repetition is unavoidable when explaining the wholesale shifts in the transport scene resulting from the formation of the first Passenger Transport Executives (PTEs) in 1969, local government reorganisation in 1974/5 and bus service deregulation in 1986. These were seismic events in the British transport industry.

Local Government Reorganisation, 1974

At this point it is appropriate to describe events which will be alluded to many times on subsequent pages. Country-wide local government reorganisation became effective on 1 April 1974 (16 May 1975 in Scotland).

Many counties in England and Wales were altered, divided or reduced in size by the formation of new and metropolitan counties. Scottish counties were merged into regions.

County boroughs, boroughs, burghs, urban and rural districts were dissolved and re-formed as districts or metropolitan districts. Many subsequently readopted the title city, borough or burgh.

Greater London and its boroughs (formed in 1965) were unaffected. The six counties of Northern Ireland became 26 districts.

Metropolitan Counties

These were established in 1974. They exercised some overall functions such as transport co-ordination. Many local activities were the responsibility of the lower-tier metropolitan district councils (which later adopted the title 'borough'), who in effect replaced the county boroughs etc in those areas.

The metropolitan county councils were abolished in 1986 after a life of only 12 years and their functions distributed among the metropolitan boroughs, transport being covered by joint boards acting through passenger transport authorities/executives.

This situation is similar to that existing in the Manchester, Merseyside, Tyneside and West Midlands conurbations from 1969 to 1974.

Unitary Authorities

Although relevant to 1959-1974 because county boroughs could be so described, the term is used in operator histories to cover recent changes.

A reorganisation resulting in many new unitary authorities (some called counties, some with the resurrected title of county borough) started with Scotland, Wales, and Avon, Cleveland and Humberside in England on 1 April 1996. Other areas in England have been altered in 1997 and more will be in 1998. Some of the few British operators still in municipal ownership may be affected. Where details are known before going to press, reference will be made on the appropriate pages.

Registration Marks

A note here on vehicle registrations may be of interest.

In 1903, and effective in January 1904,

Left:
Ipswich bought its first motorbuses in 1950 to replace trolleybuses and for many years favoured only AECs. No 45 (OPV 45) was a Regent V with East Lancs H37/28R body, one of a batch of four which entered service in 1962. Eight of the previous 44 were in fact Regal IV saloons. Depicted near the town centre Electric House terminus on 29 May 1965, the bus displays to splendid effect the then current fleet livery.

Right:
Leeds changed its City Transport livery several times during eight decades of existence. The final version is worn here by No 447 (ANW 447J), a 1971 Leyland Atlantean PDR2/1 with panoramic Roe H45/33D bodywork, one of a batch of 20 delivered during that year, and photographed on the edge of Leeds bus station on 23 May. It retained the same fleet number with West Yorkshire PTE after 1974.

HUDDERSFIELD
JOINT OMNIBUS SERVICES

6299

FUEL OIL

all English and Welsh counties and county boroughs were allotted a registration mark in descending order of population size. With a few exceptions, the distribution was:

A (London) to Y (Somerset), AA (Hampshire) to FP (Rutland).

Subsequent marks were issued to newly-formed county boroughs and all authorities as they exhausted the original allocation.

The first three-letter mark was issued by Staffordshire CC in July 1932, closely followed by Middlesex, Surrey, Kent and Cheshire by December.

Year letter suffix -A was used first by Middlesex in February 1963. Only 13 other offices issued -A. Many started with -B and a smaller number -C.

Prefix year letters began with A- (following -Y) on 1 August 1983. From the same date vehicles of unknown age were registered with marks conforming to Qnnn xxx ('n' denoting any number and 'x' denoting a letter).

In Scotland, until the 1975 reorganisation, towns were burghs. The entity of county borough denoting a stand-alone administrative unit elsewhere in the UK did not exist. For purposes such as motor vehicle licensing a line was drawn at a population of 50,000. All counties but only burghs that exceeded this figure were allotted a mark in 1903. Burghs attaining it later also received a mark eg Motherwell & Wishaw, GM in 1920; Kirkcaldy, nXA in 1963.

Aberdeen was well above the threshold. Marks were issued almost strictly alphabetically, counties first, with Aberdeenshire SA (in the series SA-SY) and Partick YS (in the series commencing at AS) coming last.

Partick was absorbed by Glasgow shortly after 1904, Govan (US) a few years later. Leith's mark (WS) went to Edinburgh when they merged in 1920.

Edinburgh and Glasgow received the prestigious S and G respectively and Lanarkshire was allotted V. Two-letter marks containing G and V were originally Scottish. Aberdeen Burgh's first mark was RS, followed by RG in 1928.

Dumfriesshire was the first Scottish authority to issue three-letter marks (ASM in 1933) and -A year letter suffix issues were only needed in 1963 by Aberdeenshire and Kirkcaldy (new office), although Motherwell also issued them.

In 1903 Ireland was a single administration and two-letter marks were allocated alphabetically (as in Scotland), counties before county boroughs. County Antrim was IA (in the series IA-IZ) and Waterford CB last with WI in the series AI-WI.

Additional two-letter marks issued after Partition in 1922 began with Z for Southern Ireland and ended with Z for Northern Ireland. There were one or two exceptions such as single letter Z issued by Dublin in 1927. Three-letter marks were first issued in Belfast in 1969 and are the current system used by all eight issuing offices.

Above:
The same fleetname style was used on motor-buses owned by both Huddersfield Corporation and the Joint Omnibus Committee. Tiny lettering in the underlining indicated the owner, although the former also carried a coat of arms. A more attractive and legible version was displayed on the front panel of flat-fronted JOC buses.

Right:
In the early 1980s York-West Yorkshire buses carried a vinyl of the city badge and the double N symbol, separated by the word YORK in NBC-style white lettering. The combination was discontinued when York City Council sold its interest in March 1986. The photograph is dated 5 June 1983.

The Republic issued three-letter marks from 1954 (only Dublin initially). These were still based on the 1903 allocation which continued in use until December 1986 after which the country started its own system based on year number prefix followed by one or two letters denoting the county or city and unlimited numbers starting at one each year (only Dublin has exceeded 50,000 to date).

Glossary of abbreviations used in the text

BET	British Electric Traction Company Limited
BR	British Rail(ways)
BTC	British Transport Commission
CB(C)	County Borough (Council)
CC	County Council
Co	Company
CT(D)	City/Corporation Tramways/Transport (Department)
DC	District Council
DVLA	Driver & Vehicle Licensing Agency
DVLC	Driver & Vehicle Licensing Centre
ECW	Eastern Coach Works
Frozen	buses held in mid-build in 1941 due to the war and 'unfrozen' – completed in 1942 or built in 1942/3 from existing stocks of components
GMPTE	Greater Manchester Passenger Transport Executive
JB	Joint Board
J(O)C	Joint (Omnibus) Committee
LMSR	London, Midland & Scottish Railway Co
LNER	London & North Eastern Railway Co
Ltd	Limited
LTO	Local Taxation Office (pre-1974)
LVLO	Local Vehicle Licensing Office (1974)
MB	Municipal Borough
MoS	Ministry of Supply
MPTE	Merseyside Passenger Transport Executive
NBC	National Bus Company
NITHC	Northern Ireland Transport Holding Co
PCV/PSV	Passenger Carrying/Public Service Vehicle
PLC	Public Limited Company
PTA/PTE	Passenger Transport Authority/Executive
RDC	Rural District Council
Selnec	South East Lancashire North East Cheshire PTE
SYPTE	South Yorkshire Passenger Transport Executive
THC	Transport Holding Company
TPTE/ T&WPTE	Tyneside/Tyne & Wear Passenger Transport Executive
UD/UDC/ UDCTD	Urban District/Council/Transport Department
VRO	Vehicle Registration Office
WMPTE	West Midlands Passenger Transport Executive
WYPTE	West Yorkshire Passenger Transport Executive

Bibliography

Fleet histories – The PSV Circle/Omnibus Society

Great British Tramway Networks – Bett & Gilham

Passenger Transport Year Books – Ian Allan Ltd

Tramway Liveries – David Voice

Trolleybus Trails – J. Joyce

Regional Tramway booklets – Light Rail Transit Association

Municipal Transport Department commemorative brochures

Also, many individual Ian Allan publications from 1950 onwards.

British Tramways by Keith Turner was published after this book was written, but enabled some facts to be cross-checked.

Index of Operators

* 17 still in municipal ownership, as an 'arm's length' limited company in April 1997 (13 are original names, four now bear other names).

Below:
The second version of Manchester's arms, seen on 14 June 1969, was in use for several years before SELNEC PTE took over in the following November.

CITY OF MANCHESTER

Aberdare Urban District Council Transport Department

Alphabetically first among British municipal transport operators, Aberdare ran services in and around the Cynon valley, Glamorganshire, and was one of only eight postwar urban district council undertakings. The town is close to the Brecon Beacons National Park. Its mines were once the source of the best steam coal in the world.

Aberdare Council opened an electric tramway in 1913 using 10 single-deck cars and a year later also commenced trolleybus operations. In 1921, when it first became required for trolleybuses to carry registration mark plates, the four roadworthy Cedes-Stolls were registered and received the then current marks L 8879-81/83 from Glamorganshire County Council. Motorbus services began in 1922, so for three years, until the trolleybuses were withdrawn in 1925, all three modes operated concurrently. The tramways, by then equipped with open-top double-deck cars, survived until 1935, being replaced by existing Bristol buses and new Daimlers.

Aberdare livery for all vehicles was originally maroon with cream relief but by the 1960s had changed to cream with bands of paler red.

It is said that Aberdare adopted the royal arms as the crest for its vehicles because an influential councillor thought they looked impressive. Years later the authority discovered that Royal consent should have been sought and belatedly obtained it.

The Department used a variety of bus types. Tilling-Stevens were the first, then Bristols. Postwar it purchased AEC, Bristol, Daimler and Guy models.

The 1974 local government changes resulted in Aberdare UDCTD becoming Cynon Valley Borough Council Transport Department, its operating territory being mainly the County of Mid Glamorgan.

A fleet of Leyland Nationals was purchased and painted cherry red, relieved only by white rubber window seals. By 1980 substantial areas of cream relief appeared. Following a change of status to Cynon Valley Transport Ltd in 1986, cream, green, orange and white formed the livery. In that year all municipal undertakings became 'arm's length' wholly-owned companies, as a result of central government legislation aimed at reducing subsidies.

In mid-1992, affected financially by the competition which followed deregulation, Cynon Valley Transport was sold to Red & White, which itself had reappeared only months earlier during the break-up of National Welsh. Red & White became a Stagecoach subsidiary in 1993 and formed Aberdare Bus Co.

In the 1996 local government reorganisation, Aberdare was merged into a new county borough, named Rhondda Cynon Taff CB.

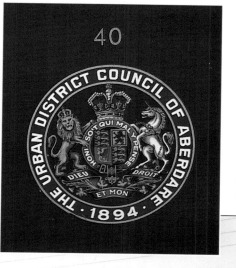

Left:
The coat of arms is that originally used without authorisation, as mentioned in the text. Photo date: 24 March 1974.

Below:
Wearing pre-1960 livery, Aberdare No 74 (GTG 867) waits in Hirwaun on 4 September 1959. It is a Bristol K6A with ECW H30/26R body, built in 1947 prior to the restriction which prevented municipalities placing orders with those manufacturers.

Aberdeen Corporation Transport Department

Aberdeen, most northerly municipal operator in the British Isles, has been called 'The Granite City' and the photograph illustrates why. Grey stone is prominent in most thoroughfares and Castle Street, the location of Aberdeen Nos 79, 25 and 17, is no exception. Now the centre of North Sea oil operations, the city, situated on Scotland's northeast coast, received its first charter in 1179 and later became a flourishing port.

The city operated trams from 1898 on taking over the 1874 horse-drawn system of Aberdeen District Tramways Co. This had used liveries as varied as yellow and cream, red and cream, green and white, blue and white and plain white.

Electric cars started operating in 1899 and were green and cream with, until 1945, a band of red, brown, white, yellow, blue, green or black as route indicator.

A company named Aberdeen Suburban Tramways operated two disconnected routes beyond the Corporation termini from 1904 to 1927, using a red and white livery. It had running rights into the city but never became part of the municipal system. The Corporation tramways flourished until 1952, new cars being built as late as 1949. However, buses took over completely in 1958.

An experimental bus and two charabancs were used on city tours in 1920 and bus services started in 1921. The fleet usually contained a few vehicles suitable for tourist services.

Bus livery continued tramway green and cream, with a grey roof until that too became cream in 1964.

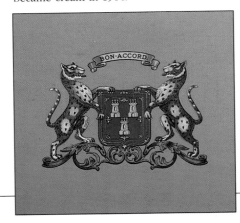

Above:
Three of Aberdeen's finest await service in Castle Street on 13 August 1962. The nearest is No 79 (BRS 579), a Daimler CVG6 built in 1946. Its body, by NCB (Northern Coachbuilders), is to H30/26R configuration. Nos 25 and 17 also shown are Weymann-bodied AECs, RT Type 0961, built in 1947 and 1946 respectively.

Below left:
Coat of arms photo date: 21 August 1972.

On 16 May 1975 the Burgh of Aberdeen and the counties of Aberdeen, Banff, Kincardine and Moray were merged into Grampian Region. The ex-Corporation fleet soon bore the name 'Grampian', a new coat of arms and an orange band on the old livery.

In 1986 the undertaking became Grampian Regional Transport Ltd, soon to spread its wings by purchasing other companies far and wide but destined to combine with the English Badgerline Group to become FirstBus in 1995.

On 1 April 1996 Grampian Region was dissolved and Aberdeen took up the role of a city unitary council.

Accrington Corporation Transport Department

Mid Lancashire is heavily populated and has supported several municipal operators, Accrington being one. The name of the town became famous as that of a type of durable red brick. It is also well known for cotton and linen fabrics but for transport enthusiasts its claim to fame was its Corporation bus livery – arguably the most dignified in Britain – very dark blue with red relief and black window surrounds. This was introduced on buses to commemorate the 'Accrington Pals', the 11th Battalion, East Lancashire Regiment, whose ceremonial dress uniform was dark blue and red with gold braid (represented on buses by gold lining-out). Black was added to mourn the horrific losses suffered by the Pals on the Somme battlefield in July 1916.

The initiator of public transport in the town was the Accrington Corporation Steam Tramways Co, which started services in 1886. Despite its name, the undertaking did not become municipally owned until 1907, although the tracks were always owned by the Borough. The steam trams, known locally as 'The Baltic Fleet', finished when corporation red and cream electric cars took over, also in 1907.

Joint routes were operated, that to Rawtenstall passing through Haslingden, which owned track but preferred the neighbouring towns to run the services. Four Accrington tramcars were based there for that purpose.

Accrington's first motorbuses went into service in 1928 and an expanded fleet replaced the trams in 1932. Lancashire CC registration marks were usual. A batch of four Leyland saloons delivered in 1952 carried a trial green and cream livery. It was not pursued as the populace, or at least that portion of it which noticed the change, maintained that it was too similar to the colours of adjacent Blackburn. A Seddon coach purchased in 1973 was outstanding in turquoise and red but succumbed eventually to standard livery.

The basic bus fleet in the 1960s was strongest in Guys, followed by Leylands. Bodies were predominantly by East Lancashire Coachbuilders, whose works is only a few miles distant.

In 1974 when it took over from Accrington CTD, Hyndburn (Borough of) Transport Department continued the dark blue and red livery. After 1986, when it became a company, minibuses were painted silver, red and dark blue. In the early 1990s a grey band was added to double-deck livery and some saloons became largely white, with red and dark blue bands being merely relief.

Stagecoach Holdings purchased the undertaking late in 1996, and it ceased to exist as a separate entity on 26 April 1997.

Left:
Coat of arms photo date: 1974.

Below:
Accrington No 23 (KTC 336C) departs from the town centre on 11 June 1967. It is a Leyland Tiger Cub PSUC1/11 built in 1965, carrying an East Lancs B43F body and was one of the last buses to have the unusual but attractive livery enhanced by lining-out. The East Lancs-bodied double-decker seen in the background has already lost it.

Ashton-under-Lyne Corporation Transport Department

Historically in Lancashire, this textile town lies six miles east of Manchester, with which it had joint tram and later trolleybus and motorbus routes. The county boundary with Cheshire passed, before 1974, within a very short distance of the town centre, and the West Riding of Yorkshire and Derbyshire were also not far away. But for those boundaries it seems possible that Ashton may have participated in the adjacent Joint Board formed by the towns of Stalybridge, Hyde, Mossley and Dukinfield (SHMD), all almost entirely within Cheshire.

Horse trams of the Manchester Carriage & Tramways Co began operating in Ashton in 1881 and an electric tram service on one route was started in 1899 by the Oldham, Ashton & Hyde Electric Tramways Co. In 1902 Ashton Corporation commenced electric operations using new track within the town and the neighbouring UD of Hurst. Part of the OA&H system was taken over in 1921 and trolleybuses were introduced in 1925. The latter were joint with Oldham, which ceased participating after a year. Ashton continued operating as far as the boundary and in 1938 introduced more modern trolleybuses to work jointly into Manchester.

Motorbuses were first acquired in 1923 and replaced trams between 1931 and 1938. Leylands and Crossleys, both single- and double-deck, were the prewar mainstay, and utility Guy Arabs arrived in 1943 and 1945. The latter proved to be very reliable chassis and were later rebodied.

Postwar bus purchases again centred on Leyland and Crossley though not in quantity, and more Guys, with rare Bond bodies, were bought in 1956. The modern trolleybuses acquired in 1938-40 were Crossleys but that make was not available at the end of World War 2 and six 'utility' Sunbeams were bought. Five more Crossleys joined the fleet in 1950, and eight Bond-bodied BUT models in 1956. They were the last acquisitions and the system closed in 1966, simultaneously with that of Manchester with which it had been intertwined.

Livery prior to 1935 was dark blue and white but then red bands (or in the case of a Crossley saloon, red streamlining) were added. It has been said that the action was taken to mark the Silver Jubilee of King George V and Queen Mary with the colours of the Union flag. Be that as it may, the livery lasted until 1954, when a lighter blue relieved by cream replaced it on both buses and trolleybuses.

Ashton Corporation buses became part of Selnec's fleet in 1969, vesting day being 1 November and full operational control passing on 1 January 1970. Vehicles taken over by the South East Lancashire North East Cheshire Passenger Transport Executive (the full title of Selnec) totalled 59, two being Leyland Panther Cubs, the others Leyland PD2s (40, mostly 1960s purchases), Leyland PDRs (13) and four Guys.

Repainting into orange and cream proceeded steadily but blue and cream could be seen, with 'Selnec Southern' logo and PTE fleet number, well into the 1970s.

After passing through GMPTE (1974-86) and GMB Ltd (1986-96) ownership with

Above:
Seen over 50 miles from home is Ashton-under-Lyne No 36 (DTE 324), a Leyland-bodied Tiger dating from 1938. It was photographed at Caldy on the Wirral peninsula, then in Cheshire, on 13 May 1962. Having visited this cricket ground on more than one occasion, it seems possible that it was retained for Transport Department Social Club use as it did not appear on the active fleet list from 1960.

Right:
Coat of arms photo date: 19 April 1969.

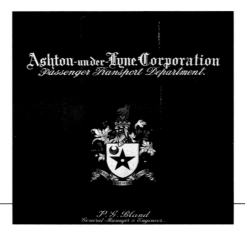

Ashton-under-Lyne Corporation.
Passenger Transport Department.

P. G. Bland
General Manager & Engineer.

liveries based on orange, local buses are now in the stripes of Stagecoach Manchester (Greater Manchester Buses South Ltd) or the overall orange of FirstBus subsidiary Greater Manchester Buses North Ltd, using 'Greater Manchester' as fleet-name.

Ashton vehicles were registered with marks from Lancashire CC.

In 1974 the Borough of Ashton-under-Lyne became a part of the Metropolitan Borough of Tameside in the County of Greater Manchester.

Barrow-in-Furness Corporation Transport

Although a mere dozen miles in a straight line separated Barrow from its nearest municipal transport neighbours across Morecambe Bay, they were 40 miles by road and a little less by rail. This isolated location at the end of the Furness peninsula which projects into the Irish Sea and bounds the west side of the bay, meant that transport enthusiasts had deliberately to go there – no just calling in on the way to somewhere else. Hence Barrow's vehicles were more familiar as illustrations in publications than 'in the flesh'.

Politically part of Lancashire but geographically separate, the Furness area became part of the new county of Cumbria in 1974 and Barrow that county's only municipal operator.

Horse buses operated in the town from 1877 for a while but did not pay. Barrow-in-Furness Tramways Co, which between 1885 and 1899 ran steam trams in maroon and cream livery, proved more successful. British Electric Traction Co bought the system and planned to electrify. In fact the last steam tram survived until July 1903, replacement electric cars operating from February 1904, also in maroon and cream. Additionally, BET operated several buses in the town from 1915.

Barrow Corporation took over the tramway on 1 January 1920 and changed

BARROW CORPORATION

Top:
A focal point of Barrow-in-Furness town centre is the traffic roundabout being negotiated by a Leyland Titan PD2/27, No 2 in the fleet at that time and registered HEO 272. The Massey H37/27F body sports an unusual glass panel in the sliding door, which when open covers the normal insignia position, hence the arms being placed further back. The year of build was 1961 and the date depicted 3 October 1964.

Above:
Coat of arms photo date: 1979.

the livery to green and cream in 1921. This was also used on the first Corporation buses, which went into service in 1923. Leyland Titan TD1s bought in 1929 introduced the dark blue and cream combination which lasted until the undertaking became a company in 1986. After peaking at around 30 cars, the tramway closed in 1932, replacement buses being Crossley Condors.

Barrow was allowed by the Ministry of Supply to buy 19 new double-deckers during World War 2, a high proportion of the fleet, and indicative of the substantial

increase in services needed by war-workers. Several times daily Barrow's buses coped with the peak loadings associated with shift-workers in the shipyards. Many thousands were employed and because the town is quite compact, some went home for their midday meal. It was therefore usual to see a dozen or more buses waiting outside the yards at noon.

Barrow was a loyal customer of Leyland and by 1961 the entire fleet consisted of that marque.

Hadwins Luxury Coaches of Ulverston was acquired with 10 machines in 1973. Red and cream livery was retained, the company being disposed of in 1977.

Barrow was a County Borough until 1974, its registration mark being EO. The town's buses carried that until 1953, then with a serial prefix letter, and from 1964 a year-suffix letter also. The Transport Department was hardly affected by local government changes in 1974 when the town became a district, but like many others, took the title of Borough.

After deregulation in 1986, livery was modified to two shades of blue with cream, and later, on some buses, to simply light blue and cream. Those also carried 'Blue Line' as fleetname.

Competition increased, the financial situation became critical and the end came in May 1989 when Stagecoach bought some of the assets. Initially the Ribble subsidiary took over the services but a month later the group decreed that Furness would in future be served by affiliate Cumberland Motor Services. Some of the 38 buses in the final fleet stayed with Ribble but others were dispersed and could subsequently be seen in several other fleets.

Bedwas & Machen Urban District Council Omnibus Department

This was the smallest of the interesting municipal operators in the valleys of South Wales. Until 1974 the twin mining towns (some would say large villages) were in Monmouthshire and thus legally part of England, although most of the inhabitants would have regarded themselves as Welsh. This ethnic anomaly stemmed from legislation in 1284, 1536 and the Wales & Berwick Act of 1746 when England was deemed to include Wales. The Welsh Language Act of 1967 was a precursor of 1974 when Monmouthshire became part of the new County of Gwent, officially Welsh. However, before that happened, Bedwas and Machen were very close to Wales as the border with Glamorganshire ran along the Rhymney River only a few hundred yards away.

The Bedwas & Machen undertaking was never involved with tramways but buses were introduced at the end of World War 1. At first there were only three Straker-Squires on a joint service but later purchases included a six-wheeled Karrier, a Gilford and Albions.

Six Bedford OWB 'minibuses' acquired during World War 2 continued the single-deck tradition. The year 1947 saw the arrival of ex-Wigan Corporation Leyland Titan TD1s, the undertaking's first double-deckers. These were followed by double-deck Albions and single- and double-deck AECs.

In the early 1960s the fleet of seven consisted of three AEC Regent Vs, one Regent III, an Albion Venturer with a rather inelegant Welsh Metal Industries body and two AEC Regal III saloons. A later purchase, a Leyland Titan PD3 with Massey body, had a claim to fame as the last side-gangway lowbridge double-decker built.

In the early 1950s the dark blue and cream livery was adorned with a UDC monogram enclosed by 'Bedwas & Machen' on a garter. By 1959 this had been replaced by the civic title on two lines, later on one.

On 1 April 1974 both towns were absorbed into Rhymney Valley District Council (Cyngor Ardal Cwm Rhymni), a Mid Glamorgan County authority and itself then a bus operator formed through the merging of the B&M undertaking with those of Caerphilly UDC and Gelligaer UDC. A livery of brown, yellow and cream was chosen, with the full Council name in Welsh (usually on the right) and English.

The Department became Inter Valley Link Ltd in 1986 and was bought by the National Welsh Co when financial problems arose in 1989. That large operator itself foundered and ceased to operate in 1992.

Previously, Red & White, a name from the past and destined to be taken over by Stagecoach Holdings in 1993, had split away from it. This subsidiary now competes with other companies in Bedwas and Machen.

On 1 April 1996 the twin towns became a part of the County Borough of Caerphilly.

Left:
In the early 1950s Bedwas & Machen employed a monogram encircled by a named belt as its device. By 1959 this had been replaced by their civic title.

Below:
This Massey body is the lowbridge rear-entrance version of that pictured for Barrow, and carries a similar shade of dark blue. Fleet No 10, registration RAX 583, it was built in 1957. The chassis is an AEC Regent V and the body configuration L29/28R. It was photographed on 30 May 1970, the fleetname close-up being captured at the same time.

BEDWAS & MACHEN U.D. COUNCIL

Capital of the province of Northern Ireland and second city of Ireland in size, Belfast was the only municipal public transport operator in that island and one of only two County Boroughs in the North.

Prior to the Corporation taking over and electrifying the system in 1905, the Belfast Street Tramways Co had run horse cars in red and cream livery from 1872. The city trams retained those colours until 1929, when dark blue and cream was introduced. That survived on trams until closure of the system in 1954, replaced by buses and trolleybuses already dressed in red and ivory not unlike the shades used in the 1920s.

Belfast Corporation had commenced motorbus operations on 4 October 1926 using six AECs with Shorts saloon bodies. Trolleybuses commenced in 1938, replacing trams on the Falls Road route and grew to number over 200, making one of the largest such fleets in the British Isles. One service entered Stormont Park and actually passed through the portico of the impressive Parliament Building – the equivalent in London would have had trolleybuses passing through the Palace of Westminster yard.

This system closed in 1968, too early to be involved in the 1973 changes when Belfast Corporation Transport became Citybus, a subsidiary of Northern Ireland Transport Holding Company. It joined Ulsterbus, which had been formed by NITHC taking over the Ulster Transport Authority in 1967.

Citybus, retaining red and cream livery (but with no fleetname until the 1990s) still runs the city services, while Ulsterbus,

Belfast Corporation Transport Department

using that fleetname on blue and cream, serves elsewhere in the province.

Near its peak in 1962 the Belfast fleet consisted of 346 buses, 13 of them single-deck, and 207 trolleybuses. By far the most numerous bus chassis was Daimler, many being ex-London Transport and new around 1945. They were rebodied by the local firm Harkness in the 1960s and retained London three-letter registrations, making for easy recognition as Belfast and all other licensing offices in Northern Ireland were at that time still issuing two-letter marks.

Most Corporation buses lasted for years in Citybus service and many were destroyed in the 'troubles' after 1969. A majority of the 1,500-plus buses burned or

Above:
Belfast Daimler No 359 (OZ 6613) passes a newer Fleetline near Donegal Square on 21 August 1965 during the 'marching season' which still disrupts public transport in the city, albeit before the current 'troubles' commenced. The chassis, a CVG6, carries locally-built Harkness 56-seat body and is one of a batch of 100, the last home-market exposed radiator Daimlers dating from 1952. Many ex-London wartime Daimler chassis ended their days in Belfast carrying similar bodies to that shown.

Below left:
Coat of arms photo date: 7 August 1976.

blown up between that year and 1996 (with replacements paid for indirectly by the long-suffering British taxpayer) were destroyed in or near Belfast, so even towards the end of the Corporation era the most elderly vehicles served those areas where respect for public property was weakest.

The City is currently (1996) one of the 26 municipal districts which replaced six counties in 1974.

Belfast issued 13 two-letter marks between 1904 and 1957, and the same number with numbers preceding letters between 1958 and 1968. They were OI, XI, AZ, CZ, EZ, FZ, GZ, MZ, OZ, PZ, TZ, UZ and WZ.

Three-letter, four-numeral marks are currently issued (by all eight Northern Ireland VROs) and many find their way onto UK vehicles, especially coaches, to disguise their age.

Left:
A livery modification accompanied deliveries of new buses in 1955. The cream band and lettering beneath the lower windows was omitted, the title and arms henceforth appearing on the blue lower panels. Leyland Titan PD2/12 No 363 (DCM 983), one of a batch of five which arrived in June 1955, was among the first in the new style. It carried an East Lancs H33/26R body and was powered by a Leyland 9.8-litre diesel engine. This particular bus had a life of 18 years in Birkenhead, being withdrawn in May 1973 by Merseyside PTE for whom it had run since 1 December 1969. It is pictured on 'foreign' territory, Seacombe Ferry terminus of neighbouring Wallasey, on 8 September 1959.

Below:
Coat of arms photo date: 4 November 1969.

Birkenhead Municipal Transport

If Birkenhead was known for nothing else, two innovations – public parks and street tramways – would suffice. The town was Britain's first for both. Birkenhead Park, opened in 1847, was a template for the more famous New York Central Park. The idea of a street tramway originated in the USA but its European debut was in this rapidly expanding town which was a centre of marine activity, with freight in the docks, shipbuilding at Cammell Lairds and passenger traffic to Liverpool less than a mile away across the Mersey.

Tram and bus services eventually radiated from Woodside terminal of the Corporation Ferries and only a few hundred yards from the Town Hall. Part of the interchange was a large railway terminus, the most northerly used by the Great Western.

George Train's Birkenhead Street Railway Co opened in 1860 and horse-drawn trams ran from Woodside past the Park. Cars were green and cream until 1876, then mahogany, red and cream. Birkenhead Tramway Co, which took over in 1877, and Birkenhead United Tramway Omnibus & Carriage Co, which ran the lines from 1889 to 1900, both retained that livery. Smaller companies operated into adjacent areas.

Birkenhead Corporation purchased the BT Co track in 1889 and leased it to BUTOCCo. In 1895 the Corporation also bought the track of Wirral Tramways, leasing it back to that company (which ran from 1877 between Woodside and New Ferry). In 1901 Birkenhead acquired those undertakings and electrified the system. The livery was changed to maroon and cream, also employed on buses introduced in 1919. Leyland G7 saloons new in 1923 carried cream and chocolate brown (known as 'Scotch purple') and this became standard. An AEC Q type double-decker in blue and cream livery arrived in 1933 and those colours were adopted for all buses, though not the trams, which ran until 1937. During World War 2 some buses were to be seen with black in place of the cream relief. Four Guy Arabs were delivered in (darker) royal blue in 1946 but that was not adopted.

The original fleetname of 'Birkenhead Corporation Tramways' was modified to 'Birkenhead Corporation Motors' on buses but in 1934 'Transport' replaced 'Motors'. Later still the Department changed to Birkenhead Municipal Transport but this never appeared in full. From 1956 simply 'Birkenhead Transport' was used on buses. This final version had in fact appeared before, in 1921 on two ex-London AEC B type double-deckers.

Birkenhead's bus fleet was largely double-deck from 1925. Four decades later it operated 225, only four of which were saloons. Rear-engines came comparatively late, a batch of Daimler Fleetlines appearing in 1964, after which orders reverted to front-engined Leyland Titans for three years. Confidence established, Leyland Atlanteans were chosen next. The last arrived after Merseyside PTE took over on 1 December 1969 and merged the fleet with those of Liverpool and Wallasey.

Until 1974 PTE buses in Wirral carried Birkenhead blue and Wallasey cream, in recognition that those Cheshire towns were reluctant to accept the use of Liverpool's dark green on their streets. A compromise reached when the communities on both sides of the river merged into the County of Merseyside was the adoption of light green and cream. Birkenhead and Wallasey became parts of the Metropolitan District (Borough) of Wirral.

Merseyside Transport Ltd (trading as Merseybus), successor to the PTE in 1986, changed to maroon and cream livery two years later. Sale of the company to its employees and financial institutions in December 1992 led to a cream and crimson corporate livery with area fleetnames, that used at Birkenhead depot being 'Wirral Peninsula'.

Birkenhead was a county borough and until 1974 used the registration marks CM and BG (with xCM and xBG serials from 1948).

Trams returned to Birkenhead on 14 April 1995 when two new Hong Kong-built double-deckers in maroon livery started running between the Ferry and Transport Museum on a Wirral Borough line extended to Egerton Bridge in 1996. Memories were also revived between May 1994 and June 1995 when Birkenhead & District, a subsidiary of Greater Manchester Buses South, ran buses in blue and cream livery in Wirral.

Right
Birmingham's postwar bodies had a continuity of appearance with those built before 1939 and the resemblance was assisted by a very attractive and characteristic livery layout. Crossleys, Daimlers and Guys were difficult to differentiate for the non-Birmingham trained eye if further away than 200yd, due in part of course to the 'tin-fronts' that all carried. Seen here on 3 April 1965 in a part of the city then being redeveloped is No 3150 (MOF 150), a Daimler CVG6 with Crossley H55R body. Most of the batch of 125 (all registered MOF) were built in 1953. The recessed driver's windscreen gave the smooth body line a curiously old-fashioned look.

Below:
Coat of arms photo date: 1969.

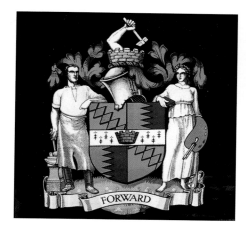

Birmingham City Transport

The dark blue and cream livery carried by Birmingham trams, trolleybuses and buses was dignified, as befitted the status of Britain's second city, the heart of the Midlands.

Several early tramway companies operated horse, steam, cable and battery cars in a variety of liveries and even after Birmingham Corporation Transport Department assumed control of some in 1904, with route electrification following, other operators survived.

Not until after its boundaries were considerably extended in 1911 did the city become the main transport provider when, the following year, it purchased the other major operator, the City of Birmingham Tramways Co. That undertaking had used several liveries, green and cream being the last.

The network of 3ft 6in gauge lines, unusual in a large British city, continued to expand into the 1920s even while one route, to Nechells, was converted to trolleybuses in 1922. This was the first such conversion in the country and also the first to be operated with double-deck, permanent covered-top (though still solid-tyred) vehicles.

Tram fleet numbers ran in unbroken sequence from No 1 to 843, though not all the earlier cars existed by the time the highest number appeared on an experimental lightweight example in 1930. The final substantial batch of trams had been delivered in 1928. Tramway abandonments started seriously in 1930 but the process was not complete until 1953. Buses were the replacements although trolleybus operations also expanded, the final batch of vehicles arriving in 1939.

Trolleybus fleet numbers reached No 90, although as Nos 1-20 were used twice, 110 vehicles were owned at various times. One batch of 11 Leylands bought in 1931 were half-cabs and fitted with that maker's characteristic radiator shells. Both features were entirely unnecessary but considered desirable as a contrast to previous tram-like bodies. The last trolleybus ran in 1951.

Bus services were started by the Corporation in 1913 with 40 Tilling-Stevens open-toppers running from Selly Oak to Rednal, extending a tram route. After World War 1, operations were cautiously extended and Tilling, Daimler, AEC, Leyland, Guy, Karrier and Morris buses were acquired. After 1930 Daimler was most frequently patronised.

World War 2 resulted in another mixed fleet and that situation continued after 1945 as the Department sought to ease vehicle shortages by multi-sourcing. This policy resulted in difficulties later, when buses using Daimler engines proved thirsty and were somewhat prematurely withdrawn. However, in 1962 when the bus fleet totalled around 1,750 of which 35 were saloons, Daimler had supplied 925, Guy 300, Crossley 270, Leyland 200 and AEC 16 double-deckers.

What we would now call 'corporate' livery developed after 1930, aided in later deliveries by 'tin-fronts'. The various makes had a very homogeneous appearance. Sand-coloured roofs adopted as camouflage in 1939 became standard.

Birmingham City Transport merged with other adjacent municipal operators as West Midlands Passenger Transport Executive on 1 October 1969. Adoption of a livery similar to Birmingham's, though reverting to a cream roof, ensured it was several years before many passengers noticed any change. Only in 1986 when the undertaking became West Midlands Travel Ltd were significant livery changes introduced.

In 1974 Birmingham became a Metropolitan District (with City title) in West Midlands county. December 1991 saw the company sold to its management and employees. It merged with National Express in April 1995.

Apart from body styling, Birmingham buses could easily be recognised by their registrations. Necessarily for such a large city, the municipal motor vehicle licensing office had, over the years, been allotted many marks: O in 1903 was followed by OA in 1913 and OB in 1915. The second letters E, H, K, L, M, N, P, X, F, G, V, J and C were subsequently issued. Incongruously, VP appeared in 1928 between OX and OF. Three-letter marks commenced at AOA in 1934.

Not a city, though possessing the requisite cathedral, Blackburn was traditionally a cotton town. Many mill buildings are now adapted for other industries. East Lancashire Coachbuilders is based in the town and over the years has supplied a large number of bus bodies to the local municipality. Blackburn is midway along a line of six former municipal undertakings, all in Lancashire and running eastwards from Blackpool to Burnley. Before 1974 there existed a seventh, Darwen, and in fact prior to 1933, when Nelson and Colne formed a joint committee with Burnley, there were nine.

The early history of the Department followed a typical course. Blackburn & Over Darwen Tramways Co, using red and cream livery, opened the first line in Britain to be authorised for road steam traction only. That was in 1881 and was followed in 1887 by Blackburn Corporation Tramways Co opening a steam operation on track leased from the municipality. Horse cars on other BCTCo lines began services in 1888.

The Blackburn company's operations were bought by the Corporation in 1898, a year before B&OD was also municipalised. Blackburn began electrification of both systems within its boundary and Darwen acted similarly with its share of the B&OD.

Electric tram services ran jointly with Darwen and Accrington for many years. The livery of green and cream was also used on buses, first introduced in 1929. Tramway abandonment started in 1938 and after being on hold during World War 2

Above:
Not all Blackburn's buses have been bodied by East Lancs but the make has been well represented, quite fittingly, as the factory is in the town. Seen here on 11 June 1967 in the town centre is No 30 (PCB 30), a Leyland Titan PD2A/24, one of a batch of 12 built in 1962. The ELCB body is highbridge and seats 35/28. The 'tin-front' design was pioneered by St Helens Corporation.

Below:
Coat of arms photo date: 18 March 1972.

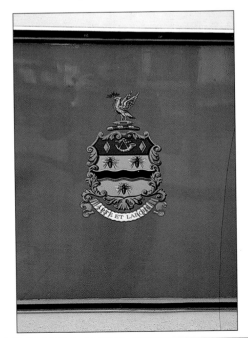

was completed when the Intack route closed on 3 September 1949, exactly 10 years to the day after that conflict started.

Blackburn cars had run four miles into Darwen until 1946, when that neighbouring borough's tram system closed. The two towns merged in 1974 and Blackburn, hitherto a county borough, gave its name to the enlarged authority, buses being operated by Blackburn Borough Transport Department. For several years the livery then included a red roof to acknowledge Darwen involvement but a reversion to green and cream followed and has survived the events since company status was imposed in 1986 and the title became Blackburn Borough Transport Ltd. In 1997 the undertaking was still council-owned.

The crest depicted was photographed in 1972 but newer buses by then carried it on a cream band alongside the title 'Blackburn'. After the 1974 merger a stylised bird logo was carried, underlined with the same title but later the crest was re-adopted.

Leylands were always predominant in the Blackburn fleet, indeed had a monopoly position until 1943 when 'utility' Guys arrived. After the war many more Arabs of the latter marque were bought until rear engines became the norm and Guy vanished as a manufacturer.

Until 1974 the town's registration marks were BV and CB (and serial prefixes).

From 1 April 1998 the local authority will be unitary, with the name 'Blackburn with Darwen Borough'.

Blackpool Corporation Transport

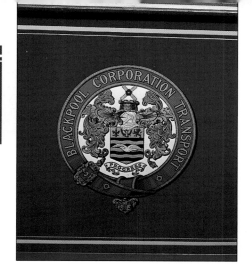

Situated in the Fylde area of Lancashire facing the Irish sea, Blackpool has always been more famous for its trams than buses. It was a tiny bathing resort in the mid-18th century but cheap railway access brought immense expansion to accommodate millions of holidaymakers from the North and Midlands of England and from Scotland. In October 1904 the town became a county borough. In 1974 the status changed to district, with the title 'Borough'.

A 2-mile conduit line built on the promenade by the Corporation in 1885 and leased to the Blackpool Electric Tramway Co was the first electric street tramway in the UK and, still in use today though not conduit, has the record for continuous operation. Some single-deck cars now haul trailers, a feature made acceptable to the authorities by the high proportion of reserved track.

The Corporation took over operation of the promenade line in 1892, converted it to overhead power supply and extended the system considerably, especially inland. The inter-urban Blackpool & Fleetwood Tramroad Co line, which opened in 1898, was absorbed by Blackpool Corporation on 1 January 1920 and that track, together with the neighbouring St Annes UDC tramway (Lytham St Annes from 1922), gave a continuous coastal line of a little over 17 miles, though it could only be experienced in full by changing cars.

Modernisation, started in 1933, has ensured survival. Indeed, between 1962 and 1992 (when Manchester Metrolink opened) Blackpool was the sole representative of the British town tramway.

Railcoach No 703 depicted is one of those mid-1930s streamliners which have carried the crowds for 60 years. The crest is shown against the red of an earlier livery.

Inland tram routes were gradually closed after the war and, apart from track to the depot, an 11-mile Starr Gate to Fleetwood line is the sturdy survivor.

Original 1885 cars were green and teak or green, sand and white, colours which continued in use after 1892, followed in 1905 by red, teak and cream. Blackpool & Fleetwood used just teak and cream. By 1928 red and cream prevailed but the streamliners introduced green and cream, which is still the current livery, although specialised all-cream and red and yellow have also been used.

Preserved Blackpool trams are to be found working on many museum lines including three in the USA.

Municipal operation of buses started in 1921 with two single-deckers which ran between Cleveleys and Thornton, both just outside the borough. A solitary open-top double-decker arrived in 1922, followed by more four years later. It was not until 1932 that a substantial number of buses were purchased. The 1933 intake were centre-entrance and by 1936 a streamline design matching the railcoaches was in service.

These buses and similar saloons gave the town a distinctive public transport image which, even when the last centre-entrance survivor was withdrawn in 1969, continued vestigially as a full-front, rear-loading, double-deck design. Front-entrance, rear-engine bus deliveries started in 1977.

Always green and cream but in varying proportions, bus livery became less uniform in the mid-1980s, when red and cream appeared on ex-London RMs and black and yellow became standard for minibuses.

Deregulation in 1986 accompanied a change to company status as Blackpool Transport Services Ltd and in 1994 the neighbouring Fylde undertaking was purchased. In mid-1997 the enlarged undertaking was still Council-owned.

Blackpool will become a unitary authority in 1998.

Until 1974 Blackpool's vehicle registration marks were FR and FV (and serial prefixes).

Above:
The coat of arms is depicted on a tram in the pre-1933 red and cream livery, seen on 10 April 1973.

Below:
Pictured on the Promenade on 23 July 1974 is Car No 703, (originally 239). Built in 1934, it was one of 27 numbered 237-263, of which those up to No 247 were open-topped until covered in 1941/2. Over 60 years later these cars (nicknamed Balloons) still carry large crowds, especially during the autumn Illuminations. Several versions of the green and cream livery have been used since it appeared on the first railcoach in 1933. In the 1990s black window surrounds have been added. Frontal appearance is now different from that in 1934 due to indicator box reconstruction. The body, bogies, motors and controllers of Car 703 are all of English Electric manufacture. The car currently seats 54 upstairs and 40 in the lower saloon. Two conductors are often necessary.

County Borough of Bolton Transport Department

But for its proximity to Manchester and Liverpool, Bolton might have achieved city status long ago. It is a substantial place, the archetypal Lancashire cotton town, and largest of a chain of former county boroughs which crowd Manchester and Salford from the north. Currently (1997) it is a metropolitan district (with borough title) in Greater Manchester county.

Civic public transport began in 1880 when the Corporation laid a horse tramway, subsequently expanded to nearly 18 miles in length. Until the Corporation took it over in 1899 and electrified it later that year, it was operated on a lease by E. Holden & Co using four different liveries: red, green, blue and amber, all with cream.

Extensions followed municipalisation until by 1924, 32 miles of track existed on 13 radial roads. The system was eventually worked by 162 double-deck trams. There were connections with the adjacent undertakings of Bury and South Lancashire Tramways Co and their cars ran into Bolton at one time. Possible links to Darwen, Ramsbottom and Rawtenstall to the north were hindered by hills, over which ran moorland roads through thinly-populated districts.

The last new Bolton trams were three all-enclosed cars bought in 1928. These were followed by eight bought from South Lancashire in 1933 when that company converted to trolleybuses. In fact, from 1944 to 1956 Bolton owned four of the

type itself, operating under SLT-maintained but municipally-owned wires within the boundary. SLT livery was carried but the vehicles were restricted to running on the route into Bolton.

Bolton's last tram ran on route T to Tonge Moor on 29 March 1947 but Car 66 (sometime 366) has been magnificently restored and currently upholds the town's civic pride by operating at peak holiday times in Blackpool.

Bolton was a very early motorbus operator, the first, a Stirling steam bus, entering service in 1904. This experiment lasted only two weeks but in 1907 further trials commenced. It was not until 1923, however, that five Leyland saloons were purchased and the bus era finally arrived. The fleet was later predominantly double-deck, chassis being mainly Leyland and Daimler, with a few AECs.

Corporation tram livery was always deep maroon and cream but buses, which originally carried the same colours, changed to maroon and red in the late 1930s, reverting to the former livery after World War 2.

By 1964 there was a move to brighten the colours and some buses were painted cherry red and cream. However, this was

Above:
With Leyland's factory being only 15 miles distant it is not surprising that a majority of Bolton's buses were built there. No 117 (MBN 172) was one of a batch of 10 PD3/5 Titans built in 1958 and bodied for 41/33 seats by East Lancs. It is seen here on 5 April 1964, swinging round near the bus station. After becoming No 6617 in Selnec's fleet in 1969 it survived only until January 1971.

Below left:
Coat of arms photo date: 29 November 1969. (On the lighter red.)

overtaken by the final development, when cream became the major colour with maroon as contrast.

The undertaking became a part of Selnec PTE on 1 November 1969, control of the fleet passing over on 1 January 1970. After passing through GMPTE (1974-86) and GM Buses Ltd (1986-96) ownership with liveries based on orange, local buses are now in the almost overall orange of 'Greater Manchester', fleetname of the FirstBus GM Buses North Ltd subsidiary.

The county borough's vehicle registration marks were BN and WH (and serial prefixes). Bolton was one of only 14 authorities to move to the year-suffix letter system in 1963, starting with '-A'. Thirteen exhausted six-character issues at various times during that year, starting with Middlesex in February. Bolton commenced with ABN 2A in December. The suffix letter changed on 1 January until 1967, so Bolton issued very few A suffix marks. The 14th, Kirkcaldy, was a new office.

Most other offices (151) commenced at '-B' during 1964 and 21 did not start until '-C' in 1965.

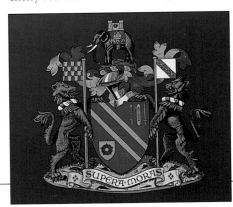

Bournemouth Corporation Transport

The Victorians' love of the seaside changed Bournemouth, a Hampshire village of 700 people in 1851, into an elegant town of 60,000, 50 years later.

Its attractions include wooded valleys and parks running down to fine beaches, a mild climate and good shops. The town was transferred to Dorset in 1974. Simultaneously it lost county borough status and became a district with the title of 'borough'. Further change, to a unitary authority, occurred on 1 April 1997.

Bournemouth became an electric tramway operator in 1902, after a change of mind caused by successful services started in neighbouring Poole from 1901 by Poole & District Electric Tramways Co (a BET subsidiary).

Poole Corporation transferred the P&DETCo lease to Bournemouth in 1904 and BCT bought 17 cars which had operated it. By 1905 Bournemouth had a system extending from Poole in the west to Christchurch in the east, requiring 132 trams. Power was supplied overhead in the suburbs but by conduit for 1½ miles in the town centre until that too was converted to trolley collection in 1911.

Trolleybuses started operating experimentally in 1933 and having been found acceptable gradually replaced trams, the final car running in 1936. At its maximum the trackless fleet was 103, all double-deck, three of which were unusual open-toppers.

One feature of the system was a manpowered terminal turntable at Christchurch. Earlier, trams to that terminus had passed over Tuckton toll bridge, the charge being included in the fare but for which passengers received a separate ticket. The trolleybus system closed in 1969 when the newest vehicles were only seven years old. They were Sunbeams, the previous batch having been BUT.

Motorbuses arrived very early, in 1906, as feeders to the trams. All those bought until 1943 were petrol-engined for quietness. After World War 2 a mixed fleet of Leyland and Guy double-deckers was used, supplemented by small Bedford WTBs from 1939, utility OWBs from 1942/3 (later converted to open-top) and Leyland saloons.

In 1940 Bournemouth had a surplus of vehicles and many were hired to towns with shortages. A German paratrooper landing between Walsall and Wolverhampton in 1942 would have been nonplussed to say the least on seeing Bournemouth trolleybuses operating there.

The bus fleet contained many full-fronted models. Open-toppers were used, single-deck, double-deck and trolleys, for holidaymakers' services.

Tram livery was always chocolate and primrose, those colours in reversed proportions also appearing on buses and trolleybuses.

The undertaking became Bournemouth Transport Ltd in 1986, adopting the fleetname 'Yellow Buses' and a primrose and blue livery. In mid-1997 the company was still council-owned.

Housed in a depot in Bournemouth is a very fine collection of preserved local buses, trolleybuses and an open-top tramcar returned from many years of operation on the Llandudno & Colwyn Bay Electric Railway followed by display in the erstwhile Clapham Transport Museum. It is now restored to original chocolate and primrose.

The county borough vehicle registration marks until 1974 were EL, RU and LJ (and their serial prefixes).

Left:
Coat of arms photo date: 27 May 1972.

Below:
Depicted in Christchurch on 29 May 1966 is Bournemouth trolleybus No 260 (WRU 260), a Sunbeam MF2B built in 1958 and fitted with electrical equipment by Crompton-Parkinson/Allan West. The H63D body is by Weymann. Thirty-nine Sunbeams were purchased between 1958 and 1962 and numbered 258-303, the first 20 having WRU-registrations. Those following were YLJ- and -LJ, the latter possibly being the only examples of trolleybuses receiving reversed registrations, which started in the 1950s as authorities exhausted forward combinations. No 303 was the last trolleybus to enter service in Britain.

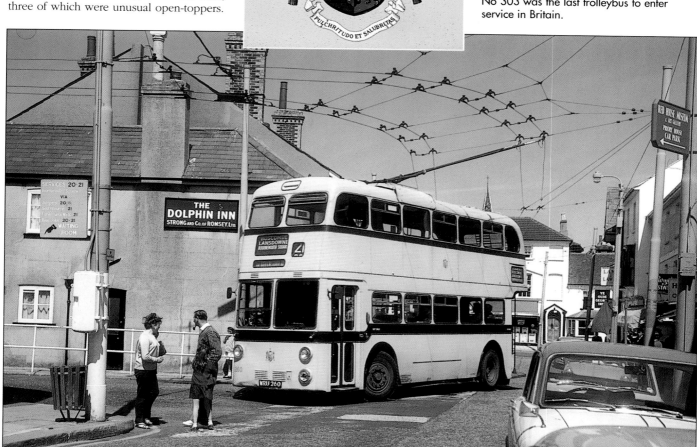

Bradford City Transport

Wool, and the cloth made from it, were the basis of Bradford's prosperity. In the early days it was one of West Yorkshire's less endearing towns but it used the wealth to acquire some impressive buildings and become an attractive city. Recently-established museums devoted to photography and transport, and adjacent Pennine villages such as Haworth, have encouraged tourism.

Having been a county borough in the West Riding of Yorkshire, Bradford became a metropolitan borough of West Yorkshire in 1974.

Public transport developed from 1882 when a private operator, the Bradford Tramways Co, later known as Bradford Tramways & Omnibus Co, commenced a horse car service on a short corporation-owned line. Also starting that year, other routes used steam traction. Car livery was brown and cream.

Another company, Bradford & Shelf Tramway, operated one route by steam, starting in 1884. Their livery was initially dark blue and cream but changed to chocolate and cream in 1892.

Electric traction experiments using overhead wires began in 1892 and in 1898 the Corporation opened a route of its own. From 1902 all the leased lines also became city-owned and steam trams ceased in 1903. Tramway expansion continued, using

4ft gauge, and by 1926 routes totalled about 60 miles. Conversion to trolleybuses started in 1928. These had been pioneered in the UK by Bradford (and neighbouring Leeds), starting in 1911, and by 1955 covered 46 miles of routes.

Bradford was one of many British cities where trams, trolleybuses and motorbuses coexisted for many years. Trams survived until 1950. Buses were not employed until 1926 but gradually numbers grew until they numerically equalled trolleybuses.

The 11th largest municipal fleet, Bradford in later years bought AEC, Leyland and Daimler buses, and new BUT trolleybuses. With true Yorkshire acumen, however, as systems in other towns closed, Bradford took advantage of bargain trolleybuses, some only a few years old, others needing rebodying. It was really the recasting of the city centre road system which sealed the fate of those swift, quiet vehicles, though some do say that with a little more flexibility by planners they could have survived. This, the last public-road trolleybus system in the UK, closed on 26 March 1972.

Bradford's final livery before being absorbed into West Yorkshire PTE on 30 March 1974 was light blue and cream, depicted as the ground for the coat of arms. This had superseded dark blue and cream, starting in 1942.

Post-1974 livery under the PTE was green and cream. After 1986, as Yorkshire Rider Ltd, buses based in the city received 'Bradford' in red.

Sale to Badgerline in 1994 produced a stronger area identity but after FirstBus was formed in 1995 local names and liveries

were reintroduced. The fleet became Bradford Traveller, with a livery based on a blue not too dissimilar to the light shade adopted following wartime operation of surplus Southend Corporation trolleybuses in that colour.

Prior to 1974 the City's registration marks were AK, KU, KW and KY (and serial prefixes).

Above:
The coat of arms is shown against the postwar light blue on 26 March 1972.

Below:
Bradford tram No 104 is one of the balcony double-deckers built for this 4ft gauge system between 1912 and 1931. Of English Electric manufacture, it was rescued from duty as a scoreboard at Odsal Rugby League ground and fully restored. Seen here on 7 July 1962, 12 years after normal tram services in the city ended, it is operating on the short stretch of track and overhead surviving alongside Thornbury Depot. These occasional outings unfortunately finished some years ago. When restored it was given the prewar dark blue and cream livery.

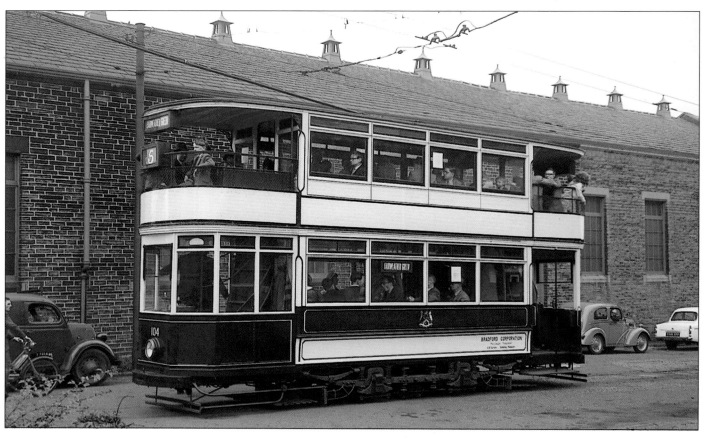

Brighton Corporation Transport

Famous for its 1787 Royal Pavilion and venue for many political party conferences, this East Sussex town situated on the English Channel coast 52 miles from London, commenced operating its own electric tramways from 1901. Earlier horse and steam lines incorporating Brighton in their title actually operated outside the boundary.

Another electric line existed between 1896 and 1901. It was the curious Brighton & Rottingdean Seashore Electric Tramroad Co, whose single car on high legs ran along the shore on twin 2ft 8½in gauge tracks set 18ft apart. At high tide the 'tram' was sometimes running in seawater 15ft deep.

Volk's Railway, an 1883 pioneer electric line, still runs along the seafront. It was 'municipalised' by Brighton Corporation in 1940.

Brighton's tramway system grew to 80 cars and closed on 31 August 1939, three days before war was declared. Municipal buses and trolleybuses, all AECs, replaced the tramcars. To Brighton went the distinction of being the last municipality to operate tramcars only, although there had been earlier unsuccessful trolleybus experiments.

Under a 1939 co-ordination agreement the Brighton Hove & District Co operated very similar buses and trolleybuses on different routes. Those vehicles carried an identical livery and fleetname but lacked the municipal arms. Trolleybus operations ended in 1961.

Between 1901 and 1920 Brighton Corporation livery was maroon and cream, followed by chocolate and cream for some years. Colours approximating to the former scheme eventually reappeared but the vehicles new in 1939 introduced a brighter red with cream. At the start of the 1970s blue and white was adopted.

Local government changes in 1974, when the town lost its county borough status and became a borough, affected the Transport Department very little and even when the post-1986 municipal company was bought by its employees the image remained recognisable. By 1996 the fleetname had become Brighton Blue Buses. The livery had passed through a two blues

Above:
Already 21 years old when this photograph was taken on 20 June 1960, Brighton No 35 (FUF 35) survived only another year as the system closed in 1961. Its AEC 661T chassis carries a Weymann H54R body with classic lines. The location is the bus station at Old Steine, only a short distance from the seafront and Palace Pier.

Below left:
Coat of arms photo date: 31 May 1972. This fleetname was introduced in 1961 when Brighton Area Transport Services replaced the 1939 scheme.

& white phase when it was Brighton Borough Transport trading as Brighton Buses, to two blues, sometimes with white and/or yellow. Further political development came on 1 April 1997 when Brighton & Hove became a unitary authority.

At that time the employee-owners of what had become Brighton Transport Ltd were considering a purchase offer from The Go-Ahead Group.

Following a decision to sell, the Group took over in May 1997 and announced an intention to merge the undertaking with subsidiary Brighton and Hove Bus & Coach Co.

Brighton's registration marks as a county borough were CD and UF (and serial prefixes).

Burnley, Colne & Nelson Joint Transport Committee

Between Pendle Hill of Lancashire witches fame and the Pennine border with West Yorkshire lie, in a line, the Lancashire ex-mill towns of Burnley (a county borough before 1974), Nelson and Colne (both previously boroughs). The last named is furthest east. Textiles have largely given way to mixed industry, heavy and light.

Burnley Corporation took over a part of the Burnley & District Tramways Co operation in 1901 and immediately commenced electrification. It had been operating steam trams since 1881, with brief reliance on horses from 1882. In addition to its own tracks, Burnley also leased lines from several adjacent authorities, including Reedley Hallows Parish Council, the only parish council in Britain to own a tramway.

The Burnley livery of dark maroon and cream was adopted by BCNJTC and, after 1974 when Colne and Nelson combined as the Borough of Pendle, was also used initially by Burnley & Pendle Joint Transport.

The first Burnley CT buses went into service in 1924.

Nelson Corporation also bought part of B&DT and its Tramways Department operated electrically from 1903 to 1933, initially using a livery of red and white, later light brown and cream. Nelson CT motorbuses appeared in 1923.

The Colne & Trawden Light Railways Co also opened electric services in 1903 and

was purchased by Colne Corporation in 1914. The livery was changed from green and cream to royal (dark) blue and cream and further altered to maroon and cream in 1922. Its rural routes closed in 1928 and the joint one in 1934, after the merger. Colne Corporation bought motorbuses in 1920 but regular services were not started until 1923.

The joint transport committee was formed in 1933 when the fleets of the three towns became one. Burnley had operated 72 trams, Colne 18 and Nelson 21. Respectively, they contributed 47, 24 and 15 buses to the new authority, plus a small number of trams. The latter were all withdrawn in 1935.

From 1933 new buses were predominantly Leylands, though Guys and Daimlers arrived during the war, and a few more Guys after it. Unusual for a municipality was a small batch of Bedford OB buses purchased in 1947. These were eminently suitable for very narrow lane routes serving villages on the flank of Pendle Hill. By 1962 the BCN fleet had built up to 147 buses.

In 1983, to mark 50 years of joint transport, Burnley & Pendle re-created the past by applying to a few modern double-deck buses the liveries of Burnley & District Tramways (black and cream), Burnley Corporation Tramways (maroon and

Above:
In 1968 buses of this operator carried the initials BCN at the front, a distinguishing feature possibly intended to enable non-enthusiast local patriots to differentiate between 'their' firm and Ribble, both using dark red livery though in different shades. On 6 October No 246 (PCW 946) rests in Burnley bus station. It is a Leyland Titan PD2A/27 with Northern Counties H64R body and dates from 1963. The original version of this livery, with a maroon band also at cantrail level, had similar proportions of dark and light to that used by Birmingham.

Below left:
Coat of arms: Burnley, Colne & Nelson crests appear left to right. The individual arms appeared on buses painted in 'heritage' liveries in 1983.

cream), Colne Corporation Light Railway (royal blue and cream) and Nelson Corporation Tramways (light brown and cream). All carried appropriate gilt lettering.

In 1986 the undertaking became Burnley & Pendle Transport Co Ltd. Pendle's portion of the assets was purchased by Stagecoach early in 1996.

Burnley originally resolved to continue as a joint undertaking with Stagecoach but in October of the same year the Council voted to sell its share also.

Before 1974 when Burnley County Borough became Burnley District (with the title of borough), the town's registration marks were CW, HG and their serials. Prior to 1933 new buses for Colne and Nelson were registered with Lancashire County and Burnley's with CW or HG. Vehicles new to BCN always received Burnley indices.

Burton upon Trent Corporation Transport Department

Still the brewing capital of Britain, Burton is in Staffordshire, midway between Stoke-on-Trent and Leicester. The town was a county borough prior to 1974, one of the smallest. Its buses carried FA and xFA registrations issued by the town's vehicle licensing office.

The transport history of Burton is not complex. Missing the horse tram era, Burton Corporation made a clean start with a 3ft 6in gauge electric system 6⅔ miles in length in 1903. Only 20 trams were needed, initially all open-top. Four more with roofs and balconies were bought in 1920.

Interest was added between August 1918 and March 1919 when eight Great Yarmouth cars were hired. As these would have been in a maroon and cream livery not unlike Burton's, few local people may have noticed.

Tramcars of Burton & Ashby Light Railways, owned by the Midland Railway and in that company's dark red (and cream) livery, had running powers over the most easterly two miles of Burton track and used it to connect Burton railway station with those at Swadlincote and Ashby-de-la-Zouch, towns in Derbyshire and Leicestershire respectively. The service operated from 1906 to 1927.

Burton Corporation tramways closed at the end of 1929, replaced by Guy single-deck buses purchased from 1927. Only saloons were operated until 1944, after which Guy double-deckers gradually became almost universal. By 1962, 45 of the fleet of 46 were Guys, only four being single-decked.

Until then only three non-Guy buses had ever been owned: one AEC Ranger, a Leyland Lioness and a wartime Daimler double-decker. In the late 1960s and early 1970s, however, Daimlers became predominant, eventually comprising 35 out of a fleet of 38.

Buses, like the trams, were painted maroon and cream until 1971 when a livery was adopted which consisted of red lower panels and a green roof, separated by cream.

East Staffordshire District Council took over from Burton Corporation as a result of political changes in 1974 and in 1977, after one bus had been given a blue roof to mark the Queen's Silver Jubilee, red, white and blue became fleet livery. This lasted until October 1985 when, possibly in anticipation of deregulation the following year, the municipal fleet merged with that of the local large independent Stevensons and adopted that company's yellow, black and white. Stevensons subsequently expanded, having at different times routes as far apart as Birmingham and Manchester. They became a subsidiary of British Bus group in 1994. That organisation was purchased by T. Cowie PLC in 1996.

Burton is currently one of a small number of Charter Trustee Boroughs which have an urban core surrounded by an extensive rural area (East Staffordshire).

Left:
Coat of arms photo date: 31 May 1970.

Below:
Burton always seemed to be a difficult town to obtain satisfactory bus photographs, the Town Hall and the informal bus station near the Trent bridge being the best locations in Corporation days. Pictured at the latter is Daimler CVG6 No 102 (JFA 602F), built 1967 with Massey H62R body. The date is 13 July 1969, shortly before red, cream and green was adopted. Half-cab, open-platform buses with F suffix registrations were uncommon, only a handful of operators by then resisting the lure of one-person operation with rear-engined vehicles (made legal in 1966). The final examples entered service in Northampton and Stockport in 1968.

Bury Corporation Transport

Famous for being the birthplace of Prime Minister Robert Peel, for textiles and black puddings, Bury is now well known as the headquarters of the restored East Lancashire Railway, usually steam operated, and as the northern terminus, from 1992, of Manchester Metrolink, the new tramway employing inter-urban ex-railway corridors with street running in Manchester.

The road transport history of Bury follows a pattern similar to other Lancashire towns in the area, with vehicles of the Bury, Rochdale & Oldham Steam Tramways Co reaching it in 1883.

Later the prefix 'Manchester' was added to that cumbersome title but after financial difficulties in 1887, new owners reverted to the original style.

Bury also had a company-owned horse tram operation on one route.

By 1903 the corporation had bought and made a start on electrifying the company routes within its boundaries, eventually operating joint or through running services to Bolton, Manchester, Rochdale and Salford, and reaching agreement with Radcliffe for leasing the lines owned by that UDC.

Over the years 60 trams were owned but, after a delay due to the war, the last one ran in 1949.

Corporation bus services started in 1925 with five single-deckers. The fleet had grown to nearly 100 when the Bury undertaking was merged with 10 others to form Selnec's fleet of 2,600 in 1969.

Although Leylands were always in a majority in Bury Corporation's fleet, some AECs were purchased and only five years from the end, two batches of rear-engined double-deckers, Daimler Fleetlines, were acquired.

The steam tramway engines and trailers had worn various colours but the Corporation used shades of red and cream until the first postwar buses signalled a new era with green and cream in 1946.

As has been detailed elsewhere, in 1974 Selnec PTE became Greater Manchester PTE, which in turn took the name Greater Manchester Buses Ltd in 1986. All retained a depot in Bury.

In 1997 the town is served mainly by buses of Greater Manchester North, a subsidiary of FirstBus, using orange livery.

Bury lost county borough status in 1974 and is currently a metropolitan district (with borough title) in Greater Manchester County. As a county borough its registration mark was EN (and xEN).

Left:
Coat of arms photo date: 14 June 1969.

Below:
Seen on 14 June 1969 in the town centre, Bury No 213 (GEN 213) built in 1958 was one of a batch of 25 (Nos 201-225) Leyland Titan PD3/6s to be purchased by the Corporation. The Weymann H41/32RD bodies had a seating capacity only one less than subsequent rear-engined Atlantean and Fleetline acquisitions.

Top:
Massey bodies were popular with the smaller South Wales municipalities but purchased in such small quantities that the business could have helped only a little in staving off the demise of that respected company. Caerphilly No 22 (YNY 922) dates from 1958 and is lowbridge height. The Massey rear-entrance body seats 29 over 28. It is seen in the council depot yard on 5 September 1959 when still quite new.

Above:
Coat of arms photo date: 24 March 1974. Clearly shown in the depiction of Caerphilly Castle is a Civil War-damaged tower which tilts by 12°.

Caerphilly Urban District Council Transport Department

Caerphilly was one of a cluster of urban districts which ventured to become bus operators in South Wales and Monmouthshire early in the 1900s.

Famous for its castle which occupies 30 acres and is the largest in Wales, the town is situated seven miles north of Cardiff, on the southern limit of the coal mining valleys. Until 1964 it possessed large railway locomotive and carriage work-shops.

Never a tram operator, the council obtained powers to operate buses in 1917 and participated in some joint routes, the longest being 30 miles from Cardiff to Tredegar.

Early vehicles were Tilling-Stevens, followed by Thornycroft, Dennis and Daimler, all saloons. Double-deckers were first acquired in 1943 in the shape of two Daimler utilities. Two Foden single-deckers arrived in 1947, followed by several double-decked Guy Arabs during 1948/9, after which Leylands predominated. Livery was green and cream.

In 1974 Caerphilly UD and Gelligaer UD, both in Glamorganshire, merged with Bedwas & Machen UD in Monmouthshire to form Rhymney Valley District Council in the new county of Mid-Glamorgan. The three bus fleets were rapidly repainted into brown, cream & yellow, the livery adopted by the new Transport Department. The council's full name appeared on the near-side of buses and the Welsh version, 'Cyngor Ardal Cwm Rhymni', on the offside.

Following deregulation in 1986 the name of the undertaking became Inter Valley Link Ltd. Livery was unchanged on full-size buses but MCW Metrorider minis acquired in 1988 appeared in two greens using 'Inter Valley Classic' branding.

Competition became fierce and Inter Valley succumbed. It was bought in February 1989 by National Welsh, itself to become insolvent before long. Most of the ex-Inter Valley buses were quickly disposed of.

On 1 April 1996 Caerphilly and the surrounding area became a unitary authority with the name Caerphilly County Borough.

This short-lived municipal/state undertaking was formed with ex-Halifax JOC and ex-Todmorden JOC vehicles and existed from 2 August 1971 to 31 March 1974, thus coming within the scope of this book.

It was managed by Halifax Corporation on behalf of Halifax, Todmorden and National Bus Company interests, and took its name from the valley of the River Calder in which both the towns lie and which permits the passage of the only low-level road through the Pennines.

When in 1969 the NBC was formed by merging the state-owned Transport Holding Company with British Electric Traction (a large bus-operating combine despite its name), British Railways' representation on

Halifax, Huddersfield, Sheffield and Todmorden Joint Omnibus Committees passed to Amalgamated Passenger Transport Ltd, a non-operating NBC holding company.

Huddersfield Corporation took over the JOC interests in its own area at the end of 1969 and Sheffield JOC was wound up at the start of 1970 with the NBC retaining some vehicles.

Halifax and Todmorden JOCs combined in 1971 as Calderdale JOC. The Todmorden operation had been wholly joint and was completely absorbed. Halifax Corporation continued to run its purely municipal services with 85 vehicles while contributing 55 to the new JOC (which in practice had replaced the Halifax 'B' fleet).

Some of them had originated with Hebble Motor Services when NBC merged most of that subsidiary's operations with Halifax JOC in March 1971.

APT's interest in Calderdale JOC amounted to 68 vehicles, some of which carried its name as legal owner. Thus the CJOC fleet totalled 135 buses.

Presumably because it was realised that the enterprise would have a limited life, and many vehicles were already in Halifax colours, green, orange and white was adopted as livery, though without a coat of arms, and ex-Todmorden buses appeared in this as repainting became necessary. Insignia was not used.

On 1 April 1974 the municipal and NBC interests in Calderdale JOC became a part of West Yorkshire PTE, and APT became dormant until resuscitated as an NBC engineering subsidiary near Lincoln in 1981.

The name Calderdale was adopted for the metropolitan borough in West Yorkshire county, which from 1974 has covered Halifax, Todmorden and the surrounding area.

Above:
Pictured in Todmorden town centre on 30 June 1973 with the recently-cleaned Town Hall as background is Calderdale No 304 (RCP 334K), a Northern Counties-bodied 74-seat Daimler CRG6LX Fleetline built in 1972. It was, therefore, never a Halifax vehicle despite the livery.

Right:
Five weeks after Calderdale JOC was formed, its No 326 (NWW 90E) turns into the bus station adjacent to the railway arch in Todmorden town centre. The date is 11 September 1971, the vehicle is a Willowbrook-bodied B43F dp Leyland Leopard new to Todmorden JOC, as No 1 in 1967 while the livery is a late development in the local scene. Todmorden arms are still carried, but the legal lettering is that of Amalgamated Passenger Transport, the NBC part of the new Joint Omnibus Committee.

Cardiff Corporation Transport Department

The capital of Wales and its largest city Cardiff has fine civic, government and educational buildings in Cathays Park. Wide roads and few gradients made it a good place for tramway operation, although some low railway bridges necessitated unusually small diameter wheels on double-deck cars to reduce overall height. The port area was very busy and handled much coal until exports virtually ceased a generation ago but the docks are now undergoing massive redevelopment to other uses as part of the Cardiff Bay Scheme.

Horse-drawn cars of the Cardiff Tramways Co started running in 1872 and Cardiff District & Penarth Harbour Tramway Co opened services in 1881. The former was part of the Provincial group and used different liveries to denote routes. The latter never actually managed to reach the second town in its title and was in fact operated by Solomon Andrews until 1887 when the Cardiff Tramways Co acquired an interest.

Cardiff Corporation took over the Cardiff Tramways Co in 1902 and ran the horse cars for a short time until electrification proceeded. Cardiff District was absorbed in 1903.

The electric trams, double- and single-deck, were gradually replaced by trolley-buses, starting in 1942. Standard livery for all modes was crimson and cream, though some vehicles ran in overall grey between 1943 and 1946 because wartime supply of pigments tended to be difficult.

The last tram ran in 1950, followed only 20 years later by the last trolleybus. Motorbuses of several makes, initially Tilling-Stevens, had been operated by the department from 1920, and by 1928 it possessed the largest municipal fleet of the petrol-engined vehicles. Only AECs and Leylands were bought in the 1930s, the former becoming fleet standard. The war years brought diversity with utility Bristols, Guys and a couple of Bedford OWBs.

Prewar, many bus bodies were purchased from Northern Counties of Wigan, a company which had its head office in Cardiff. In the late 1940s and 1950s body purchases tended to favour local factories, of which there were several.

Chassis purchases at that time included AECs, Daimlers, Crossleys and Guys.

The crimson and cream livery together with the 'City of Cardiff Transport' title was in use until the early 1970s, when orange and cream replaced it. Later, some brown

Above:
The City of Cardiff ran double- and single-decker trolleybuses, one of the former being photographed on 2 September 1962 at a terminus near the centre. It is No 277 (KBO 950), a BUT 9641T built in 1955, fitted with GEC equipment and carrying an East Lancs H49/32D body. Although not used as an exit as intended, after 1950 many Cardiff trolleybuses were equipped with a narrow sliding door at the front. This permitted Pay As You Enter to operate, with the conductor seated in the rear entrance.

Below left:
Coat of arms photo date: 30 May 1970.

was added on saloons. The title became more simply 'Dinas Caerdydd' on one side of buses and the English version, 'City of Cardiff', on the other.

As a limited company since 1986, but still local authority, owned (in 1997), the current title of the operator is Cardiff City Transport Services.

As a point of interest, from 1943 to 1950 Cardiff operated a 'non-ticket' fare collection system, very unusual for a large operator at the time. Fixed glass-fronted boxes were used to display and collect coins.

As a county borough in Glamorganshire prior to 1974, the city issued the registration marks BO, UH, KG and their serials. Between 1974 and 1996 it was a district with the title of City and was in South Glamorgan. When that county was abolished on 1 April 1996 Cardiff became a unitary authority, one of the new-style county boroughs.

Chester Corporation Transport

Now the best-preserved walled city in England, Chester was once a Roman military settlement named Deva, established to protect fertile land to the east from the native British inhabitants of what is now Wales. The remains of several Roman structures can still be visited. The Rows, double-decked shops in the medieval centre, are famous.

Narrow streets are never conducive to bus operation and in recent years, with a spreading one-way and pedestrianised layout, Chester Council have made life difficult for all operators. Much extra mileage has been generated, resulting in extended journey times.

A private horse bus connected the railway station and city centre in the 1860s and public buses started running in 1870. From 1879 to 1902 the Chester Tramways Co ran crimson and cream 4ft 8½in gauge trams on several routes, one of which, to Saltney, terminated literally yards from the Welsh border yet was only just over a mile from Chester Town Hall. During 1886 experiments were made with a tram powered by compressed air but due to inadequate pressure retention were not pursued.

Chester Corporation bought the system in 1902, electrified and regauged it to 3ft 6in and resumed services in 1903 using 12 open-top trams (later 18) in pale green and cream livery.

Buses took over when the tramway closed in 1930 and ran beyond some former termini, including a short distance into North Wales. Initially there were 10 single- and 10 double-deck AECs in green and cream. Subsequent purchases were from Bedford, Leyland, and more from AEC in prewar years, and Leyland, Guy and Daimler during and immediately after the war. Between 1948 and 1951, 10 Foden double-deckers were acquired.

Crosville, based in the town, was always a threat and when the company's Tilling group owners decided in 1944 that livery should change from maroon and cream to green and cream, Chester Corporation was not pleased, fearing passenger confusion. Before long Chester changed the opposite way, influenced, it is said, by a maroon and cream Foden demonstrator.

In 1950 two of the three cream bands were painted maroon on the few buses remaining in green livery. Maroon and cream are still the basic corporate colours in 1997.

The city's buses were originally lettered 'Chester Corporation', modified in 1957 to 'City of Chester', though 'Chester City' was tried briefly in 1974. Following the creation of Chester City Transport Ltd in 1986, a simple 'Chester' sufficed as fleetname but in 1996, to retain passenger loyalty in the face of more competition, 'City of Chester' accompanied by the arms reappeared.

All-cream livery was used on open-top buses until, in 1994, joint operation of city tours with Guide Friday necessitated a dark green skirt.

Chester's status as a county borough ceased in 1974 when, after its territory was increased by absorption of two neighbouring rural districts, it became a district with the title of city. Prior to the change, its vehicle registration marks had been FM and xFM. Both city and Crosville buses were thus registered and FM is still used by Chester VRO, one of seven marks allotted to the office. In mid-1997 the Chester undertaking remained in council ownership.

Left:
Although the River Dee separates Wales from England for part of its course, in Chester both banks are firmly English. The photograph, taken on 17 February 1968, shows No 3 (RFM 643), a 1953 Guy Arab IV with Massey H30/26R body, passing over the Dee on signal-controlled Handbridge. Also shown is Bridgegate which links sections of the heavily-rebuilt Roman city walls. Chester went through a long Guy Arab phase from 1953 to 1969, buying 47, mostly Massey-bodied, in 11 batches. The first 23 buses were rear- and the others front-entrance. Fleetlines were the double-deck favourite for the following decade.

Above:
With the coat of arms is shown a non-standard arrangement of the fleetname. This was seen on 9 February 1974. The usual wording was 'City of Chester', not 'Chester City'.

Chesterfield Corporation Transport Department

Situated in northeast Derbyshire, the Borough of Chesterfield is more famous for the twisted spire on its parish church than its close proximity to some of the most glorious parts of the Peak District National Park. The eastern suburbs are located above a major coalfield but mining is now much reduced.

A horse tramway operated from 1882 by Chesterfield & District Tramways Co met with financial problems and was taken over by Chesterfield Tramways Co in 1885. The Corporation purchased the single route in 1897 and continued to use horse cars until electrification in 1904. The initial electric fleet was 12 open-top cars (later 14) and that expanded to 17 in 1914 when three balcony cars were bought. Dark blue and cream livery was used by all three horse tram operators but electrification was marked by a change to maroon and primrose.

Top:
This view illustrates how Chesterfield's insignia and fleetname was displayed until the 1970s. The bus, No 222 (222 GRA) new in 1958, was a Leyland Titan PD2/20 with Weymann H59R body. It is standing at one of several town centre street termini on 5 May 1963. Chesterfield used livery lining-out to good effect long after many other operators discontinued it either for economy or because they considered it gave a dated image. This subtle device can still enhance a plain appearance when applied with sensitivity.

Above:
Coat of arms photo date: 1978.

Six single-deck motorbuses were bought in 1914 and services were developed until, in 1923, a joint route to Sheffield commenced. The tramway closed in 1927 and was converted to operation by single-deck trolleybuses, but they lasted only until 1938 when additional buses took over. After World War 2, Crossley, Leyland, Daimler and Guy chassis were ordered to accelerate fleet renewal.

Local government changes in 1974 had little effect, the town becoming a district but retaining its borough title. The undertaking became Chesterfield Transport Department and the green and cream livery was lightened by using less green.

A more dramatic change came after deregulation in 1986 when the council-owned company Chesterfield Transport Ltd adopted blue, yellow and white. This was also used by newly-formed subsidiary Retford & District but coaches were painted a more unobtrusive blue and ivory. Following a management buyout in 1990 the company was purchased by Stagecoach Holdings in 1995. East Midland Motor Services Ltd, also a Stagecoach subsidiary, has its headquarters in the town so a legal merger seems inevitable, and indeed in 1996 Chesterfield buses were appearing in Stagecoach stripes with the East Midlands name.

Colchester Corporation Transport Department

Colchester is the oldest recorded town in England and was the pre-Roman capital of the southeast. In AD50 the first Roman colony in Britain was established there. Later developed by Saxon, Norman and Flemish settlers, its early prosperity based on clothmaking has been replaced by employment based on engineering.

Second smallest of the five East Anglian municipal operators, Colchester was unusual because the opening of the electric Corporation Tramways in 1904 was not preceded by non-electric operations, although a scheme for steam trams existed and a short length of track was laid in 1883.

Sixteen open-top cars opened the system, supplemented by two more in 1906. These ran successfully for a quarter of a century but as in so many other towns no real financial provision was made for replacing worn-out assets and closure came in 1929.

The first Colchester buses, Dennis 'E' saloons, were purchased in 1928 to replace the trams and they carried on the maroon and cream livery.

Despite the area having many independent operators, the Corporation built up a network of bus routes before the war and these were served afterwards by a mixed fleet of AEC, Bristol, Crossley, Daimler and Guy chassis. Later, Leyland was well represented in the fleet, many with Massey half-cab rear-entrance bodies. In the 1970s Leyland Atlanteans were purchased and supplemented by Bristol REs and several ex-Salford/Selnec AEC Reliances only eight years old.

Although consistently maroon and cream over the decades, by the 1960s more cream became standard until, after several proportional changes, only a maroon skirt survived on saloons. The illustration shows the layout in use in the mid-1960s.

The Department was little affected by local government changes in 1974 but did change its title to Colchester Borough Council Transport Department. In 1986, as a result of central government legislation, it became Colchester Borough Transport Ltd and was bought by the British Bus group in 1993. This in turn was acquired by the Cowie Group in mid-1996.

In the years following deregulation in 1986 a coaching unit was established. This traded as CBT Coachways using single- and double-deck vehicles and made a striking contrast to normally-attired buses by employing shades of blue on a cream base.

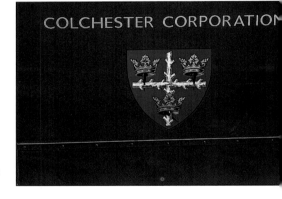

Top:
Attractive houses in Queen Street provide a background to the entrance to Colchester bus station. Seen here entering is No 30 (MWC 130) a 1963 Leyland Titan PD2A/31 with H33/28R body. Massey shape and 'St Helens' front blend nicely. Around 29 May 1967 when this view was taken, two livery developments were current. One replaced the mid-decks red with cream and the cream upper window pillars with red. The other used cream on the roof and mid-decks while the band below the upper windows became red and the title appeared on the cream waist band. The latter version became standard for a few years.

Above:
Coat of arms photo date: 8 April 1972.

Colwyn Bay Borough Council

This pleasant resort was in the north Welsh county of Denbighshire until 1974, then part of Clwyd, and on 1 April 1996 emerged from the latest local government changes as part of the unitary authority Aberconwy & Colwyn County Council which very soon elected to be known as the County Borough of Conwy.

Bus ownership started when the first of several Guy toastracks was supplied to Colwyn Bay & Colwyn Urban District Council shortly before it became Colwyn Bay UDC on 1 April 1926. The authority that year obtained powers to run a bus service, concentrating on a seasonal promenade route between Old Colwyn and Rhos-on-Sea. In later years Colwyn Bay Zoo, situated in the hills behind the town, was also served.

On 1 April 1934 the town became a borough and the buses were soon lettered 'Colwyn Bay Corporation', eventually also bearing a crest. In 1973 at least one displayed 'Borough of Colwyn Bay' and this is illustrated.

During 60 years of existence some 22 buses (or ex-coaches) were owned, none seating more than 29. No more than seven were owned at any one time.

The prewar all-Guy fleet was joined by two more in 1948, followed by three Bedfords in 1954 and two in 1960. Then followed two second-hand Bedford coaches in 1968, a hired Bedford and a Guy in 1969, a Bedford in 1973 and finally a Ford in each of 1976 and 1980.

The tiny fleet did not require a formal transport department, services being run by a traffic manager attached to the Borough Entertainments Dept.

Original bus livery is believed to have been red and cream but by 1949 was green with cream upperworks. This was reversed to mainly cream with green window surrounds in 1967. One of the 20-seat coaches arrived in blue-green and cream, the other being two shades of light green.

The 1976 Ford 'A' carried maroon and cream while the final acquisition was red and cream.

In 1974 the council, which became a district, took the title Colwyn Borough. Bus operation ceased in September 1986 shortly before deregulation but by a curious twist of fate the town regained a tiny involvement in local transport when neighbouring Aberconwy's seasonal operation passed to Conwy County Borough in 1996.

Above:
A minnow alongside Crosville, the local major operator, Colwyn Bay's fleet was five strong when this photograph was taken on 2 August 1961. It consisted of Nos 1-3 (KUN 399-401) petrol-engined Bedford OLAZs with Spurling B21F bodies and Nos 4/5 (WCA 186/729), also Bedford Spurling but with less smooth (not to say ugly) radiators. The former served from 1954 to 1968, the latter from 1960 to 1973/1. No 1 stands at the Pier entrance, midway on the promenade route, and carries, as they all did, roof brackets for advertising boards. The boards rarely appear on photographs after 1960.

Below:
In the 1970s more cream was used in the livery as shown on the coat of arms photograph, taken 7 October 1973.

Coventry Corporation Transport

The name Coventry brings to mind cathedrals, the Blitz, motor car factories, Daimler buses and the Lady Godiva legend, but not necessarily in that order.

Now one of the great cities of the English Midlands, its early prosperity was based on wool. The city became one of the four most important provincial centres in the country but wool gave way to clock-making and silk weaving until, after those skills were undermined by imports, engineering came to predominate.

A steam tramway was laid by the Coventry & District Tramways Co in 1883 but not worked until the following year. Poor profitability brought services to an end after a few years, with complete withdrawal in 1893. A town of such size was seriously inconvenienced by the absence of a public transport system and it was not long before Coventry Electric Tramways Co took over the tracks, electrified and reopened in 1895. This company was one of the earliest in the electric tramway field and its operations continued until 1912 when the Corporation purchased it.

Bus ownership was not far behind, seven double-deck Maudslays, made in the city, being bought in 1914. By 1921 tramway rolling stock had reached a maximum of 58 cars. The first route closures came in 1931.

Heavy German bombing of Coventry in November 1940 caused extensive structural damage to the tramways and rolling stock. Operating services became impossible and abandonment resulted in replacement buses being borrowed from other operators, including Manchester, London and Great Yarmouth.

Daimler buses first purchased in 1933 had been found to be very satisfactory and repeat orders, particularly after the war, gave the local product overwhelming superiority in numbers, amounting to 96% of the fleet by 1962. Metro-Cammell, another Midlands manufacturer, supplied 94% of the bus bodies.

Although maroon and cream was Coventry livery from 1933, it replaced something similar (lake) in use from 1912. That itself had superseded a somewhat darker colour (chocolate) used by the Electric Tramways Co. Acquisition of rear-engined double-deckers in the mid-1960s prompted a change to a modified layout of cream with maroon bands. The small number of coaches owned carried light blue and cream.

A change to cherry red (or crimson) and cream came along in the early 1970s but never covered the entire fleet because formation of West Midlands County on 1 April 1974 involved the merger of Coventry Transport with the five-year-old West Midlands PTE fleet. This became West Midlands Travel Ltd in 1986, was sold to its employees in 1991 and merged with National Express in 1995.

Coventry County Borough motor vehicle licensing office had used the marks DU, HP, RW, WK, VC, KV and their serial prefixes. In 1974 Coventry became a metropolitan borough using the title of city. Registrations became the responsibility of newly-established LVLOs in October, so only six months elapsed before those marks, plus AC from Warwickshire, passed to the local office.

Below:
This standard design of Metro-Cammell body was widely purchased around the country both pre- and postwar and Coventry had many. Depicted on 18 June 1960 is No 72 (GKV 72), a Daimler CVA6 built in 1949 which carried 60 seats. Deliveries in 1952 retained the same body shape but sported a Birmingham-style 'tin' front. Subsequent Metro-Cammells acquired were to the Orion design.

Above left:
By 1965 rear-engined buses were appearing in an equally attractive livery based on more cream, the coat of arms and fleetname both displayed on the lighter colour, as seen here on 15 October 1972.

Darlington Corporation Transport Department

Although associated in most minds with the world's first real railway opened in 1825, and by transport people with one of the 'bus wars' of the 1990s, Darlington is also an ancient Co Durham market town, and was until relatively recently active in building railway locomotives. It is also well known as the headquarters of United Automobile Services, once a far-flung empire but now much circumscribed. The vehicles of that company, and of Darlington Corporation, were registered with the HN and xHN marks issued by the county borough.

George F. Train's Darlington Street Railway Co, a horse tramway, ran in the town from 1862 to 1865. In 1880 Stockton & Darlington Steam Tramways Co opened a horse-drawn line in the town but never actually got around to steam operation as used in Stockton. Livery was chocolate and white.

Part of the single line closed in 1885 and the remainder passed to the Stockton & District Tramways Co, who sold it to Imperial Tramways Co in 1896. The intention was to electrify but that did not happen until the line was again sold, in 1902, to

Darlington Corporation, who operated it under the title Light Railways Department.

Dark blue and cream livery adorned the fleet which grew to 24 tramcars until they were replaced by 24 single-deck trolley-buses in 1926. These and subsequent purchases flourished until 1950 when the Corporation bought its first motorbuses. In 1961 every bus was a Guy, 38 being double-deckers and 25 saloons. Only in 1949 were double-deck trolleybuses acquired but all six were sold to Doncaster in 1952. Replacement of trolley routes had started in 1951 and was completed in 1957. Six MoS BUTs were sold to Doncaster, one to Bradford. In later years more cream and less blue became the normal livery on buses, especially double-deckers.

County borough status changed to district (with borough title) when local government was reorganised in 1974 and the undertaking became Darlington (Borough of) Transport Department. However, noticeable change came only in 1986 when the undertaking became Darlington Transport Co with a fleet strength around 60. Six were unusual 1983 Ward Dalesman saloons.

Service deregulation also came into effect that year and local competition grew until in 1994, it culminated in the municipal company going into administrative receivership. Services were taken over by Stagecoach Holdings.

The borough became a unitary authority in 1 April 1997.

Above:
Coat of arms photo date: 3 April 1971.

Below:
Until Darlington decided in the late 1970s to standardise on an all-saloon fleet, Roe was the usual builder of its double-deck bodies, and Guy supplied most of the chassis until Daimlers arrived in 1964. In the 1950s livery had been blue with cream bands beneath windows, but by 1 April 1967 when No 60 (16 CHN) was photographed, a predominantly cream layout was standard. The Guy Arab IV built in 1956 carries a rear-entrance 61-seat Roe body and awaits departure time at a town centre stand.

Darwen Corporation Transport Department

One of the smaller Lancashire undertakings, Darwen's trams and buses served a populous valley five miles south of Blackburn. To the south is Bolton but moorland inhibited a tramway link. Originally associated with textiles, the town is now better known for the manufacture of paints and wallpapers.

Prior to 1946 a 4ft gauge tram route connecting the towns was operated jointly with Blackburn. This was constructed in 1881 by the Blackburn & Over Darwen Tramways Co, the first in Britain to be authorised for, and operated solely by, steam traction. Car livery was red and cream. In 1899 the corporations of Darwen and Blackburn jointly bought the company.

Darwen took 10 engines and 10 trailer cars as its share but municipal operation was brief because electrification was completed in 1900. This permitted the use of 10 new open-top tramcars, resplendent in bright red and purple. Later, cream replaced purple. Over the years 34 trams were owned, the most modern being two all-enclosed, streamlined double-deckers

bought in 1936. These had similarities to the Blackpool cars of that era. The system closed in 1946, its life having been prolonged by the war, and the streamliners were sold to the Llandudno & Colwyn Bay Electric Railway, where they served until 1956.

Darwen buses appeared first in 1926 in the shape of four Leyland single-deckers but the fleet was small until 10 tram-replacing Leyland Titans were purchased in 1940. Subsequently more Leylands, some Crossleys and AECs with Crossley badges were acquired. Also operated in the 1960s were two second-hand coaches, a Leyland Royal Tiger and an AEC Reliance.

Bus livery continued to be bright red and cream until local government reorgani-

sation in 1974 resulted in Darwen becoming a part of an enlarged Blackburn District (borough). Darwen's bus fleet of 33 (of which 10 were saloons) merged with Blackburn's to form a new Blackburn Borough Transport undertaking using livery of green, white and red, the latter colour honouring Darwen.

Since 1986 it has been Blackburn Borough Transport Ltd and the red element is no longer used. In mid-1997 the company was still municipally-owned.

The town's name should be somewhat better known after 1 April 1998 when a unitary authority, Blackburn with Darwen borough, will be established.

Darwen's buses were registered with Lancashire County Council marks.

Above:
Like most smaller fleets with little of the financial leverage of large orders, Darwen was content to buy standard products. All-Leyland No 13 (RTJ 610) ran alongside similar chassis buses carrying Leyland look-alike bodies from Alexander, a few from Crossley, several from East Lancs and other Leylands. It is a Titan PD2/10 built in 1954, carries 56 seats and was photographed on 24 April 1960. The omission of lining-out where an advertisement is usually placed rather spoils the overall effect. Numbers were considered to be unnecessary for the limited route system operated.

Left:
Coat of arms photo date: 1963.

Derby Corporation Omnibus Department

The history of Derby, situated in the North Midlands of England, starts with the Romans. Later, the Normans made it into a market town and manufacture of cloth, beer, soap and silk followed. In 1745 Bonnie Prince Charlie's army of Highlanders reached this far south on their march to London, before having second thoughts and returning to Scotland.

Noted for porcelain in the 18th century and railway workshops in the 19th, Derby is now associated with Rolls-Royce and railway research in the 20th century. It became a city in 1977.

Public transport was provided by the Derby Tramways Co with horse trams and buses from 1880 to 1899, when the Corporation bought the system. While preparing for electrification, horse tram operation continued but 25 electric cars entered service in 1904. Gradually they took over and the last horse tram ran in 1907, although it was another 10 years before horse buses vanished. A battery bus experiment started in 1917 and finished in 1924. The first Derby Corporation motorbus was delivered the same year.

Tramway replacement commenced when trolleybuses arrived in 1932, the change being completed in 1934. In 1961 the all-double-deck fleet consisted of 99 buses and 73 trolleybuses. By 1967 the latter were gone.

Company and Corporation horse trams were painted various shades of red and white but the electric cars carried green and cream and this was also used on trol-leybuses and buses until the late 1960s. A change to blue with contrasting light grey between decks marked the introduction of rear-engined buses and eventually covered the entire bus fleet.

Local government changes in 1974 saw Derby lose county borough status, resulting in a title change to Derby Borough (later City) Transport.

In 1986 the undertaking became Derby City Transport Ltd. The local independent Blue Bus Services was purchased and operated as a subsidiary. The company passed out of municipal control in 1994 when purchased by British Bus but that group was itself taken over by the Cowie organisation in 1996.

Until 1974 Derby Council issued vehicle registrations based on the marks CH and RC. In that year the marks were reallocated to Nottingham LVLO.

On 1 April 1997 Derby became a unitary authority.

Above:
Derby No 233 (DRC 233) was one of a batch of 20 Sunbeam F4/BTH trolleybuses supplied in 1952/3. The final route extension coincided, but many were replacements for prewar Guy six-wheelers. They had Willowbrook H60R bodies and served until the system closed in 1967. Trolleybus route mileage exceeded 27 at one time. This photograph, dated 13 June 1965, shows the vehicle to be on route 60, the '6' denoting main service and the second numeral indicating a short working or variation.

Left:
Coat of arms photo date: 26 July 1981.

Doncaster Corporation Transport Department

Another railway town which originated as a Roman settlement is Doncaster. Before 1974 it was located in the West Riding of Yorkshire but is now part of South Yorkshire Metropolitan County. It is the centre of what remains of the British coal mining industry.

From 1887 until 1902 local transport was provided by a horse bus company. Corporation trams running on unusual centre-grooved rails (Hull was the only other electric operator to use them) commenced operations in 1902 and reached a maximum fleet strength of 47 in 1920.

In 1928 trolleybuses arrived and one tram route closed. The final closure, however, was not until 1935, replaced by motorbuses, the first of which started serving outlying areas in 1922.

The last trolleybuses bought were second-hand, from Darlington, Southend and Mexborough & Swinton. Many needed rebodying. Abandonment started in 1955 and was complete in 1963, when some of those bodies were only seven or eight years old. The Transport Department had them altered for use on bus chassis, a most unusual event.

Doncaster had a liking for three-axle

buses and all the early trolleys, together with several Leyland and AEC buses, were of that type. From around 1938, however, purchases were strictly orthodox. Manufacturers patronised were AEC, Daimler, Bristol, Guy and Leyland, although only the first two were in substantial numbers. Trolleybuses bought new were Karriers, while those second-hand were BUTs and Sunbeams.

From 1902 to the early 1960s Doncaster livery was maroon and cream, although in the 1940s a few saloons carried a pleasing lighter red band beneath the windows. In 1960 a lighter shade of red was tried (as illustrated) but by 1965 the favoured shade was almost scarlet.

Only two or three years prior to Doncaster CTD being absorbed into South Yorkshire PTE on 1 April 1974, a 'jazzy' livery of red with bands of mauve and white lines was adopted. The mauve ran under the lower windows to behind the door, where it rose vertically to continue horizontally around the front on both single- and double-deckers.

After formation, the PTE experimented with light coffee and cream, then mushroom and cream, before using brown and cream for some years, adding red in the early 1980s. The last combination was also used by South Yorkshire Transport Ltd, as the undertaking was known after 1986, but other liveries were used for minis, express buses, etc. Most of these colour developments were to be seen on the streets of Doncaster.

Later a geographic Mainline livery having yellow as the common colour was devised. The Doncaster version had grey and red areas. Finally, in 1992 when Mainline was adopted as the company's trading name, yellow, red, grey and blue came into use in all districts. November 1993 saw the undertaking sold by the PTA to its employees.

As a county borough until 1974, Doncaster issued vehicle registrations based on the mark DT. The town became a metropolitan borough and licensing activity, together with the mark, passed to Sheffield LVLO later that year.

Above:
Bought just before the 1948 cut-off date after which Bristol chassis were supplied only to nationalised undertakings, K6A No 99 (EDT 792) carries a Roe H56R body of a design very popular with West Yorkshire operators. Seen on 22 May 1960, it was one of a batch of four fitted with AEC 7.7-litre engines. The characteristic lateral strengthening used by Roe is clearly visible beneath the windows of both decks.

Left:
Coat of arms photo date: 21 July 1974.

Douglas Corporation Transport Department

This undertaking operates on the Isle of Man, which is roughly equidistant from England, Wales Scotland and Ireland. The island is an autonomous dependency of the British Crown (the Queen is Lord of Man), not part of the UK, and it has its own government (the parliament is called Tynwald) which has an unbroken link with Norse colonisers. It has its own laws and its motorists abroad use a separate International Identification Mark of 'GBM'. Island vehicles carry registrations MN, MAN, BMN, CMN etc. Since 1979 they have also included a prefix or suffix letter which is serial, not age-related. Since 1995 Manx plates can bear narrow characters with hyphens and show the Three Legs of Man symbol. The name of the island in any language in Celtic characters can appear above the registration. Manx trade plates take the form MN-A nnn.

Douglas is the only large town, is the national capital and, since 1896, is the equivalent of an English borough. The coat of arms, known formerly as the Corporate Common Seal, is now referred to as the 'Borough device'. The motto, in the Manx language, means 'a government within a government'.

A seasonal horse tramway on Douglas promenade is still Corporation-operated. It was started in 1876 by the Douglas Bay Tramway Co, using dark blue, cream and red livery. In 1894 the Isle of Man Tramway & Electric Power Co took over and in 1902 the service passed to the Corporation. The livery is now mostly red and cream, a few cars being blue and cream. Apart from a two-car line in South Australia, it is the last public service horse tramway in the world.

In 1896 the Upper Douglas Tramway opened, using cable-hauled cars to serve the upper town. This also came under Corporation control in 1902 but closed in 1929. Livery was teak or red and cream. One car, spliced from halves of Nos 72 and 73, is privately-owned and occasionally operates by battery power on the promenade track. It is purple and cream.

Another line, which ran from Douglas Head southward along the cliffs, was the Douglas Southern Electric Tramway Ltd. This opened in 1896 but closed in 1939 when World War 2 effectively removed tourists. The livery was crimson and white. From 1926 its owner was Douglas Head Marine Drive Co.

Other veteran tramways and railways operate on Man. The Manx Electric

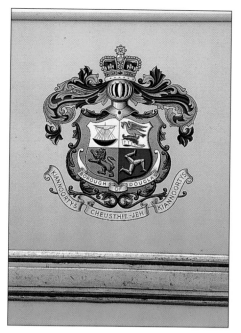

Railway, which originated as part of the IOMT&EPCo, runs to Ramsey in the north, and the steam-operated Isle of Man Railway reaches to Port Erin in the south.

The first Douglas Corporation motor buses, a Tilling-Stevens and a Straker-Squire, arrived in 1914 and many more of the former were bought until 1930. A Vulcan open-topper in 1926 was the only double-decker until six AEC Regents arrived in 1933/4. Vulcans, Leyland Cubs and more Regents followed. During the war Bedford OWBs and Daimler utilities arrived. Postwar purchases consisted of Regent III and V, Leyland Comet, Guy, Otter, AEC Reliance, Bedford VAS1 and YRQ, and Leyland Tiger

Cub models. Bus livery was primrose and red, sometimes incorporating black. This can still be seen as a 'heritage' livery on two buses of Isle of Man Transport, the state-run company which absorbed the Corporation's bus operations in 1976 and was at that time named Isle of Man National Transport. IOM Transport now also operates the MER and the IOMR and is administered by the island's Department of Tourism and Transport

Left:
Borough device photo date: 28 July 1972. Although formerly known as the Corporate Seal, the term was dropped after it was discovered that sanction by the British College of Heralds had never been obtained. It seems this came to light during a visit to the Isle of Man by the Queen.

Below:
Until recently it was thought that Douglas No 53 was built in 1946, but the year is now known to have been 1945. Externally it is typical of wartime body production when panel-beating skills were scarce so roof domes became angular. The buses were termed utilities. One of three Daimler CWA6s acquired in 1945, it has a Duple H30/26R body, seems to have survived until 15 May 1964 without serious external modification and in fact completed 25 years' service before withdrawal in 1970. It was not preserved but if it did have a subsequent life off the island its registration GMN 242 would have been replaced, as Manx marks are not valid for permanent residence in the UK. It is seen awaiting service in a yard which provided layover space near Douglas bus station. Choice of location for the park bench seems unfortunate for non-enthusiasts.

Dundee Corporation Transport Department

Several Scottish municipal undertakings fell by the wayside before World War 2 (see Appendix 2). Only four survived, of which Dundee and Aberdeen were roughly equal in size, each with around 240 buses in 1961. Edinburgh and Glasgow were considerably larger.

It was said that jute, jam and journalism (comics) brought wealth to the City of Dundee. They still do, but industry is more varied, even extending to a small oil refinery. Situated on the Firth of Tay on Scotland's east coast, local landmarks are the pre-Roman hill fort (now a memorial) on Dundee Law and the rail and road Tay Bridges.

Dundee & District Tramways Co started horse car services in 1877 on tracks owned by the corporation. Its cars had a natural mahogany finish. In 1885 steam trams were introduced, locos in red and trailers green and cream.

The company commenced electric tram operation in a small way in 1897, using dark red and cream livery. Dundee Municipality took over two years later, continuing horse and steam services until electrification was complete in 1902. The use of dark red and cream continued, surviving until replaced by green and cream in the 1920s. The latter was also used on buses.

There was a trolleybus experiment from 1912 to 1914, one of only two uses of these vehicles in Scotland (the other being Glasgow). However, buses were chosen to replace trams when the first routes were abandoned in the 1920s. They were also used in competition with the Dundee, Broughty Ferry & District Tramways Co (livery dark red and cream) which operated from 1905 and which was absorbed by the Corporation in 1931. All tram services ended in 1956.

Although prewar bus purchases varied from Thornycroft saloons in 1921 to AEC, Leyland and Thornycroft double-deckers in the early 1930s, in the three decades before 1964 only AECs and Daimlers were acquired. These included 30 ex-London Transport RTs as tram replacements.

Bus livery in the early 1960s incorporated thin red bands separating green and white but the first rear-engined buses were overall green and very drab. A later change to two greens looked better.

Scottish local government reorganisation on 16 May 1975 saw the counties of Angus (wherein lay Dundee), Kinross-shire and part of Perthshire combined as Tayside Region. This authority took over the

Above:
Dundee No 132 (BTS 472) was a Daimler CVD6 which carried a rare H30/26R body by Croft. One of a batch of 10 (124-134) built in 1951, they were the only bodies by that builder to be purchased by the Corporation. The photograph is dated 12 August 1962, a year or two before a darker livery appeared. The location is close to what was then the city bus station in Shore Terrace. Regrettably the neo-Norman arch, built in 1851 to commemorate a visit by Victoria and Albert, no longer stands. It made way for a Tay Bridge approach road.

Above left:
Coat of arms photo date: 3 September 1972. The arms are seen displayed on the darker two-greens livery by then in use.

Dundee buses, adopting an attractive livery of two blues and white. The undertaking became Tayside Public Transport Co in 1986 and was sold to its employees in the early 1990s. The name became Taybus Holdings and the livery of light blue and cream with dark blue skirt, adopted after 1986, changed to dark blue and cream in 1996. In January 1997 the employees sold Taybus to National Express.

On 1 April 1996, as a result of the Region being dissolved, Dundee became a city unitary authority, virtually a county council.

Before 1974, the burgh council issued the vehicle registration marks TS, YJ and their serials.

Eastbourne Corporation Transport Department

Most easterly of a chain of seven former municipal operators along England's south coast, Eastbourne lies in the county of East Sussex just down the road from Beachy Head. The history of the resort covers less than three centuries but it has a fine reputation for restful holidays and manages, along the front at least, to maintain a dignified charm. The very first continuous municipal bus service in Britain was operated by the Corporation between the town's railway station and the foot of Beachy Head. It began on 12 April 1903

Right:
Coat of arms photo date: 1 June 1972.

Below:
Few vehicles depicted in this book have two-letter registrations, but Eastbourne Corporation took delivery of buses with JK marks as late as 1948 (AHC was issued in 1949). No 20 (JK 9648) was an AEC Regent III 0961 new in 1947. Its classic Weymann four-bay HR body seated 56. The photograph date is 19 June in 1960, a year when open-top Leyland TD4s in white livery except for blue bonnets, and sporting names from *Alice in Wonderland*, ran sea-front services on fine days.

using Milnes-Daimlers (unregistered until it became legally necessary on 1 January 1904).

Never a tramway operator in the normal way, the town has a footnote in transport history for being host, in the 1950s and 1960s, to a 2ft gauge line with scaled-down cars owned by Modern Electric Tramways Ltd. It was in Princes Park and is now relocated to Seaton in Devon.

A network of company horse bus routes which existed in the 1890s was greatly curtailed after 1903, largely due to the corporation venture.

Eastbourne's bus-buying policy after 1912 favoured Leylands, always petrol-engined, but by 1946 there was no real choice of fuel for full-size double-deckers and diesel power arrived in the shape of Leylands, AECs and Crossleys. Wartime travel restrictions in that part of Britain reduced demand for public transport and made part of the fleet surplus. The author, who then worked in the Trafford Park Industrial Estate near Manchester, can well remember being greatly puzzled at regularly seeing dark blue and primrose Leyland double-deckers with the town name painted out. They operated on workers' services for Lancashire United

Transport around 1944/5. The mystery was compounded because LUT's address on the legal lettering on its own red buses showed its home town to be Atherton. This also happened to be the manager's name on the anonymous Eastbourne-loaned vehicles.

The prewar livery was introduced in 1931, modified with a slightly lighter shade of blue in 1946. Cream with blue bonnet and mudguards was used for open-toppers in the heyday 1950s. There was a general change to cream with one blue band from 1969 and this version lasted into the 1980s.

As elsewhere, Eastbourne was no longer a county borough after 1 April 1974 and the undertaking became Eastbourne Borough Council Transport Dept, the coat of arms being replaced by an 'EBC' logotype.

Eastbourne Buses Ltd became the title in 1986 and at the time of writing the company remains council-owned, one of only 17 survivors in the UK. It soon reintroduced a coat of arms, with the fleetname Eastbourne Buses, and extended blue to three areas in the double-deck livery.

Until 1974 Eastbourne issued the vehicle registration marks HC, JK and their serial prefixes. These marks then passed to Hastings LVLO.

Edinburgh Corporation Transport

Scotland is rightly proud of possessing one of the most attractive and impressive capital cities in the world. With an ancient volcanic peak barely a mile from the main thoroughfare of Princes Street and a castle on a crag commanding the Old Town, it hardly needs the elegance of the 'New Town' to make it the country's premier tourist area.

Edinburgh's transport history is quite complex, although the city did not legally become an operator until 1919.

Horse tram services were started by Edinburgh Street Tramways Co shortly after authorisation in 1871, using liveries such as dark red and cream and blue and cream. Tracks within the city were purchased by the Corporation in 1893 (followed by an isolated steam tram route in 1898) and leased to Edinburgh & District Tramways Co.

Also bought, in 1896, and leased to the E&D Co were the blue and cream cable-hauled cars of Edinburgh Northern Tramways Co which commenced operating in 1888. E&D also ran horse buses. It proceeded to convert all the acquired horse tram routes to cable although one entirely new line, in 1910, was built as overhead electric.

When the Edinburgh & District lease expired in 1919 the Corporation took over the system and proceeded to electrify it. Edinburgh Street Tramway tracks within the Burgh of Leith had been bought by that Corporation in 1894, operated by them in 1904, and electrified (with cars in maroon

and white livery) in 1905. Leith was absorbed by Edinburgh in 1920 and the tramways amalgamated.

Musselburgh & District Electric Light & Traction Co ran electric cars in red and cream livery (two greens from 1923) as an easterly extension of the city system. Services started in 1904 were operated by Edinburgh CT from 1928 and bought by the city in 1932.

The final fleet total of the Edinburgh system was 360 electric trams, some built as late as 1950. Policy change brought closure in 1956.

Company-owned motorbuses were first licensed to run in Edinburgh in 1898 and were operated on behalf of the Corporation by Edinburgh & District commencing in 1914. From 1922 the city ran its own vehicles, of several makes. Experience with wartime Daimlers and Guys encouraged repeat orders but Leylands replaced the trams.

For many years a sizeable fleet of coaches in black and white livery, some double-decked, ran city tours. Main fleet livery has been madder (dark red) and white from the days of the E&D cable cars in 1896 (although that company also used blue and cream and white and cream for horse cars).

In 1975 the City of Edinburgh was merged with East, West and most of Midlothian counties to form Lothian Region and that council, operating as Lothian Region Transport, took over the Edinburgh undertaking.

Between 1975 and 1986 buses displayed a Lothian coat of arms, somewhat different to the city one illustrated, and 'Lothian' as fleetname.

In 1986 the operator became Lothian Region Transport PLC, still using madder and white but with an 'LRT' logotype. The coach fleet, some now open-topped, wears a livery based on cream and blue. Town tours are operated as far away as Oxford.

On 1 April 1996 Lothian region was abolished in favour of unitary authorities and the undertaking became 91% owned by Edinburgh City Council with East, West and Midlothian Councils inheriting 3.1%, 0.4% and 5.5% respectively. Control will be through a joint transport committee.

As a licensing authority until 1974 the city issued registration marks S, SG, SF, SC, FS and WS (and serial prefixes). The last was originally the mark for Leith.

Below:
The City of Edinburgh took, and its successors still take, good care to see that buses are invariably immaculate. No 667 (ASC 667B) was nearly new, however, when photographed on Princes Street on 3 September 1964, so a shine was to be expected. It is a Leyland Titan PD3/6 with Alexander H41/29F body, the standard for Edinburgh purchases at that time. Behind is one of the Orion-bodied PD2/20s bought as tram replacements, and across the road an SMT coach proceeds to the city's St Andrew Square bus station.

Above left:
Coat of arms photo date: 11 August 1973.

Above:
There are usually exceptions to a rule and for this book Exeter No 66 (EFJ 666) is one of two preserved vehicles portrayed (the other is a Bradford tram). New in 1938, withdrawn from PSV duties in 1952 but retained by the corporation as a snow-ploughing vehicle until December 1956, it was purchased the following month by Colin Shears for the West of England Transport Collection at Winkleigh, Devon. It is seen here near Clapham Common on the HCVC London-Brighton Run of May 1965. Over 30 years later it served on a park & ride service at the Leyland Centenary Rally, June 1996, and had then been preserved for over twice as long as it had been a PSV. A Leyland Tiger TS8 with Craven B32R open-platform body, it was one of six (Nos 65-70) designed for short central Exeter routes.

Above left: Coat of arms photo date: 9 August 1970.

Exeter Corporation Transport

This city, the last place in England to submit to William of Normandy, developed from a Roman fort and eventually became the county town of Devon. Although several miles from the south coast, medieval prosperity was partly due to shipping having access to Exeter along the River Exe and later a canal. In the heyday of bus services it was noted for possibly the longest municipal route, 46 miles to Plymouth.

The year 1882 saw the opening of the first of three horse tram routes run by the Exeter Tramway Co, using cars in chocolate & yellow livery. The Corporation took over in 1904, electrified in 1905 and operated 33 green and cream 4-wheel double-deck trams until 1931. The closure followed an abrupt change in policy, as four new cars were bought as late as 1929.

The first buses, seven saloons, also arrived in 1929 and an expanded fleet of them later replaced the trams. By 1960 the fleet numbered 67, of Leyland, Guy and Daimler manufacture. Six were saloons, the others half-cab rear-loading double-deckers.

On 1 April 1970 the county borough's undertaking was sold to the National Bus Company and absorbed into local subsidiary Devon General (itself to become part of Western National before long). There then followed a period when ex-Exeter buses still received green and cream livery but carried only 'Exeter' as title, rather than 'City of Exeter' or 'Exeter Corporation'.

Repainting into Devon General livery was in progress by the time NBC corporate poppy red and white came on the scene in 1972. Devon General's fleetname and the 'Double N' logo was also applied to buses still in Exeter colours and these could be seen until 1977 at least.

Exeter was the location for NBC's 1984 experiment using frequent minibuses and its success was copied in many towns and cities. Operations in the city were sold to Devon General's managers in 1986. Several minibus fleets were developed, each with its own livery. Later, Transit Holdings was formed. In 1996 Stagecoach Holdings bought the company.

In 1974 Exeter lost county borough status and became a district with the title of city. It had already lost its vehicle licensing office (marks were FJ and xFJ) in 1972 when a joint facility with Devon County Council was established. The marks passed to Exeter LVLO on 1 October 1974.

Gelligaer Urban District Council Omnibus Department

Several small communities in South Wales ran their own public transport, as a statement of the co-operative outlook of the ratepayers as much as civic pride. One such was Gelligaer (once spelled Gellygaer), an urban district in Glamorganshire until 1974, then in Mid Glamorgan.

Neither trams nor trolleybuses were used and the first buses (hired initially) did not appear until 1928. Prewar purchases were quite adventurous for such a small undertaking, with AEC 'Q' and six-wheeled Renown single-deckers being operated. The first double-decker, a utility Daimler, arrived in 1944. Other wartime acquisitions were eight Bedford OWB 'minis' which were useful in coping with frequent peak demands caused by shift change-overs at local pits.

Livery was unusual, consisting of red, grey and dark green, great care being taken to present a clean and smart image. During the 1970s coaches were painted in a special livery of cream and aquamarine. Fleet size rose to around 30 in halcyon postwar days, normally 5 to 1 in favour of saloons. Chassis choice was AEC and Leyland but body makes were more varied.

Local government reorganisation in 1974 merged Gelligaer with neighbouring UDC operators Caerphilly and Bedwas & Machen. The combined brown, yellow and cream fleet bore the bilingual title Rhymney

Valley District Council on one side and Cyngor Ardal Cwm Rhymni on the other.

The fleetname 'Inter Valley Link' ('Cadwyn y Cymoedd') came into use shortly before the transport department (together with all others, as a result of legislation) became an 'arm's length' municipal organisation, Inter Valley Link Ltd, late in 1986. RVDC livery was retained for big buses but new minis were painted in two shades of green.

The company suffered from grave competition as a result of service deregulation and was bought by National Welsh Ltd in 1989. Its purchaser fell victim to the same market forces, becoming insolvent in 1992.

Cynon Valley District became part of the unitary authority of Caerphilly County Borough on 1 April 1996.

Above:
One of the smaller municipal fleets – usually around 30 buses – Gelligaer's was among the smartest when No 17 (KNY 454) was seen on 5 September 1959. The AEC Regal III, one of a batch of four purchased in 1950, was fitted with a Duple B35F body no larger than a modern midibus but the styling caused one to think of it as a 'big bus'. It stands on an inspection ramp outside the depot at Hengoed, and could well be freshly out of the paint shop.

Below:
Badge photo date: 31 May 1970. In the 1970s livery variants appeared in the Gelligaer fleet when larger areas of cream replaced grey. No 35, which provided the photograph, was at that time in a special scheme, mostly white, to mark a visit by the Prince of Wales.

Glasgow Corporation Transport

Scotland's largest city, founded in AD543 by St Mungo, was made a Royal Burgh in 1454 and became prosperous, firstly because of its position as a port on the western seaboard which facilitated trade with the Americas and secondly because trade required ships which the Clydeside yards provided.

Uniquely in the UK, Glasgow municipality has operated horse and electric trams, buses, trolleybuses and underground trains. The history starts in 1872 when the Glasgow Tramways & Omnibus Co, using a livery of Menzies tartan and cream, introduced a horse tram service on corporation-owned track. In 1875 a route-colour band was added. The city took over operations in 1894 changing the livery to dark red and cream (also with a route colour). Electrification commenced in 1898.

The Vale of Clyde Tramways Co operated steam trams in brown and cream from 1878 to 1893 and the associated Glasgow & Ibrox Tramway Co ran horse cars from 1879 to 1891 in blue and cream. Both were taken over by Govan Corporation, electrified, leased to Glasgow and finally absorbed into Glasgow CT when the city boundaries were extended in 1912. Glasgow also leased and operated the lines of several neighbouring districts prior to the boundary adjustments which brought full ownership.

When electric operation of the ex-GT&O lines started in 1898 it was accompanied by a livery change to orange, cream and a route colour, the latter made necessary, it is said, by illiteracy (and perhaps the cost of spectacles?). The cable-hauled Glasgow & District Subway opened in 1896. The Corporation bought this underground railway with its single circular route in 1923 but electrification was not achieved until 1935.

Motorbus operation started in 1924 using solid-tyred saloons of seven makes. The first double-deckers, open-staired Leyland Titan TD1s, came in 1928, and the first with diesel engines, Albion Venturers, in 1935. Wartime purchases were Guy, AEC and Daimler, the last two sharing orders in the first decade of peace with Albion and Leyland. One of the first production Leyland Atlanteans was bought in 1958 but it was 1962 before a fleet of these rear-engined vehicles arrived.

Modern trams (orange, green and cream, no route colour) which appeared in 1937 were built in the Corporation's workshops until 1954 but pre-1930 'standard' cars were the backbone of the fleet until 1954. At its

peak in 1948 the fleet totalled 1,208 trams, all except one being double-deckers.

Glasgow not only had the last trolleybus system to be opened in the UK, operated experimentally in 1949 and then gradually extended, but also the last tram to trolleybus conversion. This occurred in 1958 using new single-deck vehicles. The last tram ran in 1962 and the last trolleybus in 1967. The re-equipped Underground seems set to last for ever.

In May 1973 corporation operations passed to Greater Glasgow PTE which was responsible to Strathclyde Regional Council from 1975. Renaming to Strathclyde PTE occurred in 1980. GGPTE used yellow, green and cream livery. SPTE initially used the fleetname 'Trans Clyde' on orange, green and black but by 1984 green was deleted and 'Strathclyde Transport' became the title carried. The next change came in 1986 when government legislation resulted in the undertaking becoming Strathclyde Buses Ltd and, still using orange and black, adopting 'Strathclyde's Buses' as fleetname. In mid-1996 FirstBus bought the undertaking.

On 1 April 1996 further local government changes resulted in Glasgow becoming a unitary authority with the title City of Glasgow Council.

Until 1974 the Royal Burgh had issued the registration marks: G, GA, GB, GD, GG, US and YS (and serial prefixes). US and YS were originally issued in 1904 to Govan and Partick burghs respectively.

Top:
Evocative indeed, this shot taken from the top deck of an approaching tram on 18 August 1962 illustrates the combination of green, orange and cream against blackened stone tenements and grey stone setts, typical of inner Glasgow for over half a century. It is the memory retained by many people old enough to have been there then. Taken only just in time too, as the last normal day of operation for Glasgow's tramways was 1 September 1962, route 9 (Auchenshuggle-Dalmuir West) having been the sole survivor for three months. A special service between Auchenshuggle and Anderston Cross ran from 2 to 4 September, however. Car 1260 is a Coronation Mark 1 bogie car built by the City Transport's workshops in 1939. It had EMB bogies, BTH motors and seated 38/26.

Above:
Coat of arms photo date: 1973, on a standard car.

Great Yarmouth Corporation Transport Department

Yarmouth Old Town was built on a strip of land between the North Sea and the River Yare. It has been a port for over a thousand years. To the northwest the hinterland consists of the Norfolk Broads, famed for leisure boating. Great Yarmouth's chief claim to fame was its fishing fleet, source of the marine harvest which once made it the largest herring port in the world.

The main town and its Southtown suburb are connected by a bridge, once hand-raised and the reason why the town had two separate tramways, each with its own depot. A line from the town ran north towards Caister while on the other side of the Yare trams served a line south to Gorleston. Public transport started in 1875 when the line to Gorleston opened. This was owned in turn by the East Suffolk Tramway Co, the Yarmouth & Gorleston Tramways Co from 1878 (using green and cream and red and cream livery) and finally BET.

A municipal electric line, opened in 1902, was soon extended to Caister. Having bought the Gorleston route from the company in 1905 the Corporation also electrified that, services starting in the July. Livery was maroon and cream. Great Yarmouth's first motorbuses were LGOC 'B' type AECs bought in 1920. These took over the Gorleston section of tramway in 1930. The last tram route closed in 1933.

After 1930 more modern AEC and Leyland buses were acquired and Guy utilities arrived during the war. In 1934 bus livery became light blue and cream with a silver roof (later the roof also became blue). Some prewar double-deckers received a quite pleasing streamlined version.

A majority of the double-deckers bought in the first postwar decade were Leyland Titans but AECs and Daimlers later appeared. Saloons purchased were six Albion Nimbuses in 1959 and eight rare Daimler Freelines in the 1960s. The first rear-engined buses were Leyland Atlanteans acquired in 1960, Daimler Fleetlines following in 1963. A batch of AEC Reliance saloons bought in 1964 carried Pennine Coachcraft bodies but were buses for all that.

Local government changes in 1974 diminished the town's status from county borough (registration marks EX and xEX) to a district which soon took the title of borough, but otherwise the only effect was to push the boundary with Suffolk a mile or two further south. Yarmouth remained firmly in Norfolk. However, the undertaking's title changed to Great Yarmouth District (later Borough) Council Transport Department and changed again in 1986 to Great Yarmouth Transport Ltd. Services were marketed as Blue Buses.

FirstBus PLC purchased the undertaking in mid-1996 and subsequently merged it with subsidiary Eastern Counties Omnibus Company, to operate as Coastal Blue Buses using a livery of two blues and cream.

Below:
A later version of Great Yarmouth livery had a blue roof, the effect being more sombre than seen here on No 31 (AEX 331) on 24 August 1959. Then two years old, it was a Leyland Titan PD2/22 with Massey H30/28R body and the first of the undertaking's buses to bear a three-letter registration (No 30, an AEC new the previous year, 1956, was EX 9830). The location is the northern end of a Marine Parade route.

Inset:
Coat of arms photo date: 30 June 1983. By that time, the white lozenge background, illustrated, had been discontinued.

Grimsby Corporation Transport (1925-1956)

Until 1974 Lincolnshire consisted of three Parts – Holland, Kesteven and Lindsey (once known as South, Mid and North Lincolnshire respectively). They were administered by county councils. County boroughs though were free-standing authorities and Grimsby was the only one in Lindsey. (It was a borough from 1974-1996.)

Great Grimsby Street Tramways Co (a subsidiary of Provincial Tramways) served the town with horse cars from 1881 to 1901 and then with electric trams until 1925 when Grimsby Corporation bought the operation within its boundary. The cars, previously green and cream, were repainted maroon and cream and survived until 1937. Trolleybuses had taken over one route in 1926 and buses another in 1927. After trams finished, a joint trolleybus route with Cleethorpes Corporation was started. Bus and trolleybus livery was very deep maroon with relief restricted to cream window surrounds and three thin lines.

On 1 January 1957 Grimsby-Cleethorpes Transport Joint Committee took over.

The town was the southern terminus of the Grimsby & Immingham Light Railway, an inter-urban tramway built by the Great Central Railway in 1912 to provide transport to Immingham Docks. It was never part of Grimsby's system and closed in 1961.

Below:
Following the Grimsby and Cleethorpes merger in 1957 it was many years before all those buses inherited by the new undertaking were withdrawn. One bought by the Grimsby partner in 1948 was AEC Regent III No 85 (AJV 162) which possessed a Roe body. It is portrayed in Cleethorpes at Isaac's Hill on 30 October 1965 when 17 years old. Many other buses then in service were blue between decks with cream cantrail and window surrounds.

Cleethorpes Corporation Transport (1930-1956)

Cleethorpes is the twin town to Grimsby, with similar tramway history. However, in 1925 when Grimsby acquired the GGST routes in its own area and some trams, the company continued to run a joint service into Cleethorpes. Cleethorpes UDC had been operating buses since May 1930 and purchased the company system within its boundary in July 1936. The cars were still green and cream, apart from a few ex-Grimsby cars in maroon and cream. The UDC was a tram operator for barely five months before the town was chartered a borough in that November. In July 1937 the tramway was closed and trolleybuses substituted. Cleethorpes Corporation (as it then was) introduced a grey and blue livery and commenced a joint trolleybus route with Grimsby.

On 1 January 1957 the Grimsby-Cleethorpes Transport Joint Committee took over.

Below:
Insignia photo date: 12 August 1972. The shields (Grimsby on the left) were simplifications of the coats of arms employed before 1957. Full Cleethorpes insignia had supporters and the usual foliage, while Grimsby mounted its arms within a belt.

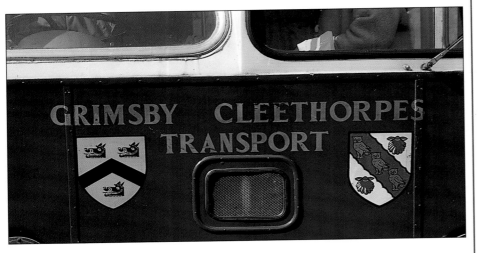

Grimsby-Cleethorpes Transport Joint Committee (1957-1986)

Grimsby is well known for its fishing industry, now diminished but still substantial. Cleethorpes is famed for its beach, promenade and water sports.

Both towns were in Lincolnshire until 1974 when they became part of Humberside. Most visitors come from South Yorkshire and the North Midlands, both about 60 miles distant.

Buses and trolleybuses were inherited from both the Grimsby and Cleethorpes undertakings when the Joint Committee assumed control on 1 January 1957. However, the electric vehicles survived only until 1960.

A livery of dark blue and cream was selected and lasted until the early 1980s, being replaced by brown and cream.

In 1986, shortly before deregulation and the undertaking becoming a limited company, an orange band and a black band were added to the lower panels. In 1988 a more radical change to orange, white and black occurred.

Five years later, in November 1993, the company was sold to Stagecoach Holdings and corporate white, red, blue and mustard livery appeared. Included in the purchase was GCT subsidiary Peter Sheffield Coaches.

On 1 April 1996 Humberside county was abolished and the twin towns became a unitary authority to be known as North East Lincolnshire Council, virtually the equivalent of an old-time county borough.

Registration marks used on Grimsby CT and G-CT vehicles prior to 1974 were issued by Grimsby CBC and based on EE and JV. Cleethorpes CT had used Lindsey CC marks BE, FU and FW. After 1974 Grimsby LVLO issued BE, EE, FU and JV serials.

Halifax Passenger Transport Department

Halifax possesses at least two especially notable buildings. One, linked to past prosperity, is the ancient Piece Hall, rebuilt in 1770 and originally the headquarters of the local wool and weaving trade. The other, built in 1974 and the very image of Yorkshire financial prudence, is the glass and concrete head office of the one-time Halifax Building Society, now a bank. The metropolitan borough is on the eastern flanks of the Pennines in West Yorkshire and furthest west of a group of towns still referred to as the Heavy Woollen District.

Corporation electric tram services started in 1898 using cars in blue and white livery, later red and yellow and finally red and white. Maximum fleet size was 143 including three single-deckers. Replacement by buses occurred over the decade 1929-1939. The system was well known for its steep gradients and also for the fact that inter-running with neighbouring systems was precluded by differing gauges.

Trolleybuses were tried experimentally from 1921 to 1926 but motorbuses, first used in 1912, were chosen for future expansion, AECs with powerful engines being a favoured make.

Bus services were steadily developed by the mainline railway companies in certain areas of Britain in the 1920s, the West Riding (as it was then) being one of them. On 1 April 1929 the Joint Omnibus Committee was formed by Halifax Corporation, the LMSR and the LNER. An 'A' fleet worked routes within the county borough boundary, the 'B' fleet services extended a limited way beyond. Both were in similar orange, green and cream livery but with differing insignia.

Notionally a 'C' fleet existed but this was entirely railways-owned (much later NBC-owned) and operated under the name of Hebble Motor Services Ltd.

These arrangements survived until 1968 when British Railways' interests (as they were from 1948) passed to the newly-formed National Bus Company subsidiary Amalgamated Passenger Transport Ltd.

In 1971 some Hebble services passed to Halifax JOC but were soon merged with the APT and Todmorden fleets in the short-lived Calderdale JOC (see Calderdale entry). Semi-municipal, that fleet bore Halifax colours but no coat of arms. It, together with the Halifax Corporation vehicles, became part of West Yorkshire Passenger Transport Executive's fleet (Metro) on 1 April 1974. Subsequent livery was green and cream.

From the same date Halifax was no

longer a county borough but part of the Metropolitan Borough of Calderdale in the county of West Yorkshire. Its registration marks CP, JX and serial prefixes passed to Huddersfield LVLO.

Green and cream livery with red lettering was also used by Yorkshire Rider Ltd, successor to the PTE from 1986. The undertaking was bought by Badgerline in 1994 and that group merged with GRT Holdings in 1995 to form FirstBus. Subsequently the fleet was given area liveries and identities, that for Calderdale being white, dark blue and yellow with fleetname 'Calderline'.

Between the Joint Omnibus Committee's formation and 1968 the badge on its vehicles differed from the coat of arms on Corporation buses. Contained within an oval belt bearing the name 'Halifax Joint Committee' were three arms, each surrounded by its title. To the left was that of the LMS, on the right the LNER, and centrally, the shield and motto of Halifax.

Below left:
Coat of arms: those buses owned entirely by the municipality bore Halifax arms underlined with the town's name, as depicted. The Joint insignia consisted of, within an oval band bearing the title, a reduced version of the Halifax arms (without supporters) together with a monogram and the badges of the LMS and LNE Railways.

Below:
Halifax No 204 (KCP 13) was one year old when seen passing the town's bus station near Wade Street on 3 October 1959. Its characteristic MCW Orion highbridge body is matched to a Leyland Titan PD3/4 chassis, a model which went into production in 1956. This bus was owned by the Corporation but the Halifax Joint Omnibus Committee 'B' fleet carried a similar livery.

Hartlepool Corporation Transport (pre-1967 Borough)

Those familiar with the local government changes in County Durham on 1 April 1967 will know that previously the borough of Hartlepool and county borough of West Hartlepool were separate bus-operating authorities. On that date they and their fleets merged, the undertaking subsequently being Hartlepool County Borough Transport Department.

Tracing the history leading to the merger reveals that there was a Hartlepool Steam Tramways Co operating in the town from 1884. It was unsuccessful and closed in 1891. The track was subsequently taken over by the General Electric Tramways Co, electrified and reopened in 1896 using cars in green and cream livery.

That same year, the Hartlepool Electric Tramways Co was formed by BET and built new lines which opened in 1900. BET also bought GET's cars and track within West Hartlepool and ran the combined system in both towns with the trams in orange-yellow and white livery. The undertaking was acquired in 1912 by West Hartlepool who also leased the track within Hartlepool from GET.

Hartlepool Borough, on a promontory north of its larger neighbour, became involved as an owner in 1925 when it purchased the 1¼ miles of GET track within its boundary and extended West Hartlepool's lease. The latter town had started trolleybus operations in 1924 and when the final tram route closed in 1927 Hartlepool participated in a joint management committee which then ran trackless vehicles in both towns. In addition to the single-deckers already operating, West Hartlepool bought another 12 and a similar number were acquired by the committee. That dozen carried both municipal emblems. Hartlepool owned the overhead equipment within its boundary.

In 1953 all trolleybuses were withdrawn and the corporations went their own ways. Hartlepool initially hired buses, then bought four ex-London Transport double-deck Bristols to operate a joint route. In practice they were run and serviced by Bee Line Roadways (Teesside) Ltd, a coach operator, and that arrangement continued when they were replaced by four new AEC

Regent Vs in 1956. These constituted Britain's smallest municipal fleet at that time, were painted blue and cream and carried the fleetname 'Hartlepool Corporation' with the town seal between the words.

On 1 April 1967 at least one of the four was already wearing the red and cream (ex-West Hartlepool) livery of the new undertaking when they joined the merged fleet (see also the following entry).

Three Bristol RE/Eastern Coach Works saloons ordered by Hartlepool in 1966 for the joint route were not delivered until after the merger.

Hartlepool Corporation was distinguished for being the only non-operating tramway owner to become a bus operator.

Left:
Hartlepool Borough used as insignia a seal featuring the hart whence its name stems. With different colouring the same device was used by Hartlepool County Borough following the 1967 merger.
Seal photo by courtesy of Geoffrey G. Fearnley

Below:
Clearly, in a fleet consisting of one batch of four buses there is little scope for choosing an illustration. No 4 (TUP 859), an AEC Regent V built in 1956, carries (it is preserved) a Roe H35/28R body and is depicted passing West Hartlepool bus station on 23 June 1961. The livery was in fact a somewhat lighter blue than the Agfa film has recorded. The Roe waistpiece, however, was painted in a contrasting very dark shade.

Hartlepool Corporation Transport (Post-1967 County Borough)

Pre-1967 details of this fleet can be found under Hartlepool Borough and West Hartlepool, whose fleets merged on 1 April 1967.

Subsequently, after the four Hartlepool Borough AECs (TUP 856-9) had been repainted maroon and cream and renumbered from 1-4 to 95-98, little changed for some time, other than a different coloured version of the Hartlepool seal replacing West Hartlepool's arms. After 1974, however, when the authority became part of the new county of Cleveland and relinquished county borough status, the undertaking became Hartlepool Borough Transport Department and the livery was reviewed. A brighter version appeared on the saloons of the largely (soon entirely) single-deck fleet. Cream mid-panels and window surrounds restricted maroon to the roof, a band beneath the windows and the skirt.

Company status in 1986 led to an expanded operating area, one route reaching Newcastle, but few new buses were purchased. The 68-vehicle operation was bought by its employees in June 1993 and sold on to Stagecoach holdings in December 1994. Buses appeared in striped corporate livery during 1995.

When Cleveland was dismantled on 1 April 1996, Hartlepool became a unitary authority (new-style county borough) but, initially at least, chose to keep the title of borough.

Between 1967 and 1974 the West Hartlepool registration marks EF and xEF were issued by the new county borough but then passed to Middlesbrough LVLO.

Above:
A month or two before the merger of West Hartlepool and Hartlepool on 1 April 1967 the former took delivery of five Eastern Coach Works B42D Leyland Leopard L1s. They were part of an ongoing change to one-person saloon operation carried to 100% by the new authority. It is of interest that the bodies were the first to be delivered to an operator outside the nationalised group when restrictions were relaxed. Seen here on 19 May 1968 is No 35 carrying a private party of what today would be called 'suits'. This bus served 98% of its life with the new Hartlepool, being withdrawn in 1980.
Courtesy Robert Kell

Left:
Though ex-West Hartlepool buses comprised over 90% of the new Hartlepool County Borough Transport Department fleet in 1967, the insignia chosen to represent it was a modified form of that used previously by the borough. The most striking difference is a background colour change to dark blue depicted here as on 3 April 1971.

Haslingden Corporation Transport Department

On the road from Accrington to Bury and cheek by jowl with Rawtenstall is Haslingden, one of the smaller Lancashire mill towns. Although industrial, it is surrounded by moors and the West Pennine foothills.

In 1887 a 4ft gauge steam tramway passed through the town. This made possible the longest continuous steam tram journey in Britain, 21 miles from Bacup to Whitehall (beyond Darwen). Four companies were involved, the Haslingden and Rawtenstall extension section being owned by the Accrington Corporation Steam Tramway Co until 1907 when it was purchased by the Corporations of Accrington, Haslingden and Rawtenstall.

Accrington electrified its portion promptly, but Haslingden ran steam trams through the town for several months, on a route between Baxenden to the north and Rawtenstall to the east, while modernisation progressed. After that Haslingden ceased to be a tramway operator, although it retained ownership of the track, depot, a tram

engine and one wagon for track and electrical maintenance. The depot was also the base for four of Accrington's red and cream trams which worked the Haslingden route until it closed in 1930. From 1910 to 1916 Rawtenstall trams also worked through Haslingden.

A Leyland saloon bus was operated experimentally between 1907 and 1909 using a dark, possibly all-maroon, livery and that manufacturer provided most of the subsequent fleet when operation resumed in 1920. Expansion from four to nine buses came in 1930. All were in light blue and cream livery which was such a contrast to the dark red Rawtenstall and Ribble vehicles which ran through the town.

In April 1968 the undertakings of Haslingden and Rawtenstall merged to form

Rossendale Joint Transport Committee, the former contributing 15 to the fleet of 60. For some years, they and neighbouring Ramsbottom UDCTD had shared a general manager. The combined fleet standardised on crimson and cream livery, very similar to the Rawtenstall colours.

In 1974 when Rossendale Borough was formed, the undertaking became Rossendale Transport and in 1986 it changed from a municipal department to an 'arm's-length' municipally-owned company, Rossendale Transport Ltd.

It remained, in mid-1997, local authority owned (see Rossendale entry).

Above:
When photographed on 11 June 1967, No 10 (PTF 207) was 14 years old, being one of a batch of two delivered in 1953. Haslingden, with a fleet size around 20, rarely bought more than two buses a year. No 10 was a Leyland Titan PD2/12 and carried a Leyland H30/26R body. After Rossendale JTC assumed control of the undertaking on 1 April 1968, it became their No 13 and served until 1972.

Above left:
Coat of arms: it would seem that the Corporation of Haslingden had faith in the ability of the populace to recognise the borough arms, for no attempt was ever made to place the town's name on the encircling garter.

Huddersfield Corporation Transport Department

Sited in the Colne Valley and on the lower slopes of the Pennines, Huddersfield is one of the principal towns in West Yorkshire and well known for the manufacture of worsted cloth, chemicals, engineered products, and as the home of a world-famous choral society. A borough from 1868 and county borough from 1889 to 1974, the town is currently the centre of the Metropolitan Borough of Kirklees.

Company horse buses were the only public transport in Huddersfield until the Corporation commenced operating steam trams in 1883, using a red and cream livery. A few horse trams were also worked. The municipality had become the first in the UK to operate trams rather than merely own the track when, having built the lines, it was unable to locate a lessee willing to work all the routes. Special and unprecedented Parliamentary powers had to be obtained. Electric trams started work in 1901 and had replaced all steam equipment by 1902. Dark red livery was employed until changed to a lighter shade in 1931.

On 1 April 1929 a Joint Omnibus Committee consisting of Huddersfield Corporation and the LMS Railway was formed. This was one of four such joint undertakings in Yorkshire. Initially the corporation served its own local area and the JOC the longer routes. Buses for the two groups carried different layouts of two reds and cream. Later, for several years the corporation technically ran only trams and trolleybuses because all buses were operated by the JOC but that changed when the trolleybus system closed and replacement buses were acquired by CTD.

Bus operation in fact had commenced in 1920 using locally-built Karriers. Double-deckers of the same make were bought for the JOC in 1930 and for a time carried the lettering 'Huddersfield Corporation & LMS Railway Omnibus Services'. A later device consisted of a disc containing town and LMS badges.

The trolleybuses started operating in 1933, painted in the same two reds and cream as the JOC buses. A change to Post Office red and cream came in 1941. Replacement of trams by trolleybuses started in 1934 and was completed in 1940. Trolleybuses were themselves phased out between 1961 and 1968.

The JOC was also discontinued in 1968, when British Rail turned its bus operating interests over to another branch of state-owned transport, the National Bus Company. In Huddersfield's case, those interests were then purchased by the Corporation.

Municipal transport in Huddersfield ended on 1 April 1974 when the fleet was merged with those of Bradford, Halifax, Leeds and Calderdale to form Metro, the operating name of West Yorkshire Passenger Transport Executive.

Metro livery was green and cream; also used, with red lettering, by Yorkshire Rider Ltd, the PTE's successor after 1986. Sale of the company to Badgerline in 1994 resulted in a stronger area image. Further change came in 1996 following the formation of FirstBus, when the fleetname 'Kingfisher Huddersfield' was adopted and carried on two greens and cream.

Before 1974 Huddersfield Municipal Licensing Office issued the registration marks CX, VH and their serial prefixes. Afterwards they were issued, together with CP and JX from Halifax and HD from Dewsbury, by Huddersfield LVLO until the office closed at the end of 1994.

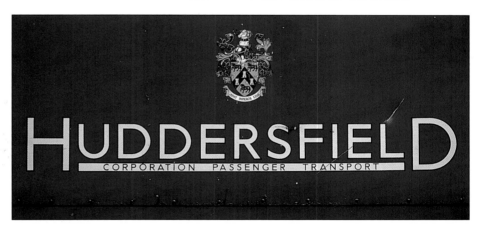

Above:
Coat of arms: a larger version of the arms alone was carried on the lower front panels of trolleybuses. 'Joint Omnibus Services' was substituted in the illustrated horizontal bar on jointly owned buses, the coat of arms being omitted. Prior to 1948 a transfer was used which showed, on a disc, part of the Huddersfield insignia on the left and the LMS arms to the right. The full title 'Huddersfield Corporation & LMS Railway Joint Omnibus Services' encircled it.

Left:
More than other similarly-equipped towns, Huddersfield's trolleybuses were evocative of swiftness and power, perhaps because their relative silence on steep gradients contrasted so greatly with the noise of diesel buses. Final day of operation was 14 July 1968 when No 638 (PVH 938), built in 1959, was seen at the railway station terminus accompanied by an overhead maintenance vehicle converted from a bus. Both were in the final procession. Details of No 638 are: Sunbeam type S7A, MVE 210CVI with East Lancashire H40/32R body.

Ipswich Corporation Transport Department

The town can trace its beginnings back to the Stone Age. It received a charter in 1200 and flourished as a port specialising in the export of woollen cloth. Among its more recent industries and enterprises were the trolleybus manufacturers Garrett, and Ransomes, Sims & Jeffries. Prior to 1974 Ipswich was a county borough and the county town of East Suffolk. It retains the latter function for the current single county formed by the merger of East and West Suffolk.

In 1880 a horse tramway, which was later operated by the Ipswich Tramway Co, was laid in the town. The original single line had been worked for a year by S. A. Graham. The company cars were in maroon and cream livery which was briefly retained when Ipswich Corporation bought the system in 1901. It ran unchanged until June 1903, then closed for five months for electrification. Services were resumed in November using four-wheel open-top cars painted green and cream.

Trolleybus experiments using Ransomes single-deckers started in 1923 and were successful. More were purchased as tram replacements, the last tramcar running in 1926.

A feature of Ipswich trolleybuses until the early 1960s was the use of unpainted aluminium, covered in a whorled pattern variously described as engine-turned, burnished or lustrous, for lower (and on double-deckers, upper) panels. Other areas were green and cream. The effect was very attractive.

The first motorbuses were not acquired until 1950 and replaced the trolleybuses in stages between 1953 and 1963. For many years only AECs were bought.

In 1974 the undertaking's name changed to Ipswich Borough Transport as a consequence of local government changes. Enlarged boundaries resulted in route extensions and expansion. A livery of cream with green roof, cantrail and skirt evolved for rear-engined buses.

Ipswich Buses Ltd took over seamlessly in 1986 and the livery was modified to two shades of green and less cream. In mid-1997 the undertaking remains an 'arm's length' possession of the borough council.

Prior to October 1974 the county borough issued vehicle registration marks DX and PV. From January 1950 their serials xDX and xPV were used.

Below:
Ipswich probably bought more utility trolleybuses, relative to the size of its fleet, than any other town. No 101 (PV 6954) was the penultimate in a batch of 12 dating from 1945. They had Park Royal H56R bodies on Karrier W chassis but not, on 28 August 1959, engine-turned aluminium panels, a livery component on most of the Ipswich buses and trolleybuses at that time which could from a distance resemble pearl.

Above left:
Coat of arms photo date: 7 August 1976.

Kingston upon Hull Corporation Transport

Historically in the East Riding of Yorkshire and still Britain's third largest seaport, Hull, as it is usually called, was between 1974 and 1996 in the trans-river county of Humberside and was a district with the title of city. On 1 April 1996 Humberside was dissolved and Hull became a city (and county), a 'new-style' county borough.

Founded in the 12th century as a quay for the export of wool, it expanded around the confluence of the mighty River Humber and tiny River Hull. Today it has an attractive modern centre and many historic buildings, some associated with the depleted fishing industry. The Transport Museum is worth a visit.

Preceded by one year by the Continental General Tramways Co, in 1875 the Hull Street Tramways Co took over horse-drawn services but not too successfully, as receivership came in 1889. The service continued with the receiver as manager until bought by the Corporation in 1896. It was then leased to a private operator until electrification which was started in 1899.

Livery used was red-brown and white, not unlike the crimson and white of the Drypool & Marfleet Steam Tramway Co, which operated on the Hedon Road from 1889. It was purchased by the Corporation in 1899 and leased back until electrified in 1901.

Corporation electric tramcars, of which there was a maximum of 179, carried crimson and white livery, unchanged until the last one ran in 1945.

Motorbuses, first used in 1909 and withdrawn in 1912 due to high maintenance costs, recommenced in 1921 and started replacing trams in 1931.

In 1932 all buses without covered tops or pneumatic tyres were withdrawn when 30 AECs were delivered in a new blue and white livery. A streamlined version of it first appeared on a batch of diesel-engined Daimlers in 1936. The last petrol buses survived until 1949.

Major tramcar replacement occurred when trolleybuses were introduced in 1937. Between then and 1964 when the system closed, a total of 116 were bought, all two-axled, of Crossley, Leyland and Sunbeam manufacture. Their replacements were Leyland Atlanteans, the first double-decker, rear-engined acquisitions.

Hull transport suffered damage in 1915 when German bombs from Zeppelins disrupted tram route P, but more serious was the attack by bombers in May 1941,

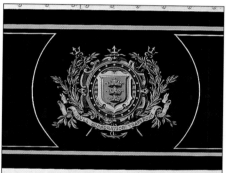

when 43 buses (35% of the fleet) were destroyed in a depot. Hirings from Leeds for several years (and other places for shorter periods) overcame the shortage. At a time when mutual help was invaluable, 32 withdrawn trams were sold to Leeds. From 1941 to 1945 bus repaints were all-blue.

The peak passenger year, as in most areas, was 1948 when over 100 million were carried.

From 1899 to 1919 trams were titled 'City of Hull Tramways', 'Hull Corporation Tramways' being used from 1920 to 1931. 'Hull Corporation Transport' followed until 1945 when 'Kingston upon Hull Transport' was preferred after trams ceased running. In 1972, anticipating 1974 when the title 'Corporation' was abolished, the departmental name changed to Kingston upon Hull City Transport and was accompanied by a revised livery with white between decks on double-deckers and from cantrail to skirt.

Deregulation in 1986 accompanied a change in status to Kingston upon Hull City

Above:
In 1961 when No 85 (HRH 85) was seen on 21 June, all Hull buses and trolleybuses carried streamlined livery, though only the latter had white front panels. Plain livery appeared in 1972, but it was the end of that decade before the previous style disappeared. The vehicle illustrated is a Sunbeam W with Roe H31/29R body, built in 1947. No 1 in the HRH registration block was issued in the normal way to a citizen who later transferred it to the then Princess Elizabeth, now the Queen.

Above left:
Coat of arms: in 1979, to celebrate 80 years of operation, Hull No 252 was painted in crimson and cream tram livery. This is the traditional ornamental version of the arms, workaday buses carrying the usual simplified shield.

Transport Ltd and various enterprises involving red minibuses, blue, crimson and white coaches, a green and cream low-cost fleet and French and Dutch subsidiaries were launched. Financial weakness eventually developed and the undertaking was bought by its employees and Cleveland Transit in December 1993. One consequence was the addition of a yellow band to the blue and white. Less than a year later, in November 1994, the joint owners sold to Stagecoach Holdings. Inevitably, that group's corporate livery followed in 1996.

As a county borough until 1974 Hull issued registration marks AT, KH, RH, and their prefix serials.

Lancaster City Transport

Once capital of a County Palatine, a virtual kingdom within a kingdom, Lancaster was earlier the site of a Roman camp and then a Norman castle which now holds the assize court and jail. The city gives its name to the Duchy of Lancaster, a royal estate with lands far beyond Lancashire. Although not the county town (Preston is), it was a bigger port than Liverpool in the 18th century. Once noted for the manufacture of linoleum, it is now more famous for its University.

A Corporation electric tramway which operated 12 cars in the south of the city from 1903 to 1930 remained physically separate from Lancaster & District Tramway Co's horse-drawn service. That, until it tapered away in 1921, ran from the city centre across the River Lune and northwest to Morecambe. In 1916 the city bought five Edison battery buses which were relatively successful and worked until replaced in 1929 by petrol-engined vehicles. The first of these had been acquired in 1917.

The livery of chocolate and primrose used on trams changed to ruby red and cream for the eventual fleet of about 40 buses.

Lancaster bought many Daimlers until 1940. Wartime deliveries consisted of an 'unfrozen' Leyland, eight Guy Arabs and a Tilling-Stevens saloon. Postwar, Crossley, Leyland, Guy, Daimler and AEC models were obtained, some second-hand. Between 1957 and 1974 only Leylands were purchased.

One unusual feature of Lancaster's buses was that the numeral component of the registration mark was also displayed as the fleet number, using transfers. In a large fleet that would not be remarkable, but in Lancaster's case it gave rise to assumptions of substantial size if strangers noticed say 710 (NTC 710) on a double-deck Leyland Titan PD2. Lancaster buses bought new were (naturally) always registered at Preston with Lancashire County marks.

In the 1974 local government changes Lancaster merged with Morecambe & Heysham Borough to form Lancaster District (with city title). The combined bus undertaking adopted the unwieldy name Lancaster City Council Passenger Transport Department.

Possibly to indicate that neither contributor was subordinate, a livery of blue and white was chosen. In 1986 the addition of a second, lighter blue accompanied the change to Lancaster City Transport Limited. Similar colours were used by the subsidiary Lonsdale Coaches Ltd.

A gradually weakening trading situation led to an abrupt takeover by Stagecoach Holdings in 1993 and Lancaster was initially served by the Ribble subsidiary of that group, using the ubiquitous striped livery. Ribble had in fact operated in the district for 70 years, though with co-operation until 1986. In 1997, responsibility for the area was transferred to Stagecoach Cumberland, using the local name Stagecoach Lancaster.

Above left:
Coat of arms photo date: 24 October 1973.

Below:
Lancaster City fleet of around 40 buses included 12 all-Crossley DD 42/3 double-deckers in the 1950s and some eventually had a service life of over 16 years. Two of the survivors, No 962 (JTD 962) of 1948 and No 572 (HTF 572) built in 1947, are illustrated resting in the bus station on 3 October 1964. The Crossley bodies had 56 seats.

Immediate prewar livery was turquoise and cream, changing in the postwar period to blue-grey and dark blue (with unpainted aluminium bonnet). By 1952 contrasting greens were in use and this scheme held sway until 1974 when, on 1 April, Leeds City Transport became a constituent of the West Yorkshire PTE fleet. By then the proportion of light green had increased. On the same date Leeds became a metropolitan district of West Yorkshire, retaining the title of City.

As Leeds District of West Yorkshire, Metro green and cream livery provided some continuity. The separate identity later submerged, only to reappear after 1986 as Leeds Area of Yorkshire Rider Ltd. This company used richer green and cream with red lettering.

In 1995, following sale of the company in 1994 to Badgerline Holdings (later FirstBus), a stronger area identity emerged, still based on green. There followed a decision to revert to local liveries. Leeds' version is white, red, orange and yellow, with fleetname 'Leeds City Link'.

As a county borough in the West Riding of Yorkshire until 1974, Leeds issued vehicle registration marks U, NW, UM, UA, UB and UG (in that order) and then, from 1934, their serial prefixes. Naturally, Leeds buses received such identities.

Above:
Very near the end of its life is Leeds Horsfield class tram No 176, one of a batch of 100 with Brush 60-seat bodies built by Leeds City Transport workshops in 1930. They had single P35 trucks, were equipped with air brakes and ran in blue and cream livery from new until around 1950. Also in the photograph, taken on 3 October 1959, can be seen a Feltham car, ex-London Transport, and several buses in and near the central bus station. Leeds tramways closed on 7 November 1959.

Below:
Coat of arms photo date: 21 July 1974. This is displayed against the livery of two shades of green then standard for buses. Half-cab vehicles usually had a polished aluminium bonnet.

Leeds City Transport Department

The history of Leeds, the largest town in West Yorkshire, is inextricably linked to wool. Sheep on the moors provided the raw material for cottage spinning and weaving in the Middle Ages and by 1800 mills and machinery were well established. The ready-made clothing industry started in Leeds about 1850, Hepworths and Burtons being long-lived pioneers. In 1996 the city gained a national museum devoted to the Royal Armouries, previously housed in the Tower of London.

Cheap road transport started in 1871 with a horse tramway run by William and Daniel Busby. Leeds Tramway Co, formed soon afterwards, took over the line in 1872 and expansion with both trams and horse buses followed, using a livery of brown and white. There were steam tram experiments in 1876 using a machine from a company in Dewsbury but regular operations really started in 1880 with the same livery. The US company of Thomson-Houston International offered to demonstrate electric trams and started on the LT Co route to Roundhay in 1891 using six single-deck cars in blue and cream livery.

The Corporation of Leeds bought the LT Co in 1894 and proceeded to electrify the entire system. It received its first new cars in 1897 and added a primrose area to the established colours. The last horse car ran in 1901 and the final steam tram in 1902.

Through running with Bradford Corporation between 1909 and 1918 involved cars with sliding sleeve axles to cope with a change of gauge at the boundary, as Leeds used 4ft 8½in while Bradford had settled on 4ft.

Tramway livery changed in 1925 to dark blue and cream, with some cars in light blue and cream from 1933. Wartime repaints received khaki-green. In 1950 red and cream for trams was adopted, rather appropriate for the ex-London Feltham cars acquired at that time. That livery lasted until the end of the system in 1959 although two experimental saloon cars received purple and cream around 1953.

Leeds shared with Bradford the distinction of being the first operators of trolleybuses in the UK, as from 1911 to 1928 those vehicles ran to the north of the city, two of the three routes extending outside the boundary.

Motorbuses were first used in 1906, eventually replacing trolleybuses and trams.

Leicester City Transport

Leicester developed from a Roman town. In the Domesday Book of 1086 it is named Ledecestre. It was a small market town in 1800 yet is home to a quarter of a million people in the last decade of the 20th century. Footwear and hosiery are the traditional trades, partly superseded by engineering today. Leicester was made a city in 1919.

Leicester Tramways Co commenced a horse-drawn service in 1874 and also used

horse buses from 1878. Their final livery was an unusual grey and biscuit, retained by the Corporation when it took over the 39 tramcars and 30 buses in 1901. Sixty electric trams went into service in 1904, clad in dark crimson and cream. The tram fleet eventually reached 178 double-deckers, all but six being converted eventually to covered-top. There were 11 routes, trunk ones surviving until after World War 2 and the last closing in 1949.

Tilling-Stevens petrol-electric buses were purchased in 1925 and other makes replaced trams on one route in 1933. Three-axle AEC Renowns acquired in 1939 permitted further substitution. At its peak the bus fleet reached over 200, only 10 of which were saloons. All were painted deep crimson with cream relief until the early 1960s, when the proportions were reversed, using three, later two, crimson bands on double-deckers. In 1984 subsidiary Gibsons was employing a similar layout using scarlet and cream.

Leicester lost county borough status in 1974 and became a district with the title city, but it was 1983 before the undertaking changed its name to Leicester City Bus and switched to red, white and grey livery. After the addition of Limited to the title in 1986, deep crimson and cream reappeared, relieved on some saloons by a yellow waistline. Minibuses appeared in silver and red while short-lived subsidiary the

Loughborough Coach & Bus Co used two greens on full-size buses and on Trippet minis.

GRT Holdings PLC (once Grampian) purchased the undertaking in 1993, adopting cream, red and maroon livery in the corporate style and this was continued when the group merged with Badgerline in 1995 to form FirstBus.

As a county borough Leicester issued vehicle registration marks BC, RY, JF and their serial prefixes. The marks were transferred to Leicester LVLO (now VRO) in October 1974.

The city became a unitary authority on 1 April 1997.

Below:
No 26 (FBC 292) bears the standard postwar livery which was just giving way to cream with three crimson bands when this view was seen on 8 August 1964. The Metro-Cammell H30/26R body of a style bought by many municipalities is married to an AEC Regent III chassis built in 1948. An attractive feature of Leicester buses was the positioning of front registration plates above the cab. This could with advantage be emulated now, when rotating brush machines seem incapable of cleaning low-mounted number plates properly.

Left:
Coat of arms photo date: 21 May 1978.

Leigh Corporation Transport

Until the 1960s Leigh, one of the most compact Lancashire cotton towns, was a forest of tall mill chimneys when seen from any direction but especially from the nearby East Lancashire Road. It is located west of Manchester, midway between Bolton and Warrington.

Fast growth from a village in the 19th century was due to proximity to coal, to canal transport and to early railway access. All were factors in bringing in raw cotton, processing it and taking away the finished textiles. Most of the chimneys are now felled and indeed those monolithic mill buildings which survive are largely used for other industries or as warehouses.

Never a tramway operator, though grateful for a South Lancashire company line through the town, Leigh obtained powers to operate buses. It bought several Straker-Squires in 1920 and started its own services. By 1940 the fleet totalled 40 and that figure doubled by 1945 due to war workers requiring transport to Risley Royal Ordnance Factory. After the war the fleet dropped back to about 55.

South Lancashire trolleybuses, which had replaced the trams in 1933, were themselves redundant in 1958, the same year that Leigh became the first municipality to purchase a Dennis Loline. This was an improvement on previous deliveries of lowbridge double-deckers with awkward upper deck side-gangways necessary to pass under low railway bridges. Even after the bridges were removed, a low lintel at the depot entrance made low height essential.

Usually, as many Lancashire United buses as those owned by the Corporation would be seen in the town centre because the main depot and headquarters of the company was only 1½ miles away.

Leigh used a livery of blue with cream relief, three bands of the latter usually appearing on double-deckers. In World War 2 some Guy Arab utilities were delivered painted in overall grey. Postwar, the shade of blue varied somewhat. Some of the later saloons were predominantly cream.

Leigh buses were registered at Preston with Lancashire CC marks.

The undertaking became Leigh District of Selnec PTE on 1 November 1969 and the town was later also served by Greater Manchester PTE from 1 April 1974, Greater

Above:
Few municipalities bought Dennis Lolines, but Leigh, which was afflicted with a low depot door lintel and several low bridges, had six. No 64 (267 WTE) seen here in the then Leigh bus station on 16 September 1969 shortly before Selnec was formed and absorbed the fleet, was a Mark III, the first of two new in 1961. It had an East Lancashire H41/31R body and became No 6964, second highest fleet number in the initial Selnec series.

Above left:
Coat of arms photo date: 25 May 1970.

Manchester Buses Ltd from 26 October 1986, and GMB North from 1994, all of whose liveries were based on orange. FirstBus bought GMBN in 1996 and overall orange is rapidly becoming the major mobile colour on Leigh's thoroughfares.

In 1969 Leigh buses received Selnec fleet numbers in the 6000 series. The last ex-Leigh double-decker disposed of by GMPTE in March 1980 was also its last AEC double-decker. This was No 6905, a Renown, but the final Leigh survivor was No 6061, a Leyland Leopard sold in November 1981.

The borough of Leigh became a part of the metropolitan district (borough) of Wigan in the county of Greater Manchester on 1 April 1974.

Lincoln Corporation Transport

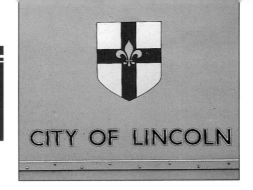

CITY OF LINCOLN

Approaching Lincoln across the plain is a great experience as the hill-top cathedral draws near. The town on the flat ground is less impressive but many historic buildings survive. Steep Hill, leading to the cathedral and castle is lined with ancient shops and a little to the north is Newport Gate, the only Roman gateway in Britain still used by traffic. Lincoln today has engineering industries of which one, Ruston & Hornsby, has produced diesel engines. A few, including one in a Lincoln Guy Arab, were fitted to buses as an experiment in air-cooled machines.

The year 1882 saw horse-drawn cars of the Lincoln Tramway Co reach Bracebridge, a southern suburb. Bought by the Corporation in 1904 and electrified by 1905, the route was energised with the Griffiths-Bedell surface contact system using studs in the road. This was replaced by orthodox overhead wire and trolleypoles in 1919. The electric trams introduced a livery of green and white, replacing red-brown and cream on the horse cars.

Other tram routes were planned but not built and it was left to buses, initially Dennis saloons, to serve the higher parts of the city, starting in 1920. Trams were withdrawn in 1929 and replaced by Leyland Titan TD1s. The first of these, arriving in 1928, was also the first production TD1 chassis with open-staired lowbridge body. The Titans were able to pass under the city's ancient Stonebow Arch, a fact used in Leyland advertising at that time. Bus livery was green and cream and during earlier postwar years the area of cream waxed and waned. By 1965 only the roof and lower panels on double-deckers and roof and window surrounds on saloons were green. In the mid-1970s Leyland Atlanteans displayed cream on only a cantrail band and on the front between decks but the early 1980s saw green reduced again, this time to roof, cantrail and a shallow skirt.

Local government changes in 1974 affected the Department little – even the county borough registration marks FE and VL (and serial prefixes) used on its buses continued to be issued by the local LVLO after Lincoln became a district council with the title of city. Politically it changed from an independent authority squeezed between the Parts of Lindsey and Kesteven (two of the three county divisions of Lincolnshire) to simply being in Lincolnshire when the three merged.

In 1985 the displayed title, which had been 'City of Lincoln' for many years became 'Lincoln City Transport'. This was shown on white relieved by bands of different shades of green, initially two, later three, with a green skirt. As many as 22 taxicabs entered the fleet and operated in the three-stripe livery for a few years after the department became Lincoln City Transport Ltd upon deregulation in 1986.

As a consequence of that change the company was sold to its employees in 1990 and purchased by Yorkshire Traction in 1993. It is kept separate from Lincolnshire Road Car Co, also owned by YTC.

Below:
Lincoln railway station was a focal point for city bus services in 1965 and No 69 (CFE 565) is seen leaving its vicinity along St Mary Street on 29 October. It is a Leyland Titan PD1A built in 1947 and fitted with a Roe H31/25R body. The predominantly green livery seems more appropriate than the largely cream version introduced in the early 1980s. Lincoln had route numbers, but the vestigial blind aperture available on No 69 did not permit their display.

Above left:
Coat of arms photo date: 6 June 1971. Lincoln used possibly the simplest heraldic insignia of any British municipality.

Liverpool Corporation Passenger Transport

With a declining population, yet experiencing a resurgence in developments intended to improve its physical image and encourage industry and tourism, Liverpool remains, as always, especially interesting to the student of public transport. Both its cathedrals were completed after railways started to contract yet before the great transatlantic liners gave way to aircraft. More sea freight is now handled by one large container terminal than was dealt with by a whole chain of docks 40 years ago. Those were linked by the Overhead Railway until 1957. Many older docks are now closed and filled in.

Horse buses were operating in Liverpool by 1830 and there was a horse tramway in 1859, one year earlier than Birkenhead's famous street line, but it ran on a dock railway parallel to the public road. A short-lived street railway also ran in the Old Swan district in 1861/2.

Not until 1869 were serious operations started by the Liverpool Tramway Co using cars in maroon and white livery. The Liverpool Omnibus & Tramway Co also started the following year and both were absorbed in 1876 into the Liverpool United Tramways & Omnibus Co which used multifarious liveries in its 21-year life. The tracks were acquired by the Corporation in 1880 but leased back until 1897 when the operations were purchased.

Electrification started in 1898 and was completed in 1901, although one short horse line outside the then city boundary in Litherland survived until 1903. The only through running on Liverpool metals by another operator was from 1903 to 1905, when the Lancashire Light Railway Co worked cars from St Helens to the Pier Head. They were in dark red and cream livery not unlike that then used by

Liverpool Corporation Tramways (except on first class cars which were cream and white).

Liverpool cars, of which there were 744 at one time, were orthodox in design until 1933 when modern bogie streamliners ('Green Goddesses') were introduced, bringing with them a new livery of green and cream. Similarly styled but single-trucked 'Baby Grands' followed in 1937. After World War 2 a 1932 policy to develop the tramways was reversed and the last route closed in 1957 (the last tram being painted white).

The Woolton Motor Bus Co was purchased in 1911, but buses were a side-line for many years. Clerestory-roofed Karrier and Thornycroft saloons were operated before the first machines of modern (for the 1930-60 period) appearance, AEC Regents with Weymann double-deck bodies, arrived in 1935.

Postwar deliveries were spread over AEC, Crossley, Daimler and Leyland chassis, many fitted with bodies finished in the Department's workshops. After 1963 Leyland Atlanteans became the fleet mainstay, following trials also involving an AEC Regent V and an AEC Bridgemaster.

One small batch of half-deck airport coaches were in blue livery. Later, deliveries of rear-engined saloons carried reversed colours, green relief on cream.

December 1969 saw the undertaking merged with those of Birkenhead and Wallasey to form Merseyside Passenger Transport Executive. Liverpool Area retained dark green and cream livery (unlike Wirral Area which had blue and cream) but in 1974 Merseyside County was created, Southport and St Helens joined the PTE and an all-district scheme of lighter green with larger areas of cream was created. Brown window surrounds and skirt were added in 1978.

Deregulation in 1986 introduced the 'Merseybus' trading name of Merseyside Transport Ltd and, two years later after an experiment with two shades of green, a maroon and cream livery appeared.

Local government ownership ended when management and employees bought the company in December 1992. The name became MTL Trust Holdings and a year later a corporate livery of cream and crimson evolved, accompanied by area fleetnames. That used in Liverpool remained Merseybus, though a low-cost operation became Merseyrider.

When, in 1974, Liverpool became a metropolitan district (with city title) the function of issuing registrations moved to an LVLO. Marks issued by the city were K, KB, KA, KC, KD, KF, LV (in that order) and serial prefixes after 1934.

Above left:
Fleet No E1 (371 BKA) was not a typical Liverpool bus. In 1958/9 the city acquired three competing models: the AEC Regent V depicted, a Leyland Atlantean and an AEC Bridgemaster. E (experimental) numbers 1-3 were allocated. The Atlantean won, but both AECs remained in the fleet. E1, seen here on 12 September 1959 when only a week or two old, passed to Merseyside PTE in 1969 and was not withdrawn until 1973. It had a Park Royal FH40/32F body and is shown at Mann Island with the Mersey Docks & Harbour Board offices on the left. This road is now a cul-de-sac but in 1959 the trams had been gone only two years and track is visible.

Above:
Coat of arms photo date: 22 November 1969. Delivered in cream with green window surrounds during 1968/9 were 110 Leyland Panther and 25 Bristol RELL saloons. This insignia was also used on green livery.

Llandudno Urban District Council

Not the largest but certainly the most attractive resort on the North Wales coast, Llandudno is favoured with two rocky headlands which define the main bay. The town is built on an isthmus and a smaller beach is known as West Shore. Basically Victorian in architectural style, recent developments have been subdued, preserving an atmosphere now rarely found elsewhere.

The larger promontory, Great Ormes Head, is circled by the five-mile Marine Drive and it was on that road the first UDC Dennis toastrack buses operated short tours in 1928. Local inter-urban transport was provided by the Llandudno & Colwyn Bay Electric Railway Co's trams until 1956, and by Crosville Motor Services buses (now Crosville Cymru Co), but the Marine Drive route was a seasonal niche operation which the Council found very profitable.

In 1950 an inland circular tour was started, followed in 1951 by a stage carriage service up the Great Orme using two Fodens specially equipped with low gearing and sprag brakes to cope with a 1 in 3½ gradient. Later in the 1950s a peak fleet size of 17 was attained. Original livery was maroon, with some cream soon added, but in 1968 a change to dark blue and cream accompanied delivery of two Dennis Pax buses. Fleet numbers were never used.

The council became a tramway operator in 1949 when it purchased the four-car, two-section, cable-hauled Great Orme Railway, retaining the deep blue livery with white roof. In 1962 the colour was modified to a lighter blue, still with white roof but adding white to the (unglazed) window surrounds.

On 1 April 1974 the local authority became Aberconwy District (Borough) Council, part of Gwynedd county in place of the abolished Caernarfonshire. Livery changes followed: buses became light red and grey; trams were painted light blue and cream and lettered 'Great Orme Tramway', reverting to the name used from its opening in 1902 (the cars were then yellow and white) to 1935.

The Transport Act of 1985 compelled local authorities to form 'arm's length' companies to run their municipal transport undertakings. Probably due to its summer-only operation and tiny fleet of five buses, Aberconwy was permitted to be an exception and is now the sole surviving municipal operator. The name became Grwp Aberconwy, otherwise Aberconwy District Council Transport.

By 1991 a slightly darker blue, still with white upperworks and dark roof, was in use on the trams, which are decorated with ornate primrose lining and lettering. Four small Bedford coaches, all second-hand since 1990, became very dark blue with chrome trim. They are lettered 'Great Orme Tours'.

On 1 April 1996 Aberconwy merged with neighbouring Colwyn (from Clwyd county) to form a unitary authority which chose the name Conwy County Borough Council. Ownership of the buses passed to it.

Above:
Municipal Fodens were uncommon, the single-deck version doubly so. Llandudno had two 1951 PVSC6 models fitted with Metalcraft bodies described in enthusiast shorthand as FB35F, but they were very coachlike in appearance. Withdrawal was not until 1968. Llandudno and neighbouring Colwyn Bay were the only municipal undertakings not to use fleet numbers, so the identity of the vehicle portrayed here is plain AJC 91. It was 8ft wide, 29ft long and had sprag gear on the back axle to prevent runback on the very steep route which climbs out of the town onto Great Ormes Head. The location is the Great Orme Tramway's Halfway station and part of one of the council-owned unglazed cable cars can be seen on 4 August 1961.

Left:
Coat of arms: the armorial bearings illustrated were granted by letters patent on 14 July 1959 and replaced the earlier style displayed on some buses in the 1950s.

Lowestoft Corporation Transport Department

LOWESTOFT CORPORATION

Holiday resort, fishing port, ship builder, Norfolk Broads boating centre – and home to the lamented Eastern Coach Works Factory – Lowestoft is all of these. This Suffolk town has no glorious history despite its Scandinavian name, but had a lifeboat 21 years before the RNLI was formed. The North Sea is the town's eastern boundary and in fact a slight prominence, The Ness, is the most easterly point in England. Not far from the town is the East Anglia Transport Museum at Carlton Colville.

Victorian plans for company tramways coming to nothing, Lowestoft Corporation obtained powers to build its own and work on a north-south line crossing the borough from boundary to boundary started in 1903. A three-quarter-mile branch served the railway station and reached the depot.

Services started later the same year using 11 open-top double-deck and four single-deck trams. Four more double-deckers arrived in 1904. Livery was choco-late (dark maroon) and cream. Car 14,

heavily restored, can be seen at Carlton Colville.

Five Guy saloon buses arrived in 1927 to operate as tram feeders but the trams, abandoned in 1931, were replaced by AEC Regents with local United (later called ECW) double-deck bodies. No more buses were bought until six Guy Arabs with Massey double-deck utility bodies arrived in 1945. Two of them remained in service until 1965. Bus livery was maroon and dark cream.

Postwar deliveries consisted of AEC Regent II, III, and Vs, followed by two Leyland Titan PD2s, all double-deckers, in 1965. Total fleet size rarely if ever rose above 20 buses.

A batch of 10 AEC Swifts carrying ECW dual-door saloon bodies was delivered shortly before the undertaking was renamed Waveney District Council Transport Department as a consequence of local government changes in 1974. The new name lasted less than four years, for in December 1977 the Council chose to cease

operating. The buses were sold, the Eastern Counties Omnibus Co took over the routes and also accepted delivery of an outstanding municipal order for two Bristol VRs with ECW double-deck bodies.

Currently in 1996, Lowestoft, as the core town in the mainly rural Waveney District, has the honorary title of a Charter Trustee Borough.

Above:
Coat of arms photo date: 2 June 1971.

Below:
Large gilt transfers were used on Lowestoft buses until 1963 when a new delivery of AECs introduced a neater style. No 6 (FBJ 374) was the highest numbered Guy Arab II utility bought in 1945. Its Massey H30/26R body had been modified, especially around the windows, by the time this photograph was taken on 26 August 1959. The location is the terminus at Corton Road, northern end of a cross-town route to Pakefield.

Luton Corporation Transport

Largest town in Bedfordshire and from 1964 to 1974 a county borough, Luton has a history as a market town dating to the 12th century and was known as a centre of hat manufacture. In the 20th century, however, it is the motor industry which is synonymous with it. General Motors made Bedfords in the town until the marque was discontinued but production of Vauxhalls remains a high volume operation. Close to the town lies Luton Hoo, a mansion in 1,500 acres of parkland built as a stately home for the Earl of Bute and now an art museum. Luton was a district with the title of borough from 1974 to 1 April 1997, when it became a unitary authority, also a borough.

Horse bus owners were active in the town in the early 1900s but the tramway

and replaced the trams. It also bought two local bus operators, Excel and Bluebird.

As the town grew so did the bus fleet, which at one time after World War 2 totalled nearly 70 Bristol, Crossley and Leyland double-deckers, all registered with Bedfordshire CC marks. Bristol RE/ECW saloons were acquired in the late 1960s and these carried xXD-x or xXE-x registrations, marks which had been used by London CC from 1920 to 1963, then reallocated to Luton when it gained county borough status on 1 April 1964.

Luton bus livery was red and cream until the 1960s when red alone was used. In January 1970 the undertaking was sold to the United Counties Omnibus Co and the fleet repainted in that operator's green and cream, soon to be superseded by NBC corporate leaf green and white.

A new company, Luton & District, was split off from UCOC in 1986 and adopted red and cream colours for its home town fleet, later adding black. Other names were employed in neighbouring towns. Ex-London Country areas taken over used a

green base. Luton & District was later bought by the British Bus group which in 1996 was acquired by T. Cowie PLC.

'The Shires' is the corporate name used since 1995, its local fleet having the identity 'Luton & Dunstable' together with blue and yellow livery.

Below left:
Coat of arms photo date: 1969.

Below:
Luton No 153 (WTM 153), a Leyland Titan PD2/31, was new in 1959. Its MCCW L55R body is painted overall red, a livery brightened by the addition of a cream band on some contemporary Bristol REs. Prior to and during the early 1960s, double-deckers also had a cream band at cantrail level. The scene is a town centre group of kerbside stands on 16 February 1969, less than a year before Luton Corporation sold the undertaking to United Counties.

history of what was a relatively small place began in 1908, when J. G. White & Co Ltd, a lessee of the Corporation, which owned the tracks, commenced electric operation of three short routes.

The cars, in green and white livery, showed, however, 'Luton Corporation Tramways' on the rocker box. In the following year the lease was transferred to Balfour Beatty & Co and two more routes opened. Only 13 tramcars were ever operated, 12 open-top double-deckers new in 1908 (of which four were given top covers in 1929) and one single-decker bought from Glasgow in 1923. That same year the Corporation withdrew the lease and began operating the system directly, retaining the same livery.

After declining an offer for the system from the Eastern National Omnibus Co in 1932, Luton purchased Daimler motorbuses

Lytham St Annes Corporation Transport Department

Sedate southern neighbours of Blackpool, St Annes and Lytham face Southport across the Ribble estuary and are noted for spacious seafronts consisting of Fairhaven Lake in the former place, and wide greensward at the latter. Prior to 1922 they were separate local authorities. In 1974 the enlarged district was renamed Fylde (Borough), adopting the historic name for the whole of that part of Lancashire. The town is now widely known as home to 'Ernie', the Premium Bond prize draw computer.

The first tramway there was built by the Blackpool, St Annes & Lytham Tramway Co and leased to the British Gas Traction Co which ran 16 cars (later 20) on compressed coal gas from 1896 to 1898. BGT encountered financial problems and BStA&L, by then a public company, took over operation of the gas cars until 1903 (with ex-Farnworth UDC horse cars on the sandy northern section). Following electrification of the 6¼-mile line, 10 new trams came into service. Somewhat earlier the Blackpool Electric Tramways (South) Co had been floated to buy the system but nothing came of it.

The next development came in 1920 when St Annes Urban District Council bought the operation and put the name 'St Annes Council Tramways' on the cars. In 1922 the Borough of Lytham St Annes was

formed and the departmental name became Corporation Tramways.

Through running into Blackpool started in 1905 using inland tracks to reach the centre. Blackpool had running powers to Lytham but used them only on special occasions. Lytham St Annes trams were permitted to use Blackpool Promenade to reach Gynn Square from 1926, the cars making a nice colour contrast, as blue and cream in various shades had been used since around 1900.

Blackpool Corporation regularly hired 20 Lytham crossbench trams to cope with Illuminations traffic and then blue could be seen as far north as Bispham The electric fleet eventually numbered 56.

Buses were first bought in 1923 and in 1937 an enlarged fleet of Leylands replaced all the trams. They were in darker blue and white. Those colours have given continuity for a century, for they were also used (with a short-lived primrose band) when the undertaking became Fylde Borough Transport in 1974.

'Blue Buses' was adopted as the fleet-name when Fylde Borough Transport Ltd was formed in 1986, and a livery of two blues eventually appeared on a part of the fleet. The undertaking was sold to its employees in December 1993 but, unusually, reverted to public ownership when

purchased by council-owned Blackpool Transport Services Ltd in 1994. Although services were integrated, blue livery was retained for traditional Fylde routes until mid-1996 when repainting into green commenced.

Top:
Unlike neighbouring Blackpool, Lytham St Annes takes a delight in being sedate and abhors brash publicity, so the sign on its bus depot was uncharacteristic. With the Blackpool boundary literally yards away it was a demonstration of independence. Few of the borough's buses were single-deckers and No 22, a Leyland Tiger PS 1 built for Lancaster CT in 1947, was its only postwar half-cab. It passed to Lytham St Annes in 1959, and is depicted on 27 October 1964 shortly before withdrawal. The 36-seat body is by Crossley and has that maker's built-up rear window frames. In this case they seem to be a styling feature, though on the double-deck version they provided additional support for the platform. No clue to the original owner is provided by the HTB mark as both Lancaster and Lytham St Annes registered their buses with Lancashire.

Above:
Coat of arms photo date: 7 April 1973.

Maidstone Corporation Transport Department

Situated on the River Medway in the 'Garden of England' and adjacent to the North Downs is Maidstone, the county town of Kent. It was established in Saxon times and became a port for the shipment of food to London. Later, Flemish refugees expanded weaving and linen thread production, and hop growing and paper making became important.

Maidstone's municipal electric tramway opened in 1904, the town having missed the horse tram era. There were eventually three routes worked by 17 open-top, four-wheeled trams and one single-decker, all in light brown and cream livery. The system was replaced by trolleybuses, the first of which went into service in 1928 in the same livery. Trams were finally withdrawn in 1930.

Extension of the trolleybus system continued as late as 1963 and additional vehicles were obtained from closed operations at Llanelli, Brighton and Hastings. Postwar trolleys were two-axle, latterly all Sunbeam and BUT.

Motorbuses went into service in 1924 and some prewar double-deckers were Crossleys. Wartime deliveries were Guy 'Arab' utilities with slatted wooden seats (known to some as 'bum slashers'). Daimlers and several batches of Leyland Titan PD2s followed. In 1962 buses outnumbered trolleys by 29 to 24 and by 1967 they reigned supreme.

The trolleybus replacements were Leyland Atlanteans, the first rear-engined order. They introduced a new livery of light blue and ivory and were the largest vehicles operated since some 1928 Ransomes three-axled trolleybuses. After 1974 the coat of arms was omitted from bus panels, replaced by 'Maidstone Borough Council' on the waist of double-deckers and the cantrail of saloons.

Around 1980 some secondhand vehicles were purchased. They operated for a time in the liveries of erstwhile owners Lancaster (mid-blue and white) and Nottingham (lilac coach colours).

A year or two later brown and cream was reintroduced, followed by brown and yellow. When the undertaking became Maidstone Borough Council (Holdings) Ltd in 1986 it adopted the fleetname 'Boro'Line Maidstone', together with a blue, yellow, red and grey colour scheme.

By then 30 of the 40 buses in the fleet were Bedfords, though double-deckers were quickly acquired to take advantage of the new freedom to operate outside the borough. This resulted in operations in Bexley and Dartford, with one route extending to Central London.

Fleet size reached nearly 130 in 1990 but the following year financial troubles arose, which led to Maidstone & District Motor Services buying the assets in May 1992. M&D became part of the British Bus group in 1995. That conglomerate was bought by T. Cowie PLC in 1996.

Right:
Coat of arms photo date: 2 February 1974. An ivory painted disc was employed to accentuate the appearance of the arms on both the brown and blue liveries. Trolleybuses, all withdrawn in 1967, were not repainted blue.

Below:
When other trolleybus operators were converting to diesel buses in the 1950s Maidstone took advantage of some youthful bargains which included No 89 (BDY 818), a Sunbeam W/BTH 209 built in 1948 and bought from Hastings Tramways (a subsidiary of Maidstone & District) in 1959. Its Weymann HR body seated 30/26. When seen on 25 June 1960, the Barming route terminated at Fountain Inn, but was later extended to the Bull Inn.

Manchester Corporation Transport Department

Industrial capital of the north of England, Manchester was once the third busiest port in Britain, thanks to ships as large as 12,500 tons sailing 35 miles up the Ship Canal to docks in Salford and Stretford. The city is the largest metropolitan district in Greater Manchester county (formed in 1974) but it is still 'Lancashire' to its old folk. Originally based on the Roman fort of Mamucium but developed largely in Victoria's reign, the main industry of cotton goods manufacture was supplemented by engineering many years ago. In Liverpool Road there still exists the first railway station in the world, eastern terminus of the Liverpool & Manchester, the first successful passenger line, opened in 1830.

Manchester's road transport history begins in 1824 when John Greenwood started a horse bus service from Market Street to Pendleton, outside the boundary. That business and others like it grew and

Above:
17 December 1961 was the day a PSV Circle private hire matched the performance of the last prewar Daimler and Leyland in the Manchester fleet. The former, seen here, is No 4266 – originally No 1266 (GNC 61), a COG5 built in 1940 and fitted with an MCT/Crossley H28/26R body. Until its first full repaint around 1946, streamlined livery was carried. Hyde Road Works is the location and the weather could have been better. For those of tender years, the 1d mentioned in the advertisement was an old penny (0.417p). Also in use that day on a trip which included a run by both buses along the newly opened M62 (later renumbered M63) was TD5 No 3914 (ex-914).

Below left:
Coat of arms photo date: 19 June 1973, when tram No 765 was newly restored in Birchfields Road depot. The style illustrated was in use until around 1960, replaced by a redrawn, more compact version which incorporated a tilting helm (steel helmet used in jousting) resting on the shield.

came together in 1865 when the City Omnibus Co joined with Greenwood to form the Manchester Carriage Co.

Horse trams were introduced in 1878 by the Manchester Suburban Tramway Co and bore the fleet name 'Manchester & Salford Tramways'. In 1880 the two firms merged to become the Manchester Carriage & Tramways Co. Rapid expansion of routes followed and Manchester Corporation gradually took over the system within its boundaries and electrified between 1901 and 1903.

The city also provided tram services on metals owned by 11 adjacent urban district councils (also successors to MC&T), some of which were later absorbed by boundary

changes. Trams in the liveries of seven other towns could be seen in Manchester as a consequence of inter-running agreements. Cars owned by its twin city of Salford were often in the majority on Manchester's Deansgate.

Buses were introduced in 1906 as tramway feeders but did not become numerous until after World War 1. The tramway system reached its maximum extent as third largest in Britain in the late 1920s with 950 cars and 123 miles of track. During the 1930s however, buses took over some routes and abandonment accelerated when trolleybuses arrived in 1938.

Livery from Manchester Carriage days was always red and cream, enhanced from 1937 on buses, and then trolleybuses, by streamlining (curved cream flashes on red panels). A World War 2 shortage of pigments resulted in cream being replaced by grey on bus repaints from 1942 to 1945. This also made the vehicles less visible to marauding German aircraft.

Local manufacturer Crossley supplied a significant proportion of Manchester's buses and trolleybuses until 1951, though from 1934 Leyland was increasingly patronised and Daimler streamliners appeared in 1940. Top-deck streamlining was discontinued from 1946 on the first postwar Crossleys and dropped entirely in 1947, a development foreshadowed by the 1945/6 delivery of semi-utility Daimlers in plain livery.

The last tram ran in 1949, abandonment delayed by the war. Trolleybuses lasted until the end of 1966, as did those of inter-running Ashton CTD.

Blue and cream livery for airport buses first appeared in October 1946 on a prewar saloon. In 1967 a delivery of Leyland Panthers introduced a brighter version of the standard livery with cream roof and skirt, and 1968 brought the double-deck version of the Mancunian body style, where red was confined to the roof and from cantrail down to wheel arch peak. This was short-lived as on 1 November 1969 Selnec PTE absorbed the Manchester undertaking and 10 other municipal fleets. Subsequently Selnec became Greater Manchester PTE in 1974 and Greater Manchester Buses Ltd in 1986. This was split in 1993 to form GM Buses North and GM Buses South, acquired in 1996 by FirstBus and Stagecoach respectively. The former uses overall orange livery and the fleetname 'Greater Manchester'.

Trams reappeared on Manchester's streets in 1992 when Metrolink (Greater Manchester Metro Ltd), in which GMPTE is a stockholder, commenced operating. The first car carried the same fleet number, 1007, as the final corporation tram in 1949. Livery is pale grey and aquamarine.

As a county borough until 1974 Manchester issued registration marks N, NA, NB, NC, ND, NE, NF, VM, VR, VU, XJ and their serial prefixes.

Merthyr Tydfil Corporation Passenger Transport Department

Prior to the Industrial Revolution Merthyr was a quiet market town. By 1801 it was the largest town in Wales. Iron-making, helped by plentiful coal deposits, was the reason. By 1900 it was only the fourth largest town and heavy industry was expanding nearer to the coast. A county borough from 1 April 1908 (registration marks HB and serial prefixes), it was in Glamorganshire, subsequently in Mid Glamorgan and in the further reorganisation of 1 April 1996 became a unitary authority reverting to the title of county borough.

The town is at the head of the Taff Valley, most northerly of the nine erstwhile municipal transport undertakings in the area and noted for once running a 25-mile joint bus service to Cardiff – a long route for the valleys.

From 1901 to 1939 the Merthyr Electric Traction & Lighting Co (owned by BET) operated trams in green and cream livery (initially maybe in dark red and ivory). They ran on unusually narrow streets, one

in Pontmorlais being less than 15ft wide. Originally there were 13 saloons and three open-top, double-decker trams. Some were later given ex-Birmingham & Midland Tramways open-top bodies and three additional cars came from Birmingham CTD.

Merthyr Corporation began operating buses on two routes in 1924 and soon opened six more. Chassis used were Leyland, AEC, Dennis and Thornycroft, with Bristols following in 1929. No 1 of eight 1924 Leylands completed 100,000 miles in its first three years and when withdrawn in 1937 was the oldest municipal bus in South Wales.

The first double-deckers came in 1938 and replaced the company trams when they were withdrawn. Wartime deliveries were Daimler, Bedford and Bristol, the latter in maroon, red and cream. Bristols were favoured postwar, although Fodens were bought too. Leyland became the majority make after 1954, always in traditional maroon and cream livery. Around 1970 the proportion of maroon on saloons was reduced to a broad mid-panel band but a more drastic change came after 1974 when orange and cream was adopted and the title became Merthyr Tydfil Borough Council PTD. Brown was later added to those colours and in 1986, when the undertaking became Merthyr Tydfil Transport Ltd, a fanciful logo was adopted which presented the letters 'MTTC' in a form resembling a ship in full sail. Presumably to demystify passengers the words 'Merthyr Tydfil' were later added on cantrails.

Top:
The utility H30/26R body of No 41 (HB 6017) had been severely modified by 4 September 1959 when it was captured on Kodachrome. Built in 1945, it was the last of a batch of six Bristol K6As bodied by Park Royal. Merthyr liked the chassis and patronised the marque further until prevented from doing so by the nationalisation of Bristol in 1948.

Above:
Coat of arms photo date: 30 May 1970. By then this more prominent corporate title had replaced that encircling the arms as shown on No 41.

By 1989 white bands on two blues became the favoured colours but before the entire fleet could be so attired, financial difficulties overtook the company. It passed into the hands of administrators in July 1989 and ceased trading in August.

Left:
Guys with Northern Counties bodies, many featuring standee fenestrations, were popular with Middlesbrough. When this view was taken on 23 June 1961 over half the fleet were of that combination, in high and lowbridge versions. Few undertakings by then went to the expense of gold lining which so enhances the bus portrayed, No 36 (DXG 136), an Arab III built in 1954. It is high-bridge with a rear entrance. The lower vehicles were necessary to serve the route to the Tees Transporter which is hampered by a railway bridge.

Below:
Coat of arms photo date: 5 August 1973.

Middlesbrough Corporation Transport Department

Originally in the North Riding of Yorkshire but between 1974 and 1996 a part of the county of Cleveland, Middlesbrough is situated on the River Tees's south bank and connected to the north bank by a municipally-owned transporter bridge capable of carrying buses. A village before 1830 when an extension to the Stockton & Darlington Railway brought coal for shipment to its docks, the town held 40,000 people by 1870. Later, a local iron ore source encouraged the establishment of a large steelworks, now no more.

Despite its title, the horse trams of the Middlesbrough & Stockton Tramways Co (which operated cars in red livery from 1874 to 1878) never linked those towns and neither did its successor the Imperial Tramways Co (red and cream livery). Steam trams painted chocolate and cream were tried in the town from 1896 to 1898 but the link had to await electrification in 1898, by which time the local name Middlesbrough, Stockton & Thornaby Electric Tramways had been adopted. Still in red and cream, the cars were operated by that company until 1921, when the three municipalities

named in the title bought and divided the system. Middlesbrough received 32 trams which were then repainted dark blue and cream.

Imperial had commenced operating buses in Middlesbrough in 1913 and they also passed to the corporations in 1921. The fleet was augmented in 1931 to permit tramway closures, completed in 1934.

Although the Transport Department did not operate trolleybuses directly, the Teesside Railless Transport Board, which from 1919 ran into the town from the east, was jointly owned by Middlesbrough and the Urban District Council of Eston. It used a green and cream livery not unlike Stockton's and added motorbuses in 1924.

After World War 2 the Middlesbrough fleet, still in dark blue and cream enhanced by gold lining-out and crests on both decks, became strong in Guy 'Arabs' with a minority of Leylands.

Teesside County Borough was formed on 1 April 1968 from the County Borough of Middlesbrough, the Borough of Stockton-on-Tees and the Urban District of Eston, and retained the former authority's registration marks DC, XG, and serial prefixes. It formally absorbed the fleets of the two towns and TRTB, although repainting of all three into a common turquoise and cream livery had been proceeding for over a year, albeit with pre-merger insignia and titles. Upon merging, the title 'Teesside Municipal Transport' appeared on all buses and trolleybuses, although on the latter it was short-lived as,

despite a route extension barely three years earlier, the system closed in April 1971. It was the last extension anywhere in Britain (in the 20th century).

When Cleveland county was carved out of North Yorkshire and County Durham in 1974 the undertaking became Cleveland Transit (Langbaurgh, Middlesbrough & Stockton-on-Tees Joint Transport Committee was the full title) with a green and primrose livery. In 1986 this became Cleveland Transit Ltd and changed to green, white & yellow.

In December 1993 the company bought the Kingston upon Hull undertaking but the final development came in November 1994 when the group was purchased by Stagecoach Holdings. By the end of 1995 replacement of the local livery by corporate stripes had begun, and early in 1996 the subsidiary was renamed Stagecoach Transit.

On 1 April that same year Cleveland county was abolished and Middlesbrough became a unitary authority, technically a county but calling itself a borough.

Left:
Coastal resorts which maintain oversize fleets to cope with inflated holiday demand are noted for the longevity of some of their rolling stock. Morecambe & Heysham fell into that category when No 25 (DTB 64) and other petrol-engined AEC Regent Is built in 1937/8 were still in good shape a quarter of a century later. The location is Heysham Road depot, the date 14 October 1961 and the occasion an Omnibus Society visit. Park Royal built the body of No 25 (and four similar buses with 56 seats) which was withdrawn soon afterwards. Their replacements, which arrived in 1960, were five Massey-bodied Leyland PD2s, the first non-AEC buses bought since 1932.

Below:
Coat of arms photo date: 5 August 1973.

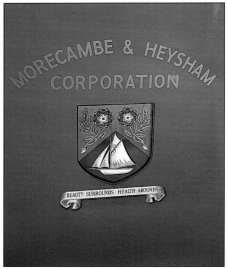

Morecambe & Heysham Corporation Transport Department

These resorts in north Lancashire front onto Morecambe Bay and have views across to the Furness area and the mountains of the Lake District. Nearby in the other direction is the city of Lancaster. Morecambe is the larger of the two and still has a thriving visitor trade. Heysham (pronounced Heesham) is a large marine village really, quiet until the 1960s when the harbour was improved and eventually became the main port for Isle of Man services. A nuclear power station sited well away from the village is housed in a monolithic structure visible for 40 miles.

The Morecambe Tramways Co ran maroon, teak and white horse cars in Heysham and Morecambe (urban district and borough respectively) from 1887. Morecambe Corporation built a three-quarter-mile extension in 1898 but leased it to the company. The original track from the Battery northwards was sold by the company in 1909 together with 14 cars, and Morecambe Corporation became an operator (using maroon and cream livery). The line was never electrified and survived until 1926, the last horse tramway in England.

The Heysham section was converted by the company to Leyland petrol-engined trams in 1912 and ran until 1924. Most cars were in maroon and white livery with a few in green and white. Heysham UDC purchased the line and scrapped it, replacement motorbuses being run by Heysham & District Motors Ltd.

The Lancaster & District Tramways Co began operating into central Morecambe from the city in 1890 and replaced the horse cars with motorbuses in 1921. These were subsequently bought out by Ribble.

Morecambe Council started running buses in 1919, their fleet being merged with that of the Heysham company in 1929 when the towns amalgamated to form the Borough of Morecambe & Heysham. Livery from 1919 to 1932 was red and white.

The new corporation bought only AECs from 1932 until 1960 and was the last buyer of petrol-engined double-deckers in the northwest of England. Some purchased in 1938 lasted until the early 1960s and were the last in Britain. Green and cream livery was employed from 1932, the proportion of cream increasing over the years and becoming a lighter shade on Leylands bought in 1960. A few AECs were converted to open-top and painted cream with green mudguards. In 1973 two new Seddon saloons carried a 'last fling' livery of blue and light green.

The 1974 local government reorganisation resulted in amalgamation with the smaller Lancaster fleet and the new undertaking, using blue and white livery, took the title Lancaster City Council Passenger Transport Department. This changed to Lancaster City Transport Ltd in 1986, the corporate colours being subsequently modified to two blues and white.

Difficult trading circumstances in 1993 led to the operation being taken over by the Ribble arm of Stagecoach Holdings with the usual livery implications. Ribble has traditionally operated in the surrounding districts and the conglomerate at that time saw no sense in establishing yet another local affiliate. However, as Ribble was becoming a little unwieldy after absorbing the Burnley & Pendle and Hyndburn operations the area was transferred to Stagecoach Cumberland in 1997 and local identity Stagecoach Lancaster came into use.

The name Newcastle derives from a Norman castle built on the site of a Roman fort but the people have stronger links with forebears from across the North Sea, both Germanic and Viking. The fine city centre was planned and built between 1825 and 1840, supplemented by some good post-World War 2 structures. It lies on the north bank of the River Tyne, Gateshead being its southern neighbour. Until 1974 it was a county borough within Northumberland, the Tyne being the boundary with County Durham. Romans built the first bridge – now there are several of which the latest is dedicated to the Metro, the Tyne & Wear light rail system opened in 1980. Another carries the Great North Road towards Scotland.

The Newcastle & Gosforth Tramways & Carriage Co ran horse cars from 1878 (and four steam trams for a short time) on tracks owned by the Corporation. The latter took

Below:
Over 150 trolleybuses were in service in Newcastle when No 513 (LTN 513) was caught by the camera on 20 July 1963. Three years later all had gone. Such a waste of equipment and materials is difficult to understand now, especially with current knowledge of how air pollution can be minimised by efficient generating station chimneys. The block of Sunbeam S7 three-axle vehicles, of which No 513 was one numbered 30, were all built in 1948 and carried Northern Coachbuilders H70R bodies. NCB was a local firm then favoured by operators in the northeast of England. The swish of tyres on tarmacadam and the hum and occasional click of trolleywheel on wire are evoked by such pictures.

Right:
Coat of arms photo date: 31 October 1969.

Newcastle upon Tyne Corporation Transport & Electricity Undertaking

over and electrified the system, opening the first sections in 1901. The fleet increased to 300 cars, all in a complicated livery of dark maroon, yellow and cream.

Corporation buses commenced running in 1912 but serious tramway replacement did not start until the mid-1930s and then mainly by trolleybuses, the first of which arrived in 1935. At that time the three branches of the municipal transport service carried different liveries. Trams were as described above, buses were dark blue and cream, while trolleybuses were yellow and cream with three chocolate bands. The change to yellow and cream with maroon wings on buses started with a delivery of AECs in 1949.

Tyneside Tramways & Tramroads Co cars in green and cream worked into Newcastle from 1910 to 1930 and Gateshead company trams ran jointly with the Corporation into County Durham. The final Newcastle tram route closed in 1950 but Gateshead cars ran into the city for another year in crimson and white livery.

Having peaked at around 200 vehicles in 1963, the trolleybus system was wound down and closed in 1966. Such closures, involving scrapping of many sound vehicles, were influenced by previous nationalisation of the electricity industry, as hitherto

the traction demand assisted the economics of municipally-owned generating stations.

Tyneside PTA was created by the Transport Act of 1968. Its operational arm, the PTE, came into existence on 1 October 1969 and took over Newcastle's fleet on 1 January 1970, together with that of South Shields Corporation. The Sunderland Corporation fleet followed in 1973 although that municipality did not expire until absorbed into Tyne & Wear metropolitan county on 1 April 1974. The PTE changed to the new name, still retaining yellow and cream livery. Newcastle became a metropolitan district with the title of City.

From 26 October 1986 the PTE buses undertaking became Busways Travel Services Ltd, an 'arm's length' subsidiary of the PTA, and was sold to its employees in 1989. Livery remained basically yellow and cream but incorporated bands of colour denoting operating area, maroon in the case of both Newcastle depots, which ran with 'Newcastle Busways' and 'City Busways' fleetnames. The company became a part of Stagecoach Holdings in 1994 and buses started appearing in that corporate livery in 1996.

As a county borough Newcastle issued vehicle registrations, its marks being BB, TN and VK (and their serial prefixes). They passed to the local LVLO in 1974.

Newport Corporation Transport

Until 1974 Newport was a county borough in Monmouthshire, then legally linked to England due to some medieval gerrymandering. In that year it became a district of Gwent county (with borough title) and definitely part of Wales. On 1 April 1996, as a unitary authority, it became one of the new-style county boroughs. Newport was a market town until coal and iron from the valleys started to pour through its docks to export markets in the 1820s. Today, with one of the few remaining large British steelworks nearby to provide employment, it has a population of 130,000. The River Usk is of course bridged as it passes through the town but can also be crossed further downstream by a transporter bridge. This has recently been overhauled and is one of only two examples in public use in Britain (the other is at Middlesbrough),

As in many towns, public transport started with a horse tramway, opened by the Newport (Mon) Tramway Co in 1875. The corporation bought it in 1894 but, after building a three-mile extension, leased it to Solomon Andrews & Sons until 1901.

Following electrification in 1903 and further extensions, the fleet built up from 29 to 58 cars. The green and cream 1875 livery was retained until 1903 apart from a few cars in blue and cream from 1901. The Corporation adopted cherry red and cream for its electric trams, modifying to deep maroon and cream from 1920.

Municipal motorbuses commenced operations in 1924, the first being Karriers. Tramway abandonment started in 1928 and the last route closed in 1937, supplanted by Leylands.

World War 2 brought utility Guys and Daimlers, peace brought more, plus Leyland Titans and some Dennis saloons, all green and primrose.

A change of title to Newport Borough Transport in 1974 coincided with the purchase of Metro-Scanias. Those were followed by Scanias, still the most favoured make in the 1990s. Livery changed to

cream with green. In 1986 the undertaking became Newport Transport Ltd which remains, in mid-1997, in municipal ownership.

The original county borough had DW as its registration mark and all buses bought prior to 1974 bore that or a three-letter serial. The mark is now one of 10 issued from the nearest licensing office in Cardiff, so current Newport buses usually carry marks originally allotted to that city, Glamorganshire, Merthyr Tydfil or Monmouthshire.

Above:
Cardiff Central bus station was a good place for bus photography. The sun was at a suitable angle for many hours, most buses faced it, there was ample space and many operators ran in. The service from Newport was one and pictured here on 3 September 1959 is No 170 (PDW 15) a Leyland Titan PD2/40 built the previous year. Its Longwell Green H30/28R body has, as a front recognition point – unintentionally no doubt – a bowed paint line. The coachbuilder was popular with Newport, 50 of its bodies, nearly half the fleet, being in use at that time.

Left:
Coat of arms photo date: 6 April 1980. As illustrated, by that date the arms in use on No 170 have been modified by reducing the shield size and adding supporters.

Northampton Corporation Transport

Principally known for footwear manufacture, Northampton in the southeast Midlands of England is an ex-county borough (that status having been withdrawn in 1974) and is the county town of its shire. It owes its spacious town centre to the good planning of rebuilding which followed a great fire in 1675.

Local transport history followed the usual pattern; a horse tramway started in 1881 (Northampton Street Tramways Co) was supplemented by horse buses on other routes in 1894. The Corporation bought the operations in 1901 and ran municipal electric trams from 1904. Company livery was dark green and cream but some red and cream and blue and cream cars appeared after 1893. The Corporation used red and cream for the electric cars and also probably for improved horse buses used on a route not railed until 1914.

Municipal motorbuses arrived in 1923 and started to replace the trams in 1926, final change-over occurring in 1934. Red and white livery on the buses was touched up with grey on some during World War 2. Later, cream replaced the white.

Tramway fleet size had peaked at 37 but buses, serving a wider area, at one time totalled nearly 100. The town was a confirmed Daimler user, other makes being rare between 1939 and 1974. In the latter year Leyland Nationals were purchased, Bristol VR double-deckers following in 1977 and subsequent years.

Half-cab, rear-loading Daimlers as depicted formed almost all the postwar fleet. They were purchased as late as 1968, the honour for the youngest vehicles to that layout being shared with Stockport's Leyland Titan PD3s.

When the town became a district with the title of Borough in 1974 its transport undertaking was little affected. The name became Northampton Transport, with Limited added in 1986. However, central government pressure on local authorities to sell their 'arm's length' companies led to Northampton accepting an offer from Scottish-based GRT Holdings in 1993. The most noticeable developments at that time were the addition of a second shade of red to a Grampian-style livery and an interchange of vehicles within the group (such as ex-Northampton buses running in Edinburgh for the affiliated SMT). GRT merged with Badgerline in 1995 to become FirstBus.

What would now be regarded as silliness developed when Northampton was allocated the registration mark DF in December 1903, as befitted its place in the population ranking used for A to FP in England and Wales. These letters were then an acronym for Damned Fool – virtually swearing by the standards of the time – and public ire caused an early rethink. DF was withdrawn in 1905 and replaced with NH, well beyond the original extent of issue but, perhaps because it could be seen as an abbreviation of the name Northampton, selected to mollify the motorised citizenry. The second town mark, VV, issued from 1930, caused no such problems and in fact when DF was reallocated to Gloucester CC in 1926 there was no public outcry. Serial prefixes of NH and VV appeared from 1947.

Left:
Coat of arms photo date: 7 July 1973.

Below:
No 218 (LNH 218) was one of a batch of 12 Daimler CVG6s delivered in 1959. These were not the first Northampton batch to have the Manchester (fibreglass) front which, although ugly, must have been serviceable as the feature appeared on all the Corporation's double-deck purchases until -G suffix (1968) when Daimler phased out production of front-engined chassis. On later orders the maker's name scroll was replaced, above the radiator, by the well-known fluted symbol. Repaints in the 1970s received cream window surrounds on both decks. Northampton was a frequent customer of Roe for HR bodies which, on the example seen here, seated 59. At that time, the bulk of the fleet comprised that type.

Nottingham City Transport

Situated in the northeast Midlands, Nottingham received its first charter in 1155 and was made a city in 1897. The population is now over 250,000. Nottingham has a plethora of associations: lace, bicycles, Robin Hood, tobacco, Boots, castle, Luddites, Sherwood Forest, sheriff, whereas most cities would claim fame with just one or two.

When in 1897 Nottingham Corporation acquired the fleet of horse trams which the Nottingham & District Tramways Co had operated since 1877, it inherited a mixture of liveries – all-yellow, red and white, dark blue and white and all-green. Some of the cars received Nottingham Corporation Tramways lettering on maroon and cream livery but all had been withdrawn by 1902 following rapid electrification. The first electric trams, also maroon and cream, commenced operating on 1 January 1901 and the system expanded until 1915, having 200 cars at one time.

Municipal motorbuses made an appearance in 1906 but became unreliable by 1909 and, following several months' reliance on horse buses, were replaced by a tramway. A more permanent service using motorbuses commenced in 1920 but trolleybuses, introduced in 1927, were more favoured as tramway replacements for the usual reasons – worn out track but overhead wiring still serviceable, and a power supply providing profits for rate relief.

Green and cream Nottinghamshire & Derbyshire Tramways Co cars ran into the city from the northwest between 1913 and 1932, as did blue and cream replacement trolleybuses from 1933 to 1953. These in turn were supplanted by motorbuses in similar livery.

Nottingham City tramways closed in 1936 but the trolleybuses thrived for many years before succumbing in 1966. Livery for trolleys and buses was green and cream and remains so for the latter.

The bus fleet was traditionally strong in AECs and around 25 more were added on 1 April 1968 when neighbouring West Bridgford Urban District Council Transport Department was absorbed. That undertaking's maroon and dark cream double-deckers had run over the River Trent into the city since 1914 from what was really a southeast suburb.

Since World War 2 Nottingham has favoured a distinctive style of double-deck body. One feature which could with advantage be copied elsewhere is downward-tilted front destination screen glass to avoid sky reflections and improve legibility. Buses sold out of service to other operators are thus easy to identify even without reference to the Nottingham registration marks which they bear.

Country-wide municipal changes in 1974 had little effect locally. Formerly a county borough, Nottingham became a district council with the title city and the undertaking became Nottingham (City of) Transport, changing again to Nottingham City Transport Ltd in 1986. In 1992 the council acquired the South Notts Bus Co. The city council has held out against political pressure to sell the undertaking and is currently (1997) still the owner of the largest municipal bus company in Britain with a fleet exceeding 400.

Until 1974 it issued the registration marks AU, TO and TV (and serial prefixes). They are now among 12 marks issued by the local VRO.

Bottom:
Postwar, early major motorbus purchases had been AEC as exemplified by No 273 (XTO 273), a Regent V with Park Royal H62R body from the 1956 tranche. It is caught heading west out of the city on 22 August 1958. The similarity between the shape of this body and some of those built by Park Royal for London Transport RTs is noticeable, only the higher radiator line breaking the comparison. However, from 1957 Leyland provided Nottingham's alternative supply.

Below:
Coat of arms photo date: 19 May 1973.

shade of red named pommard came into use and the red cantrail band was omitted. During World War 2 white was covered with grey on some buses and in the late 1940s two shades of maroon and white appeared on a few.

Many ex-Oldham vehicles passed from Selnec into Greater Manchester PTE ownership in 1974. A few, ordered by OCPTD but delivered to Selnec with booked Oldham 'ABU nnnJ', registrations survived until 1983, missing GM Buses ownership by only three years.

The 1986 company adopted a similar orange-based livery to that previously used. After central government pressure led to division of the undertaking in 1993, GM Buses North Ltd was formed and purchased by FirstBus in 1996.

The new company uses the fleetname 'Greater Manchester' on a livery almost entirely orange, and has its head office in Oldham.

Oldham became a metropolitan district and assumed the title of Borough in 1974. The same year the administration of vehicle registration passed to Manchester LVLO (now VRO). Oldham's mark, BU, became one of 14 allocated to that office.

Oldham Corporation Passenger Transport Department

Still visualised by some non-northerners as a place of clogs and shawls, Oldham, in Lancashire until 1974, has modernised as much as any neighbouring Greater Manchester town and has busy shopping precincts, pedestrianised/bus-only streets, an attractive centre around the old town hall and parish church and not a clog or shawl in sight. Situated on the western slopes of the Pennines, a damp climate encouraged the change from wool to cotton cloth manufacturing during the 18th century. Many of the huge cuboid multi-storied mills built then have gone. Oldham was the first parliamentary seat of Winston Churchill, then a Liberal, but earlier, in 1832, William Cobbett had been the town's first MP.

The county borough of Oldham came late into the municipal transport field by purchasing in 1900 the horse tram services started in 1880 by the Manchester Carriage & Tramways Co which ran on tracks built and owned by the Corporation. Also taken over, in 1901, were the routes within the town (again on municipally-owned track) of the Bury, Rochdale & Oldham Steam Tramways Co. Electric trams first ran in late 1900, horse and steam services ending in

1901 and 1902 respectively. Eventually 150 electric cars were operated. Some of the routes ran in adjoining urban districts.

The Manchester company livery had been red and white, the steam trailers brown and cream, but Oldham chose maroon and ivory after a trial with blue and white. There was joint through running with Manchester, and Oldham cars could be seen in that city throughout World War 2 and until the smaller system closed in 1946. Ashton trams also ran into Oldham on a joint route from 1921 to 1925. Trolleybuses replaced them but after a year Oldham's two vehicles were withdrawn, leaving Ashton to continue as far as the boundary. That experiment followed an earlier one with a battery-electric bus between 1917 and 1919.

A short length of track owned by the neighbouring Middleton Electric Traction Co was acquired in 1925 together with eight single-deck trams. The 1921 division of the Oldham, Ashton & Hyde Electric Tramways Co had no impact because, despite the title, it ran through Ashton only to the Oldham boundary.

Petrol-electric Tilling-Stevens motorbuses were tried in 1913 but withdrawn in 1917 and it was 1924 before Leylands were bought, the first of many.

Post-World War 2 purchases included some Crossleys and Daimlers but basically Oldham remained loyal to Leyland. When the undertaking was absorbed into Selnec in late 1969 it had 193 buses, all of that make: 16 saloons, 120 Titan PDs and 57 Atlanteans.

The bus fleet was painted crimson and white until the mid-1960s when a lighter

Above left:
Cannon Street bus station in Manchester on 9 April 1960 is the location of this Agfacolor view of Oldham No 452 (PBU 952), a Leyland Titan PD2/30 with Roe H35/28R body. It was the last of a batch of 24 delivered in 1958. According to the indicator blind it will head for Wrens Nest, Shaw, a destination unfamiliar to most Mancunians. Behind the hoarding is a bombed site, then still undeveloped after the 1940 Blitz, but now a pleasant open space. On the far side of that is the curiously named Hanging Ditch. Barely 100 yards from where this bus was stood, and behind the camera, there exploded on 15 June 1996 one of the largest terrorist bombs yet suffered anywhere. No 452 became Selnec No 5352 in 1969 and was withdrawn in 1973.

Above:
Coat of arms photo date: 25 May 1970.

Plymouth (City of) Transport

With a city centre largely replanned and rebuilt after severe bomb damage suffered in February 1941, Plymouth, in the county of Devon, is one of the more attractive cities in Britain, with a long nautical tradition of great interest to visitors. Its origins do not reach much further back than AD1000 and not until the 14th century did it gain much importance. In 1439 the town was freed from monastic rule and was the first in England to gain a charter by Act of Parliament.

Municipal transport started early, for in 1892 the Corporation bought Plymouth Tramways Co, operator of horse-drawn services only since 1890. The company had taken over a defunct steam-hauled line which opened in 1884 and ran into difficulties in 1885. This was the Plymouth, Devonport & District Tramways Co which had brown-liveried tram engines pulling brown and cream trailers but the succeeding horse cars were red and cream, colours initially retained by the Corporation.

The city electrified its lines between 1899 and 1907 and soon ran 54 cars, originally in red and primrose livery. Over the years alternative colour schemes were tried but primrose/yellow and white (1922-7), brown and white (1927-30) and maroon and white (1930-45) seem to have been dominant.

In 1914 the County Borough of Devonport and the Urban District of East Stonehouse were merged with the County Borough of Plymouth, and in 1915 Plymouth Corporation Tramways took over the BET-owned Devonport & District Tramways Co. This had operated electric cars in chocolate and yellow from 1901 (some were repainted green and cream in 1914).

The municipal merger had vehicle registration implications. Devonport had been allocated DR as its mark in 1903 but due to neighbouring Plymouth having most of the local automotive dealers in its boundaries, issues had only progressed to 268 by 1914. The mark was then suspended by Plymouth which was currently issuing CO, and resumed from DR 269 in 1926, being succeeded by JR in 1932.

Another local tram operator, Provincial Group-owned Plymouth, Stonehouse & Devonport Tramways, had worked horse cars from 1872 to 1901 and electric trams until 1922, always using green and cream livery. In the latter year the company was purchased by Plymouth and contributed 15 cars to the city fleet, making 125.

Corporation bus services started in 1920 but it was 1930 before Leyland Titan TD1 and Dennis Lance double-deckers arrived and replacement of tramways began. The change-over was nearly complete in 1939 but the opportunity to save imported fuel spared one route until 1945. One is led to ponder on the influence that consideration would have had on nationwide tramway scrapping policies, if in 1930 war had been seen as inevitable.

Postwar bus deliveries were predominantly Leyland, red and cream livery being used except for a short-lived change to dark maroon and cream around 1980.

Municipal change in 1974 affected Plymouth little (although it ceased to be a county borough and became a district with the title of City) but company formation in 1986 saw a title change to Plymouth Citybus Ltd. Adoption of a red, white and black livery followed. In mid-1997 the company remained municipally owned.

Above:
Plymouth possessed an entirely-Leyland double-deck fleet in the early 1960s and No 78 (MCO 678) was typical of deliveries in the previous decade. Consisting of a Metro-Cammell Orion H30/26R body on a Leyland Titan PD2/12 chassis, it was the last-numbered of a batch of 24 built in 1956, of which one was converted to open-top in 1958. A similar bus from the 1955 delivery stands nearby in this view taken in Plymouth bus and coach station on 28 August 1963.

Left:
Coat of arms photo date: 28 October 1976.

PLYMOUTH CITY TRANSPORT

Pontypridd Urban District Council Transport Department

This town lies at the junction of Taff Vale and the Rhondda Valley. The confluence of their respective rivers is in the centre, near an 18th century, 140ft stone bridge built by a self-taught local man and featured in the municipal insignia. Although the heart of a coal producing area, Pontypridd was and is just as famous for chainmaking, producing such monsters as those used to secure the *Queen Elizabeth 2*. Originally in Glamorganshire, the town became part of Mid Glamorgan in 1974 as the core of Taff Ely District (Borough). On 1 April 1996 it merged into Rhondda Cynon Taff unitary authority, a new style county borough.

The Pontypridd & Rhondda Valley Tramways Co opened a line in the town in 1885 but it was later operated, with horses, by Solomon Andrews & Sons. In 1899 it was purchased by BET and electrification was planned. The UDCs of Pontypridd and Rhondda, in whose areas the undertaking operated, each bought half in 1904. The former electrified and opened its sector in 1905 using maroon and cream livery. From 1919 services operated jointly with the Rhondda Tramways Co. One tram route was replaced by the first Pontypridd UDC motorbuses in 1930. Services run by

Tresillian Motors and Amalgamated Bus Services had in fact passed through the town since 1920/1.

Trolleybuses to convert the other two tram routes were purchased by the UDC in 1931. Subsequent deliveries, including wartime Karriers, were in service until the system closed in 1957. Livery, also used on buses, was dark blue and cream.

Bristol chassis were popular with Pontypridd but the 1948 nationalisation of that supplier precluded acceptance of further non-BTC orders and some customers had to look elsewhere. Utility Guy Arabs had proved rugged and reliable, so it was to that make that the undertaking transferred its affections until 1961. Then four AEC Reliances arrived, followed, from 1965, by several Regent Vs.

In the run-up to local government reorganisation Pontypridd livery changed to bright blue and white, still bearing the PUDC badge. The latter was replaced by the name 'Taff-Ely', still on those colours, after 1 April 1974. The new Borough Council Transport Department replaced

Bristols with Leyland Nationals starting in 1976, the paint scheme being all-blue apart from a white roof.

In 1986 the title changed to Taff-Ely Transport Ltd and at that time the fleet totalled 23 (with one double-decker). In 1975 it had been 42 (20 double-deckers). A relentless slide to insolvency followed, due to deregulation. In September 1988 the company, with 20 buses, was bought by National Welsh, itself to fall victim to the maelstrom in 1992. For a short while though, as part of the takeover agreement, Freight-Rover minibuses operated in the town by National Welsh, were in a blue livery with red, yellow and white bands and bore the fleetname 'Taff-Ely Bustler'.

Below:
The medium-sized Pontypridd fleet contained Bristols, Guys and a few AECs when No 55 (HTX 510) was panned cutting a corner on 1 September 1962. It was one of a batch of six Bristol K5Gs with Beadle H30/26R bodies built in 1949 to an order pre-dating the non-BTC ban. Undertakings placing smallish orders tended to buy unusual bodies at that time, possibly because the large manufacturers could sell everything they could make and gave preference to big orders. When photographed, No 55 was fitted with replacement windows, half-drops having given way to slide-openings.

Left:
Badge photo date: 24 March 1974. The central feature is a bridge, locally cherished, described in the text. It was usually surmounted by the initials PUDC in large gilt letters.

Portsmouth (City of) Passenger Transport Department

A name almost synonymous with The Royal Navy to many people, Portsmouth remains a major naval base despite fleet reductions and it cherishes such historical links as Nelson's ship *Victory*, still the flagship of Portsmouth Command. Before 1415 this Hampshire town was a minor port on a marshy island. It developed rapidly after, for in that year King Henry V founded the navy. Today it is home to 200,000 people, has a busy ferry port and enjoys the spacious leisure area of Southsea Common and promenade.

Below:
Portsmouth's last trolleybuses were replaced by the city's first Leyland Atlanteans in 1963. No 238 (BBK 238B), seen here in Southsea on 30 May 1966, is one of a subsequent batch built in 1964. Weymann 76-seat bodies were fitted and traditional livery with gold lining retained until, in the early 1970s, more white became standard, the lining was omitted and a more ornate coat of arms adopted. No 238 has a PDR1/1 Mark 2 chassis.

Inset:
Coat of arms photo date: 29 May 1972. Vehicles in traditional livery bore arms consisting of the shield and motto which are the central features in the version illustrated.

The Landport & Southsea Tramway Co, the oldest statutory tramway undertaking in the British Isles, obtained a private Act of Parliament in 1863 and opened a line in 1865 using horse cars in three liveries – yellow, green and chocolate, all with white relief. That undertaking, built primarily as a link for train and steamer passengers, became in 1882 part of Portsmouth Street Tramways Co (owned by the Provincial group), which had started in 1874 using trams painted red and white. Also operating a short line in the city from 1878 was General Tramways of Portsmouth Ltd which became a part of PST in 1883.

The newly-formed Corporation Tramways Department took over the company operations within Portsmouth on 1 January 1901 and commenced electrification. The first electric tram ran nine months later and the last horse cars (still in the old liveries) were withdrawn in 1903. By 1913 there was a fleet of 100 electric cars, all painted red and cream.

The Portsdown & Horndean Light Railway, with cars in green and cream, had running rights in the town to the Guildhall (from 1924) and Southsea pier (1927). That undertaking closed in 1935.

The first Corporation motorbus, a Thornycroft J, arrived in 1919 and by the early 1930s Crossley and Leyland TD double-deckers were in service (several later prewar Leylands are preserved). Some utility Daimlers arrived during World War 2 but postwar purchases were, apart from two batches of Crossleys in 1948/9, largely Leyland. All were in crimson and white livery.

Trams were replaced between 1934 and 1936 by 100 AEC trolleybuses and some bus routes were also later converted using 15 BUT trolleys which joined the fleet in 1951. However, in 1960 the City Council chose to abandon the system and the last trolleybuses were withdrawn in 1963.

Portsmouth was made a city in 1927. Municipal changes in 1974, when it ceased to be a county borough and became a district with the title of City, hardly affected the transport department, even the title remaining unchanged.

However, deregulation in 1986 accompanied adoption of the name Portsmouth City Transport Ltd which passed to a consortium led by Southampton Citybus in 1988. That resulted in the name 'Citybus' appearing and the white and crimson used by the local municipal company gave way to red and cream.

A year later the concern passed to the Stagecoach group which commenced painting buses into corporate striped livery with 'Southdown-Portsmouth', later simply 'Portsmouth', as the fleetname.

In 1991, however, after regulatory pressure, the city operation was again sold. This time it went to Transit Holdings who rapidly replaced big buses with minis. These traded as Blue Admiral in the city (blue with white and red areas) and Red Admiral (red with white and blue areas) in the hinterland.

In 1996 FirstBus came on the scene, combining those two sub-fleets with Peoples Provincial, all in red and cream livery.

On 1 April 1997 Portsmouth became a unitary authority.

As a county borough, Portsmouth issued the registration marks BK, TP and RV (and serial prefixes) until 1974.

Preston Corporation Transport Department

Now one of Lancashire's largest towns and its administrative centre, Preston is on one of the two major highways from England to Scotland and was often 'in the wars'. As recently as 1745 it was occupied by a Scottish army. Still the main industry, cotton became important when the first mill was opened in 1786 and Arkwright's spinning frame vastly increased productivity. The town has some fine buildings which add dignity to the celebration, held every 20 years, of Preston Guild. It also has a large bus and coach station, once the world's biggest. Ribble Motor Services takes its name from the river on which Preston stands and its headquarters is in the town.

The Preston Tramways Co opened a service in 1879. In 1882 W. Harding & Co leased track laid by the Corporation and started other services. The horse cars used were painted yellow and cream. In 1886 the town bought the original line and added that to Harding's lease from 1887. The lease expired on the last day of 1903 and although the Corporation Tramways Department assumed ownership the following day, in fact Harding ran horse buses for them while lines were electrified. The new trams, in maroon and yellow livery, started work in June 1904.

Most of Preston's cars were built at a works only a mile from the Town Hall. This was owned by Dick, Kerr & Co, later known as the United Electric Car Co and from 1918 as English Electric. It was the most prolific tramcar production facility in Britain.

Of the 350 buses which Preston purchased between its first in 1922 and 1986, only three (Bristol LHs) were not Leylands. This loyalty was based primarily on quality, also influenced by the fact that many townspeople worked at the Leyland factory only five miles distant. The first were G7s and carried 'Preston Corporation' as the fleetname but thereafter only the town's crest was displayed. Double-deck, open-stair TD1s arrived in 1928.

Conversion of tram routes to bus operation started in 1932 and the exercise was completed in December 1935. Thirty new double-deckers were bought as replacements.

Until 1971 all except two of the town's buses had been registered with its county borough marks of CK or RN (or serials), but some were bought second-hand that year. In 1972 Preston Licensing Office merged with that of Lancashire CC which was also in the town.

Bus livery was originally crimson and deep cream but postwar the relief shade

Above:
Kodachrome 25 film abetted by bright sunlight has contrived to show the old livery of Preston as a more cheerful shade of maroon than the gloomy colour perceived on cloudy days. The single cream band version was current from 1956 until blue and cream was adopted 10 years later. No 108, illustrated, was first of a batch of 20 (Nos 108-127, DRN 291-310) and is a Leyland Titan PD2/1 with H30/26R body by the same maker. It was new in 1950 and served until around 1970. The photograph was taken on 22 July 1963.

Below left:
Seal photo date: 1971. Locally, PP is said to denote Proud Preston.

became lighter. In 1966 a change to blue and ivory was made and later reversed with blue as the relief.

In 1974 when the town became a district with the title of Borough, the undertaking became Preston (Borough of) Transport Department and the fleetname 'Borough of Preston', still accompanied by the same town crest.

The Government's policy of establishing 'arm's length' municipal companies that were not a drain on the rates brought another change, to Preston Borough Transport Ltd, in 1986. Simultaneous deregulation of service controls led to the introduction of minibuses and the fleetnames 'Preston Mini', 'Preston Bus' and 'Preston Coach' appeared. Fierce local competition developed but was eventually beaten off. In 1993, as a result of more government persuasion, the undertaking was sold to its management and employees.

Ramsbottom Urban District Council Transport Department

A small market town on the River Irwell and confined by Pennine foothills, Ramsbottom was in Lancashire until 1974. Once it was well-known in transport circles as being among the smallest local authorities to run its own buses. Since transfer into Greater Manchester county as part of the Metropolitan Borough of Bury and losing its fleet to Selnec PTE, its main claim to fame is as a station on the reopened East Lancashire Railway. The family of Sir Robert Peel established calico printing in the town in 1783 and the nearby Peel Tower commemorates him as the Prime Minister who repealed the Corn Laws and established the first modern police force. The present-day town and district, quite picturesque in places, is working hard to become a tourist area.

Although tramway operating powers were obtained by the council (and the depot had Ramsbottom Tramways engraved on a stone), it was trolleybuses which brought electric traction to the district. These very early single-deckers operated for 17 years from 1913 to 1930 (officially withdrawn in 1931) on a three-mile route from Edenfield to Holcome Brook. They were replaced by motorbuses, adding to a fleet built up since 1922.

After early Thornycrofts very few non-Leyland chassis were among the 60 buses operated between that year and the final order, which was for a Titan PD3/14. It was delivered carrying Ramsbottom livery, fleet number and crest in the first days of Selnec's existence and was the only brand-new half-cab to be operated by a PTE.

At that time the trunk route was 10 miles in length from Rawtenstall to Bury via Ramsbottom. Saloons were used until 1947 when lowering the roadway beneath a local railway bridge permitted future orders to be mostly double-deckers. In 1960 the fleet was at about its largest, a total of 17, 10 of which were single-deckers and two of those were 21 years old.

Maroon and cream Ramsbottom buses Nos 1-12 passed to and were operated by Selnec. Some of the earlier models were never repainted before withdrawal and, indeed, one in maroon very nearly lasted into GMT ownership in 1974. Of the 10 which transferred to the enlarged PTE, three were not withdrawn until 1981, only five years short of GM Buses Ltd ownership and deregulation.

The only second-hand bus ever owned was No 12, an Albion Nimbus bought in 1968, new to Halifax Corporation but passing via Warrington CTD.

In its later years the Ramsbottom fleet was managed jointly with the nearby Rawtenstall and Haslingden undertakings, although each retained its own livery and depot.

Ramsbottom buses were registered with Lancashire CC marks.

In 1997 buses in the area are mainly in the overall orange livery of 'Greater Manchester', the FirstBus subsidiary trading as GM Buses North Ltd. This enjoyed a short PTE-owned existence from December 1993 (when GM Buses was divided) until March 1996. This livery gives continuity of a sort right back to the Selnec sunglow of 1970.

Above:
No more typical example of a municipal all-Leyland bus could be found than Ramsbottom No 25 (HTE 820), a 1947 Titan PD2/1 with H30/26R body. Standing in Rawtenstall bus station on 11 June 1967, it awaits departure on the joint route through its home town to Bury. It was one of six identical buses (Nos 20-25) which were Ramsbottom's first double-deckers. Most were withdrawn before the fleet was absorbed by Selnec on 1 November 1969 but No 21 was still in stock on that date. It was, however, withdrawn before the end of the year.

Left:
Coat of arms photo date: 29 November 1969.

Rawtenstall Corporation Motors

Situated on the upper River Irwell, prime tributary of the mighty Mersey, Rawtenstall is in east Lancashire just south of a stretch of moorland called the Forest of Rossendale. Its traditional industries are footwear and textiles, particularly the manufacture of felt. In recent years some tourism has developed, mainly as a consequence of the restored (and often steam-hauled) East Lancashire Railway terminating in the town. The southern terminus is Bury.

Starting in 1881 Rawtenstall was served five times a day by horse buses of the Bacup Carriage Co and in 1887 the Accrington Steam Carriage Co extended its tramway service to the town. Two years later the subsidiary Rossendale Valley Steam Tramways Co started to build an extension to Bacup.

Rawtenstall Corporation entered the field in 1907 with an Orion omnibus but this and the Ryknields bought the following year proved unsuccessful and were withdrawn. The Ryknields were apparently painted blue and cream.

Sections of the RVST route, owned from 1900 by BET, were acquired by the Corporation in 1908 and operated for a few months while electrification proceeded. The last steam tram ran on 22 July 1909, and was Britain's last urban operation of that mode. Two tram engines were kept as snow ploughs. Electric cars had started on

an adjacent section on 15 May the same year. Livery was maroon and cream, used also on the bus fleet until 1968.

From 1910 to 1916 Accrington Corporation trams could be seen in the town working a joint service as far as Bacup, five miles to the east and approached via long valleys. By 1921 Rawtenstall's tram fleet numbered 32.

Corporation buses were introduced in 1924 and, being successful, started replacing some trams in 1929, the remainder going in 1932. Nearly all buses purchased were Leylands. A single utility Guy Arab, delivered in 1943, was rebodied in 1951.

Although the Department was titled Rawtenstall Corporation Motors, only the first two words appeared as fleetname which, postwar, was in a very elegant style. Buses were registered with Lancashire CC marks.

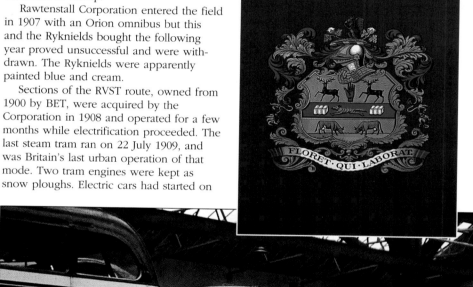

The General Manager was also responsible for operating the neighbouring undertakings of Haslingden (from 1949) and Ramsbottom (1951). Formation of a joint operation with Haslingden occurred in April 1968, Rawtenstall contributing 45 to the fleet of 60. Buses were lettered 'Rossendale Joint Transport Committee' initially, but by 1971 'Rossendale' surmounted by the arms of both boroughs was in use. Livery was crimson and cream, not unlike Rawtenstall's maroon.

In 1974 the Borough of Rossendale was formed and the undertaking dropped the words Joint and Committee from the title, simply using the fleetname 'Rossendale' but no insignia. Later the word was accompanied by a logo representing two green hills and continued in use after 'Limited' was added to the title in 1986. The livery of some buses was then enhanced by the addition of one green band.

In 1996 the company remains in the possession of the local authority and has a greatly expanded operating area. There is a second depot, in Rochdale, and its buses are seen as far south as Manchester.

Left:
Coat of arms photo date: 21 May 1978.

Below:
When seen inside Rawtenstall's depot on 17 June 1960 No 46 (DTD 250) had been withdrawn for three years but was still owned and used as a mobile polling booth, presumably in an outlying hamlet with no school or other suitable premises. It is a standard all-Leyland product of 1938, a 36-seat Tiger TS8.

Reading Corporation Transport

Roman farms and villas dotted this part of mid-southern Britain but it was the 19th century before the market town of Reading, which had grown up around a 13th century abbey, experienced much development. Situated close to attractive stretches of the Thames Valley and Chiltern Hills, this Berkshire town, a county borough until 1974, now has industries centred on biscuit making, brewing and engineering.

The Reading Tramway Co operated a maximum of 13 horse cars from 1879 until purchased by the Corporation in 1901. The horse lines were worked municipally until 1903 when, following electrification, 30 new four-wheeled, open-topped trams in crimson and cream livery took over. Six bogie cars arrived the following year and this fleet provided the backbone of local transport for over three decades, the last being withdrawn in 1939.

Buses were first operated in 1919, but the tramway replacements were trolley-buses. The first went into service in 1936. In their turn they became inconvenient for road planners and municipal economists alike and the last one ran in its home town in 1968. Some had extended lives else-where, particularly on Teesside.

AEC was a major supplier of both bus and trolleybus chassis for many years

though soon after World War 2 double-deck Crossleys and petrol-engined Bedford 'midis' were purchased. The last two batches of trolleybuses were Sunbeams.

In the 1960s the Reading bus fleet included many Dennis Lolines and double-doored standee type Bristol REs and AEC Reliances.

Somewhere along the line livery changed from what has been described as crimson and cream to what was then called maroon and cream. This was a common occurrence with fleets employing dark reds and is perhaps mainly attributable to different paint manufacturers' names for similar shades, or perhaps removal of lead from formulations.

Reading Transport became the under-taking's name in 1974, and the relief element in the livery was lightened to what was described as white but could equally well have been cream or even ivory.

In the mid-1980s double-decked MCW

Above:
Dennis Lolines were purchased in three batches by Reading between 1962 and 1966. All were Mark IIIs and carried East Lancs bodies classified as LD68F. No 44 (ADP 944B) was one of 10 acquired in 1964 (others were eight each in 1962-6) and is seen here on 18 October 1972 in Station Hill, the bus/rail interchange. Reading Corporation Transport was a devotee of plat-form doors on buses since 1950. Lolines had them as standard.

Below left:
Coat of arms: 18 October 1972.

Metrobuses and Leyland Titans (the only rear-engined Titans to be supplied new to a municipal fleet) operated a frequent express service to London, taking advantage of revised regulations for coach travel which became effective in 1981. They ran under the name 'Goldline London Express'. The fleet at that time totalled nearly 150.

'Limited' was added to the title in 1986. Part of the Beeline company's operation was bought in 1992. About that time a turquoise band was added to the Reading Bus livery and later a green band was used on those vehicles operating in Newbury. Latterly, coaches have appeared in a livery of metallic blues.

At the time of writing (mid-1997) Reading is one of 17 undertakings which remain municipally owned.

Until 1974 Reading County Borough issued the registration marks DP and RD (and serial prefixes). In April of that year the town became a district with the title of Borough.

Rochdale Corporation Transport Department

As a Lancashire town, Rochdale received world fame as the birthplace of the Co-operative movement, John Bright and Gracie Fields. Its gothic-style town hall would be prized in many a metropolis. The population of 100,000 is less employed in the cotton industry now, but that material was responsible for the town's initial growth. The climate tends to be moist 400ft up in the Pennine foothills, and that is an advantage when handling delicate thread. The county borough became a metropolitan district (borough) of Greater Manchester county in 1974.

One association the name Rochdale has for transport enthusiasts is the late lamented Yelloway Motor Services whose headquarters were in the town centre. The town's buses and Yelloway coaches were always registered with Rochdale's DK or serial prefixes until 1974. Currently the mark is issued only when specially requested from Manchester VRO.

Horse buses were running in Rochdale in 1856 and a regular service to Oldham six miles away started in 1870. The (Manchester,) Bury, Rochdale & Oldham Steam Tramways Co started operating in the town in 1883 using a variety of liveries, that on trailers included green and cream.

In 1899 the Corporation took a decision to have its own electric system and construction started in 1901, the first route opening in 1902. Also in 1902 the Steam Tramway Co was served with notice to sell its tracks to the Council. Possession was taken in 1904, the last steam working occurring on the Littleborough section in 1905. Electrification of those lines followed and leases were secured on tracks owned by several neighbouring but non-operating urban district councils. In the Borough of Bacup, Rochdale even maintained a small depot and some track was also leased from the Borough of Heywood. It was not until the Middleton Electric Traction Co was bought out jointly with Manchester in 1925 that Rochdale trams ran through to that city.

Guy and Dennis saloons were the Corporation's first buses in 1926 but the next three years saw significant development in double-deck design which, coupled with imminent expensive track repairs, led to Rochdale's being the first major municipal tramway abandonment in the northwest. The maximum number of trams operated at any one time was 88, although over 100 had been owned by the time Crossley double-deckers replaced the survivors in 1932.

AEC was the major bus supplier to the Corporation between 1945 and 1954 but Daimlers also were purchased, Fleetlines introducing the rear-engined type in 1964.

Rochdale tramway livery was dark brown and pale yellow, also used on early buses. Later, dark blue and cream was

Above:
Coat of arms photo date: 14 June 1969.

Below left:
Until around 1946/7 (when Bury and Salford went green) Rochdale's livery was a blue jewel in a sea of reds – Manchester, Salford, Bury, Bolton, Oldham, Ramsbottom, Rawtenstall – not to mention LUT, Ribble and North Western – all ran into or near the town. No 319 (TDK 319) stands in Bury town centre on 3 October 1959. It is an AEC Regent V D2RA built in 1958 with Weymann H33/28RD body, one of a batch of four (Nos 319-322) having platform doors. In later years the livery was made commonplace by reducing dark blue to one band at cantrail or waist level, all else being cream.

adopted. By 1960 the layout was basically cream with blue relief.

The undertaking was one of 10 in Manchester's satellite towns which merged with the big city fleet on 1 November 1969 to form South East Lancashire North East Cheshire Passenger Transport Executive (Selnec).

Several vehicles ordered by Rochdale were delivered to the PTE, one batch of AEC Swifts even receiving their 'booked' TDK-J marks in 1971/2. Soon sunglow orange and cream came to the streets of the conurbation and many of the 128 buses relinquished to the PTE by Rochdale survived to receive slightly darker orange in Greater Manchester PTE ownership after 1974. No genuine Rochdale survivor achieved GM Buses ownership in 1986 but a batch of Fleetlines actually ordered by RCTD lasted until 1984/5, only a year or so short.

In 1986 the PTE formed an 'arm's length' company, GM Buses Ltd, to take over operations. It continued the orange-based livery. Following its division in 1993 the company covering Rochdale, GM Buses North Ltd, was sold to FirstBus in 1996 and the buses now carry a virtually entirely orange 'livery' and bear the fleetname 'Greater Manchester'.

Rossendale Joint Transport Committee

This fleet became operational on 1 April 1968 when the committee assumed control of bus services previously operated by Haslingden (15 vehicles) and Rawtenstall (45). The relevant pages provide details of those.

Both contributory fleets were entirely Leyland except that each owned a non-PSV BMC personnel carrier. A livery of light blue and cream was carried by the smaller predecessor, while ex-Rawtenstall buses were maroon and cream. Those vehicles not earmarked for early disposal were gradually repainted into crimson and cream.

Initially buses were lettered 'Rossendale Joint Transport Committee' in full, but later the name 'Rossendale' surmounted by the two boroughs' crests was adopted (both types are illustrated).

Leyland Leopard saloons ordered by both participants were delivered to the JTC (it was then common for two years to elapse between order and delivery – hence subsequent inroads by foreign makers offering better time-scales).

New buses were bought by the Committee in 1971/2/3, all being Leopards with East Lancs bodies.

Rawtenstall's general manager had supervised the Haslingden fleet since 1949 and Ramsbottom's since 1951. The joint committee's manager continued the arrangement with Ramsbottom until 1969,

when the latter was absorbed into Selnec PTE.

Rawtenstall and Haslingden boroughs merged to become the district of Rossendale (taking the title of Borough) on 1 April 1974 and the JTC became Rossendale Transport (Department). On that date 27 single- and 25 double-decker buses (of which 21 were new to the committee) changed owners. Subsequently the undertaking bought Bristol RESL saloons followed by Leyland Atlantean double-deckers.

The livery continued as crimson and cream with the latter becoming predominant on double-deckers. 'Rossendale' was still used as fleetname but was later accompanied by a logo representing two green hills.

In October 1986 the undertaking became a limited company, the fleet expanding to cope with the more extensive operating area which deregulated services encouraged. Rochdale became well served by Rossendale buses and eventually a depot was established there. Even Manchester, 18 miles away, was reached by services passing through Bury. A slightly different livery of cream and red, some-

times with a green band in addition to the logo, was introduced. Coaches are ivory, red and crimson.

Ellen Smith (Tours) Ltd, a prominent Rochdale firm, was purchased around 1991. In mid-1997 Rossendale Transport remained municipally owned.

Above:
Coat of arms photo date: 11 September 1971. This is the second version, used from about 1970 to 1974.

Below:
The newly formed operator's first new buses arrived within days of the merger in 1968. They were five Leyland PSU4/2R Leopards with East Lancashire B44F bodies. Three (Nos 52-54, JTF 152-4F) were a Rawtenstall CT order, two (Nos 55/6, LTD 995/6F) were intended for Haslingden. Illustrated is No 53 bearing the original fleetname. It waits in Rawtenstall bus station on 25 April 1968. Still relatively new, it passed from the Joint Transport Committee to the ownership of Rossendale Borough Transport on 1 April 1974.

Rotherham Corporation Transport Department

The written history of Rotherham describes a market town established in Saxon times near the confluence of the Rivers Rother and Don. It was in the 19th century that the town developed into one of the centres of very heavy industry in Yorkshire, having coal resources nearby to fuel iron and steel production. Having been in the West Riding of Yorkshire until 1974, it exchanged county borough for metropolitan district status (and chose to have the title of Borough) and became part of South Yorkshire county. Its registration marks had been ET and xET.

For a time in the 1920s it was possible to travel by tram from the north of Barnsley to the south of Sheffield, over 20 miles, with changes, using the cars of five operators. The fourth was Rotherham Corporation.

Pre-municipal horse tramways were never started in Rotherham, leaving the Corporation a clean sheet to open electric lines on routes most suitable to cater for recent development. The first opened in 1903 using 12 double- and three single-deck cars. A through joint service with Sheffield began in 1905 and later a joint route to Rawmarsh and Mexborough was opened with the Mexborough & Swinton Tramways Co. At one time the cars of all three operators could be seen together in Rotherham centre.

Rotherham owned track in Tinsley until 1925, although that rural district had been absorbed by Sheffield in 1911.

Trolleybus and motorbus operations were started by the Corporation in 1912 and 1913 respectively, within 11 years of trams appearing. The first trolleybus route was quite isolated until 1924 and it was not until 1929 that the more flexible and quieter vehicles replaced some tram services. By 1936 only the route to Sheffield survived, operated by 11 single-ended, double-deck trams until 1949. New in 1934/5, these cars resembled trolleybuses on rails. They turned on loops at the termini, with a reversing triangle for a short working.

Until 1955 the trolleybus fleet, which had expanded to nearly 50, consisted entirely of very fast single-deckers. In that year 20 were rebodied as double-deckers and the system was reduced in extent. It closed in 1965.

Rotherham trams had carried maroon and pale yellow livery, changed to dark blue and cream in 1919. The unidirectional batch were cream with blue relief.

The bus fleet developed steadily from 1913, Bristol chassis being bought as the mainstay between 1923 and 1949. When that marque became unavailable due to nationalisation, Daimler and Crossley found

Above:
No 35 (FET 338) was one of 20 single-decker Rotherham trolleybuses rebodied as Roe H72R double-deckers in 1956. It is seen in Rotherham on 22 May 1960. The Daimler CTC6 chassis with Crompton-Parkinson electrical equipment, was built in 1949. Although rebodying improved the operating economics by allowing longer headways, it delayed abandonment of the system by only nine years.

Below left:
Coat of arms photo date: 13 August 1956.

favour. Postwar trolleybuses were all Daimlers. Fleet livery was blue and cream.

On 1 April 1974, as a result of the formation of South Yorkshire, Rotherham's buses joined those of Sheffield and Doncaster to form SYPTE's fleet. As repainting became necessary, experimental light coffee and cream and later mushroom and cream were tried. Steel blue and smoke grey would have been more symbolic! Eventually a darker coffee colour was chosen.

By 1986, when the undertaking became South Yorkshire Transport Ltd, a more attractive red, brown and cream was uniform. Several liveries were then introduced for different types of service, with local variants of a standard layout for the Mainline fleet (yellow, blue and red, or yellow, blue and black in Rotherham). In 1992 Mainline was adopted as company name and a new standard livery of yellow, red, grey and blue came into use in all areas. In November 1993 Mainline was sold to its employees.

St Helens Corporation Transport

Coal and later glass have been the industries which made St Helens, and the latter remains a major employer. Now a metropolitan district (borough) in Merseyside, it was until 1974 a county borough in south Lancashire and had the registration mark DJ (and xDJ of course).

Although the town had a population of 100,000 then, it did not become a municipal transport operator until 1919. The previous history was unusually complex, starting with horse buses in the 1860s, horse trams of the 'old' St Helens & District Tramways Co in 1881 and followed by steam tramways of a 'new' StH&DTCo in 1890.

In 1897 the Corporation, contemplating operation, purchased the company track including some in Haydock, Prescot and Whiston districts, but decided against and leased it back.

Yet another company, the New St Helens &DT was formed in 1898. It had some managerial connection with the Lancashire Light Railways Co (which owned the Liverpool & Prescot Light Railway) and South Lancashire Tramways. The shares of both LLR and SLT were bought in 1900 by a new company, South Lancashire Electric Traction and Power.

Electric trams first ran in the town in 1899 and steam operation ended in 1900. Briefly, from 1903 to 1905, there existed a through tram service from St Helens to

Liverpool Pier Head using Lancashire Light Railway cars.

Lancashire United Tramways Co assumed responsibility for operations in 1906 following voluntary liquidation of SLETP in 1904. The New StH&DT and LLR remained separate companies, although closely associated. Both used dark red and cream livery from 1899 to 1913 and green and cream from 1913 to 1919. Fleet numbers were in a common series. In 1919 St Helens Corporation rescinded the track lease, bought the 36 NStH cars and commenced operating. The seven LLR cars passed to SLT (LUT). The corporation tramway system operated until 1936, having been gradually replaced by buses and trolleybuses.

County Carriers (later known as St Helens & District Motor Services) had, with encouragement from the Corporation, started bus services in non-tram served areas from 1914. Directly controlled operations commenced in 1921, using two buses

hired from Bristol T&CC. The first owned buses, several Guys and a Bristol, were bought in 1923/4 and ran in blue livery until 1925.

StH&D Motors was taken over by the Corporation in 1927, the same year that trolleybuses went into service. The first trolleys were single-deckers but double-deckers followed in 1931. That year a 14-mile route to Atherton started, operated jointly with South Lancashire Transport which had also introduced trolleybuses.

By the start of World War 2, 52 St Helens trolleybuses comprised 57% of the total fleet and to cope with wartime demand 8ft-wide Sunbeams diverted from Johannesburg (and utility Guy Arab motorbuses) were acquired. BUTs were the last bought, in 1951, and the system closed (as did SLT's) in 1958.

Replacement buses were largely Leyland and AEC, some of the latter being RT type. The last double-deckers came in 1967. From that time only AEC Swifts, 66 in all, were purchased.

St Helens CT ran trams in the company green and cream from 1919 to 1921, then in red and cream. Buses after 1925 and all trolleybuses (except those delivered painted in overall grey in 1942) were also red and cream.

The undertaking became part of Merseyside Passenger Transport Executive on 1 April 1974. Initially some buses, including rear-loaders drafted in from the Wirral to St Helens, continued to be painted red and cream but it was not many years before Merseyside light green and cream (brown added later) prevailed. Merseyside Transport Ltd, trading as Merseybus, was formed in 1986 and in 1988 maroon and cream livery made an appearance (following a two-greens trial).

The company was sold to its employees in 1992 and became MTL Trust Holdings Ltd. A local identity, MTL St Helens Rider, existed briefly in 1993/4 using traditional red and cream livery. It was overtaken by the formation of St Helens-based MTL Lancashire Travel. This area identity initially continued to use maroon and cream but adopted corporate cream and crimson when it appeared in 1994.

Above:
Leyland Titan PD2/27 No 55 (MDJ 555E), one of a batch of six (Nos 50-55), stands outside Shaw Street depot (now the capacious premises of St Helens Transport Museum) on 23 February 1974, five weeks before Merseyside PTE became its owner. The East Lancashire H37/28R body, united with the chassis in 1967, is adorned with what has become known as a 'St Helens front'. This entire batch were eventually repainted in PTE green and cream though retaining their St Helens fleet numbers, and all were withdrawn in 1980.

Below right:
Coat of arms photo date: 5 May 1970.

Salford City Transport

Like its twin city Manchester, Salford was one of the earliest towns to be affected by the Industrial Revolution and only in recent years has the legacy of cramped housing cheek by jowl with factories been cast off. The major 'Manchester Docks' were in fact in Salford, 35 miles from the seaward end of the Ship Canal, and handled vessels up to 12,500 tons. Salford Quays, a marvellous amalgam of new businesses, entertainment, housing and marinas has replaced the wharfs. Soon Metrolink trams will link the area with Manchester and Eccles.

Salford's charter is older than Manchester's, but they share honours in historic transport as John Greenwood's 1824 horse omnibus traversed the former to reach the latter. Subsequent horse bus/tram developments ran in parallel, Salford laying tracks in 1876, leasing them in 1877, municipalising in 1901 and opening its first electric tram services that same year. Later the undertaking leased lines in adjacent districts and from the South Lancashire Tramways Co. It also obtained powers to run on the private tracks of Trafford Park Estates.

Oddly, due to geography, many Salford tram routes ran across the River Irwell into Manchester to unload/load and turn, Deansgate being the focus. Joint routes were operated in the 1920s with SLT, Manchester and Bury.

At its maximum the tram fleet totalled 224 and, despite serious maintenance problems during World War 2, a small number remained in service until replacement buses were delivered in 1947.

Predecessor Manchester Carriage & Tramways Co livery had been red and cream, but Salford used maroon and cream on its electric cars until 1912 and thereafter red and cream. Due to paint shortages in the war, red-brown, all-red, grey and cream, all-grey and other odd combinations appeared on buses and some trams.

Buses were first acquired in 1920 but the fleet expanded in the 1930s and included some Dennis double-deckers of decidedly fussy frontal design. There were also Crossleys, but most of the fleet were Leyland and AEC. Despite a chronic shortage of reliable vehicles in the early 1940s, Salford was not allocated utility buses by the Ministry of Supply.

Routes joint with Manchester, Bolton and Lancashire United etc started in 1927 but many succumbed to the 1930 Road Traffic Act.

Initial postwar deliveries, AEC, Crossley and Leyland, retained red and cream livery (some with silver roofs). A new regime

determined to improve the image out of all recognition and introduced green and cream with silver roofs in 1947. This was similar to the colours used at the new manager's previous post but seemed inspirational at the time. Following delivery of Leyland Titan PD1s in the new colours, 210 Daimler CVG6s, including six saloons and a coach, were ordered and arrived in 1950-52. These formed a very uniform but smart fleet. Later the silver roof and some cream bands were omitted. A reversed scheme of green bands on cream was used to mark the 1953 Coronation and the undertaking's 60th anniversary in 1961. The title had changed from Salford Corporation Transport to Salford City Transport in 1947.

The management abhorred external advertising on buses, a coat of arms appearing on both decks. Manchester permitted such advertising and it was said that Salford's newest buses, in pristine condition, were always put on a route which passed the office window of that undertaking's manager. The point about visible pollution was, sadly, not taken.

In 1962 fleet numbers reverted to 101 (after having reached 560) and the following year two each of rear-engined Fleetline and Atlantean models were bought. Subsequent orders were mixed – front-engined rear loaders and rear-engined front loaders – until 1967. Deliveries in 1968/9 were all the latter.

Salford was the second largest of the 11 municipal undertakings merged into Selnec PTE on 1 November 1969 and many of its

Above:
Some of the first postwar Metro-Cammell-bodied buses delivered to Salford arrived in traditional red and cream but were rapidly repainted by the new management. The all-Leyland tram replacements which arrived later the same year were, however, already in green and cream. Titan PD1 No 309 (CRJ 309) is one of the first batch with H30/26R bodies. It is depicted heading west on the A6 at the Woolpack, Pendleton, a location now changed out of all recognition. Salford buses had a hard life on the city's unyielding and uneven granite setts until tarmacadam covered the main roads in the 1950s. Despite that, No 309 had quite a long life, not being withdrawn until 1963. It is depicted two years earlier, on 28 October 1961.

Below left:
Coat of arms photo date: 29 November 1969.

buses were still serving when Greater Manchester orange and cream replaced PTE sunglow and cream in 1974. Some of those transferred survived until 1982.

Salford's registration marks BA, RJ and serial prefixes were transferred to Manchester LVLO in October 1974. Earlier, on 1 April, Salford changed from a county borough to a Greater Manchester metropolitan district with the title of City, and absorbed the neighbouring borough of Eccles and other districts.

Salford's thoroughfares now see both the overall orange livery of 'Greater Manchester' as the FirstBus subsidiary GM Buses North Ltd proclaims itself on the buses, and the corporate colours of GM Buses South Ltd (Stagecoach Manchester). This is a consequence of the 1993 division and 1996 sale of the 1986 arms-length GM Buses Ltd.

Sheffield Transport Department

The city was a self-contained steel manu-facturing complex specialising in cutting tools. Iron ore, water power, charcoal, coal and gritstone for sharpening – it was all locally available. Now many of the steel mills have gone and at least one of the sites is a shopping city served by South Yorkshire's Supertram which began oper-ating on 21 March 1994.

Horse buses began working in the city in 1852 and horse trams of the Sheffield Tramway Co joined them in 1873. When the track lease expired in 1896 the City Council became one of the first municipal tramway operators; horse at first, with elec-tric commencing in 1899. The last horse car ran in 1902. A service joint with Rotherham Corporation started in 1905.

Motorbus operations commenced in 1913, delayed by difficulty in finding machines which would reliably cope with the hilly routes. After World War 1, bus services expanded, especially in areas lacking tram routes.

As a result of the LNER and LMSR obtaining bus operating powers in 1928, Sheffield Joint Omnibus Committee was formed in 1929. The whole area was divided into three route groups referred to as A, B and C.

'A' were entirely within the city boundary and served by corporation buses; 'B' were routes serving adjacent districts, vehicles being 50% railway-owned; and 'C' were run by wholly railway-owned buses and coaches. 'C' included long routes such as that over the Snake Pass to Manchester.

Buses in the 'B' and 'C' fleets were oper-ated by the Corporation on behalf of the JOC and Railway companies.

Trams owned in 1940 totalled 444 and only a few routes had by then been converted to buses. In 1951 a policy deci-sion to replace them was taken, though new cars arrived as late as 1952. The system closed in 1960, two years earlier than originally envisaged.

Horse trams carried a variety of liveries, the original being crimson and cream, and the Corporation did not change it. They chose cream and royal blue, sometimes cream and two blues, for the electric fleet (and later for all buses including 'B' and 'C'). Only during World War 2 did liveries vary, some buses and trams appearing in brown and cream, grey and white or overall grey. In 1952 there were unsuc-cessful experiments with all-green and two shades of green.

Postwar the bus fleet was very varied in manufacture and type, being mainly AEC and Leyland but including some Crossley, Daimler and Guy models.

Ownership was denoted by a small letter near the fleet number. In 1959:

'A' block was Nos 200-900,

'B' blocks were Nos 1-199 and 1251 onwards,

'C' block was Nos 1142-1207.

All trams were corporation-owned, fleet numbers duplicating some used for buses. After 1960 rear-engined double-deckers became the staple of the city bus fleet.

On 1 January 1970, the Joint Committee (since 1948 Sheffield and British Railways) was dissolved, some routes and vehicles passing to NBC subsidiaries. Sheffield, formerly in the West Riding of Yorkshire, became a metropolitan district of the new county of South Yorkshire on 1 April 1974 and retained the title of City. On the same day the second phase of PTE creations merged the fleets of Sheffield, Rotherham and Doncaster into South Yorkshire PTE. Successively, light coffee, mushroom, and darker coffee, all with cream as contrast, were tried, before, in the early 1980s, red, brown and cream became standard.

During 1986 the undertaking became South Yorkshire Transport Ltd, subsidies evaporated, and fares rocketed.

A variety of minor liveries were used for mini, express, bendybus, etc operations. There were geographic variants for the Mainline fleet. Yellow and red was used on Sheffield-based vehicles. The complexity was partially reduced in 1992 when yellow, red, grey and blue became standard in all areas and Mainline was adopted as company name. In November 1993, following central government pressure, Mainline was sold by the PTE to the company employees.

Pre-1974 the city issued the registrations W, WA, WB, WE, WJ and their serials.

Below left:
Pictured near Millhouses on 22 May 1960, only four months before the system closed on 8 October, is Sheffield tramcar No 528. It was one of 35 seating 62 built by Roberts in 1952 and rode on a Maley & Taunton four-wheel truck. The full batch were numbered 502-536 and they were the last trams to be built for Sheffield. Restored cars from the city system can still be travelled on at Crich and Beamish.

Below:
Coat of arms photo date: 13 August 1972 (as displayed on a bus).

South Shields Corporation Transport Department

South Shields is a mixture of port and seaside resort, frequent shipping movements in and out of the River Tyne being visible from its long beach and promenade. The ex-County Durham town was once used by the Romans as a granary to support the legions on Hadrian's Wall not far away. In the 19th century the town had a thriving coal export trade but this is now replaced by timber importing.

The South Shields Tramways Co started running horse cars on corporation-owned lines in 1883 but ceased in 1886. The South Shields Tramways & Carriage Co restarted the service in 1887 adding horse buses, but sold out to BET in 1899. These trams, still horse-powered, operated until 1906 when

the Corporation took over and electrified the system. Its fleet built up to 60 cars before closures commenced in 1938. A single tram of modern design was purchased as late as 1936. One route, the sleeper track to Cleadon, survived until 1946. Between 1908-11 and again 1924-7 a joint service between the towns was run with the Jarrow & District Electric Traction Co.

Edison accumulator buses started work for the Corporation in 1914 and it was 1919 before petrol-engined models replaced them. The bus fleet still only totalled 10 following the delivery of four diesel-engined Daimler saloons in 1934.

Trolleybuses, introduced as tram replacements in 1936, were all Karriers until Sunbeams arrived after the war. More Karriers followed. The system closed in 1964, some of the final vehicles to be operated having originated with St Helens.

Postwar bus purchases consisted of double-decked Daimlers supplemented by Guys and one batch of Crossleys painted in a blue and primrose version of Manchester's striking double streamline style.

Tramway livery between 1906 and 1938 was basically maroon and cream but other colours were briefly tried. The trolleybuses arrived painted blue and primrose, subsequently used also for buses and trams. During the war a few trolleybuses were all-grey.

Buses and trolleybuses, except the few second-hand, were registered with the county borough's mark CU until 1958, when this slow-issuing authority finally reached ACU. The mark was transferred to Newcastle LVLO in 1974.

Above:
Trolleybus No 205 (BDJ 77) was one of a batch of eight new to St Helens as Nos 174-181 (later renumbered 374-381). South Shields allocated Nos 201-3/5-9 when they were bought after their original operator's trolley system closed in 1958. They were Sunbeam F4 type with East Lancashire H29/26R bodies built in Bridlington. The photo location is the Pier Head on 20 July 1963, the year before South Shields also went all-diesel.

Below left:
Coat of arms photo date: 31 October 1969.

In 1969, just prior to the formation of Tyneside PTE on 1 October and the merging of the town's fleet with that of Newcastle on 1 January 1970, South Shields received a batch of ECW-bodied Bristol RE saloons and these ran well into the Tyne & Wear PTE era, which commenced on 1 April 1974. On that day the town became the Metropolitan District of South Tyneside (in Tyne & Wear county) and adopted the title of Borough.

Both PTEs used Newcastle's yellow and cream livery and this was given a local identity colour on cantrail and skirt (blue for South Shields) after Busways Travel Services Ltd took over on 26 October 1986.

The company became part of Stagecoach Holdings in 1994 and repaints into corporate striped livery started in 1995.

As light rail is a modern version of street tramways, it is relevant to mention that Tyne & Wear Metro has operated into South Shields since 1984. This remains PTE-owned and until recently used that organisation's yellow and cream livery.

Southampton Corporation Transport

This Hampshire city, a port for nearly 2,000 years, has seen many invasion fleets sail. It saw the Pilgrim Fathers' *Mayflower* depart for North America and has welcomed the world's largest liners. One of the relics of Norman times is the Bargate, the arch of which determined the height and roof profile of many of Southampton's trams.

Horse-drawn cars were introduced in 1879 by the Southampton Tramways Co using track leased for the customary 21 years. The corporation purchased the assets early, in 1898, to facilitate electrification of the two routes. Work started promptly, making the city a horse tramcar operator for less than two years as the first electric services started in January 1900. New routes were opened and expansion continued after World War 1, the final significant line opening in 1930. Early cars were of the open-top knifeboard type. Later covered-top double-deckers were low-height with specially profiled roofs. Bargate was bypassed in 1938.

Tramway replacement became policy about 1934 and a route changed to buses in 1936. After World War 2 substitution proceeded rapidly. The last tram ran on 31 December 1949, almost the 50th anniversary of electric services.

One year before the end, the first privately inspired step in the tramway preservation movement occurred when the Light Railway Transport League (now Light Rail Transit Association) acquired open-top Car 45. This is now one of the gems at the National Tramway Museum, Crich, Derbyshire.

The first bus trial by Southampton was in 1900, too early for the machine (an 11-seater) to carry a registration mark. However, the trial was not successful and the department did not become a bus operator until 1919.

For some years the city emulated siblings such as Liverpool by building its own tram and bus bodies, but this ceased in the 1930s. Covered-top buses were not built until 1929.

An unusual responsibility for the department was operation of the Floating Bridge from the city to Itchen, across the river of that name.

To replace the last trams and prewar bus fleet, 185 Guy Arab double-deckers and 12 saloons, all with Park Royal bodies, were bought between 1946-55. Three Albion 'midis' followed in 1956. Leylands and AECs started to replace the Guys from 1960. The first rear-engined buses arrived after 1970.

Tram livery was always red-based. The earliest electric trams were red and white, some with primrose added from 1923. Some prewar buses, however, were blue and cream. Wartime saw the use of overall grey. Postwar Guys were crimson and cream with a silver roof but Leyland Atlanteans introduced a lighter red with more cream.

Above:
The city fleet's large Guy contingent is represented by No 69 (LOW 215), a Gardner 6LW-powered Arab III built in 1954. A Park Royal H30/26R body was fitted and appropriately, as the design work was done locally, a Cave-Brown-Cave cooling/heating system is fitted. Its air intakes can be seen near the front indicator boxes. When caught on film, No 69 was crossing Civic Centre Road on 30 May 1966.

Below left:
Coat of arms photo date: 4 April 1983. The example shown, although an exact replica of the transfer used on buses, was in fact seen on restored tram No 45.

Southampton became a city in 1964 and the undertaking's name changed to City of Southampton TD. It altered again to Southampton City Transport Ltd in 1986, with 'Citybus' as the fleetname.

Some buses appeared in plain red with a black skirt but a subsequent lightening to red and white accompanied a policy of 90% single-deck (minis incorporated some orange). Coaches using 'Red Ensign' as a fleetname are a darker red. The undertaking was sold to its employees in December 1993. Purchase by FirstBus was completed in mid-1977

Using Southampton Guys as testbeds, the Cave-Brown-Cave bus heating system was developed by a Southampton University professor of that name in the 1950/60s. Frontal appearance was not enhanced.

Southampton county borough registration marks until 1974, when it became a district council with city title, were CR, TR, OW and prefix serials.

The city became a unitary authority on 1 April 1997.

Southend-on-Sea Corporation Transport

The position of Southend on the north side of the Thames estuary decided its past dual role as 'Blackpool of the South' – a playground for London's masses and a residence for those able to commute to the capital. Its name is derived from being the south end of the parish of Prittlewell. Nowadays the Essex town has fewer visitors and is more self-contained. Many pensioners choose the quiet life of its suburbs.

A well-known feature is the longest passenger pier in the world which is served by a corporation-owned railway. This ran as a horse tramway from about 1850 to 1881 and was electrified in 1890. In 1949 seven-car trains resembling Blackpool streamlined single-deck trams were bought. Following a period of closure it now operates again and in 1995 acquired a battery railcar for winter use.

The town tramways were never horse-drawn. In 1901 the council opened electric lines built under light railway orders, although subsequently entitling them Southend-on-Sea Corporation Tramways. What was probably the earliest tramway sleeper track in England was laid in 1913 as part of a boulevard route, partly through shrubbery. This was popular with visitors who rode single-deck 'toastracks' on circular services. Enclosed double-deckers served workaday town operations, however, until the last route closed in 1942.

Southend had grown large enough to become a county borough by 1914. One year earlier a trial with motorbuses finished prematurely when they were commandeered for war service. Nothing further was done until 1932, when single- and double-deck AECs were purchased.

Trolleybuses, originally single-deckers with open cab and centre entrance, came into service in 1925. The first double-deckers were built with 'piano fronts' and mock radiator grilles. Later models were more orthodox. The system closed in 1954.

Motorbuses had to be able to pass under a low bridge and double-deckers were therefore always lowheight. In the 1960s/70s the fleet included AEC Bridgemasters and Leyland Lowlanders, both unusual for a municipality. Open-top buses were popular on the seafront services for many years.

In the 1980s the undertaking, since 1974 named Southend Transport, took advantage of coach deregulation to operate several services to London. They were primarily for commuters and the yellow and blue vehicles became a familiar sight in the capital.

Tram livery was green and cream from 1901-7 and again from 1925, two shades of green being used between those periods. Bus and trolleybus colours changed to light blue and cream (cream with a blue band on open-toppers). When the undertaking became a limited company in 1986 a red band was added. An unusual development somewhat later was the use of ex-London Routemasters but most were phased out following the purchase of the company by the British Bus group in 1993. T. Cowie PLC took over the entire British Bus organisation in 1996.

Southend's registration marks from 1914 to 1974 (when it became a district council with the title of Borough) were HJ, JN and prefix serials.

Left:
Coat of arms photo date: 7 April 1972.

Below:
A total of 273 Leyland/Albion Lowlanders were built, Southend and Luton being the only municipalities to buy them. Southend No 325 (7089 HJ) is an LR7 model built in 1963 with Alexander H41/29F body. The scene is the promenade near the Gas Light & Coke Company's famous conveyor used to transfer coal inland from a jetty, and the date is 28 May 1967. No 325 is clearly badged as a Leyland despite being classed as an Albion in some literature. The Lowlander was in effect a low-height Leyland PD3 but usually carried an Albion badge in Scotland, where most of the orders for it originated. Bodybuilders seemed unable to provide a well-proportioned front end, not helped in Southend's examples by a relatively deep indicator box array.

Southport Corporation Transport Department

Southport is a sedate place, proud of tree-lined Lord Street, its wide shopping thoroughfare. It is probably still uncomfortable about its 1974 status change from a county borough in Lancashire to the northern end of the Metropolitan District (Borough) of Sefton in Merseyside county. The southern end is Bootle (also an ex-county borough), 12 miles distant across largely open country. Southport has a large pleasure beach and a long pier on which a railway has run since 1863. Now standing a few miles offshore is the Lennox oil/gas production platform, Australian-owned and part of the Irish Sea petroleum industry.

Public transport dates from 1873 when the Southport Tramway Co began a horse car service. The Birkdale & Southport Tramway Co also opened lines in a different area in 1883. The Corporation purchased the tracks of both companies within the borough in 1896 (changes effective 1 January 1900) and Birkdale UDC also acquired the STC lines in its own area, leasing them back. The company continued horse-drawn services in Birkdale until 1902. Southport Corporation gave the STC, by then BET-owned, a 21-year lease and the company set about electrification. Horse cars continued until the first trams came into use in 1901. Separately the Corporation electrified the ex-BST lines, hiring company horse cars meanwhile until the July 1900 electric opening. Southport CT took back the STC lease in 1918 and merged the fleet with its own. The last tram ran in 1934.

Southport was made a county borough in 1905 and absorbed Birkdale in 1912. The registration marks of the town's licensing office were FY, WM and serial prefixes until 1974.

The first corporation bus, built locally by Vulcan, was bought in 1924 and seven more saloons and 12 double-deckers followed by 1931. Next were Leylands and starting during World War 2, four batches of Daimlers, the first being utility type and painted light brown. Two Guy Wolf minis acquired in 1936/7 overlapped in service with 12 unique, twelve-seat, open, ex-army Bedford QLs bought in 1946/7 to operate a beach service to Ainsdale, five miles down the coast.

Many Leyland Titan PD and Panther batches followed, the final purchases being 10 Atlanteans and eight Nationals in 1974. The latter were delivered only three months before the undertaking was merged, together with St Helens, into Merseyside PTE. Among the Southport fleet at that time were three open-top ex-Ribble single-deckers and several open-topped Titan double-deckers.

Gradually the non-open-toppers were repainted into green and cream, later with brown trim. Conversion to Merseyside Transport Ltd in 1986 led to a livery experiment with two shades of green in 1987 and

adoption of maroon and cream in 1988. Trading as Merseybus, the company was sold to its employees in December 1992 and adopted the title MTL Trust Holdings.

In 1994 it pleased Southport people by adopting the local fleetname 'Southport & District' and putting the old municipal coat of arms on buses based in the town. All have been painted in the new corporate cream and red, reminiscent of corporation livery. These colours go back to 1880 as the Birkdale & Southport Co used various shades. The Southport Tramways Co used green and cream for horse and electric cars and the Corporation settled for maroon and cream on trams but bright red and cream on buses.

Above:
Southport became convinced in 1961 that front-entrance double-deckers had advantages. One was the possibility of operating without a conductor. No 49 and several others with similar layout were converted to OPO in 1970. The buses then carried a board, mounted above the front registration plate, which stated 'Please Pay Driver'. An angled window above the bonnet gave the operator more room to turn to collect fares. No 49 (WFY 49) was one of a batch of four Leyland Titan PD2/40s with Weymann Orion H37/27F bodies delivered in 1962. Seen on 10 May 1964 in front of Canning Road depot flanked by a Crossley and Leyland-bodied No 87, it is in the livery still used for open-toppers today. The Southport undertaking was absorbed into Merseyside PTE on 1 April 1974, No 49 being withdrawn the following year.

Left:
Coat of arms photo date: 19 May 1973.

Stalybridge, Hyde, Mossley & Dukinfield Transport & Electricity Board

Four West Pennine textile towns which formed a transport undertaking known as SHMD lie east of Manchester. They were independent boroughs earlier in the 1900s but currently form part of the Metropolitan District (Borough) of Tameside in Greater Manchester county.

Until 1974 Hyde and Dukinfield were in Cheshire, Stalybridge part Cheshire part Lancashire, while Mossley was mostly Lancashire with portions historically in Cheshire and the West Riding of Yorkshire.

By 1890 private horse bus routes linked the towns but the Councils agreed in 1901 to foster municipal enterprise and co-operate in forming an SHMD Tramways & Electricity Board. After starting electric services in 1903 with hired Ashton Corporation cars, the undertaking's own trams took over in 1904.

Eventually 64 cars were owned, 20 being single-deckers, and 10 further double-deckers came via Hyde Corporation and were briefly used when the Oldham, Ashton & Hyde Electric Tramway Co was bought by local councils in 1921. Hyde's share of the company track was leased to the board. Other tramways which at some

time operated cars on SHMD rails were Manchester C&T Co (horse cars until 1903), Manchester, Ashton and Stockport Corporations. The board's tramcars also ran into those towns.

Buses were operated from 1925, only Thornycrofts being purchased until 1936. Then Daimlers were favoured until 1954. SHMD buses were a common sight in Ashton, Oldham, Manchester and Stockport and, in 1929 on short-lived joint express routes, reached Stretford and Urmston.

Although trolleybuses were never owned, SHMD constructed overhead wiring in Stalybridge and Hyde and this was used by Manchester and Ashton until 1966.

The tramway, which had been progressively cut back from 1928, was reduced to two routes by 1939. A 'last tram' ran on 29 May 1945, three weeks after VE Day. Stockport and Manchester cars still ran into Hyde, however, until 1947.

SHMD tramway liveries were crimson and buff 1904-7, dark green and crimson 1907-13, all-maroon on a few cars in 1911 and green and cream 1913-45. Some World War 2 repaints appeared in two shades of grey.

Trams were originally lettered 'Joint Tramways', then 'SHMD Joint Tramways' and finally 'SHMD Joint Board' – all with a monogram crest. Early buses showed 'SHMD Joint Tramways', then 'SHMD Joint Board', sometimes with a monogram. 'Transport' replaced 'Tramways' in the title and after 1945 the monogram was replaced by a superb device incorporating the crests of the four towns, accompanied from 1965 by the full name at waist level.

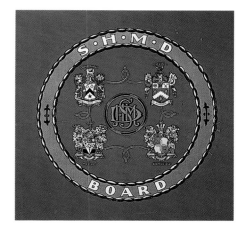

Buses were always green and cream, originally a dark green. In 1937 a light green streamline curve, or flash, was added but removed after 1945 when roofs became silver. The mid-1950s saw a change to a lighter green with two bands of cream relief (on double-deckers). Ten years later the waistline cream was omitted. The final development was extended cream, from waist to cantrail. Also in the mid-1950s several Atkinson buses were purchased, including the unique double-decker, but Leylands and Daimlers predominated. The very last vehicles acquired were Bristol RE saloons and Daimler Fleetline double-deckers.

SHMD buses, demonstrators apart, were always registered with Cheshire County Licensing Office at Chester, 40 miles distant.

The Joint Board became a component of Selnec PTE in 1969 and many of its buses passed to Greater Manchester PTE in 1974. Concurrently, the four boroughs were merged with Ashton to form Tameside Metropolitan District (borough).

The orange-based liveries of Selnec, GMT and their 1986 successor GM Buses Ltd, have now been replaced locally by the all-orange of 'Greater Manchester' (FirstBus subsidiary GM Buses North Ltd) and the stripes of Stagecoach (GM Buses South Ltd). These came into existence after the 1993 division and 1996 sale of the GMPTE 'arm's length' 1986 company.

Above:
Coat of arms photo date: 19 April 1969. Upper left – Stalybridge, upper right – Hyde, lower left – Mossley, lower right – Dukinfield.

Left:
Hyde bus station on 19 July 1969 is the setting for this view of SHMD No 80 (280 ATU), a Daimler CVG6 with Northern Counties H36/28R body built in 1957. It passed into the ownership of Selnec as No 5680 in 1969, being placed in the Southern division fleet, and was withdrawn in 1975. Windows giving standing passengers an eye-level view of progress along the route were an optional feature of NC bodies from 1950.

Stockport Corporation Transport Department

Stockport was a cotton spinning town in the 19th century but today is more concerned with engineering. It stands at the point where the River Mersey is formed from its upper tributaries and in fact the river now flows under a shopping centre and Mersey Square. Prior to 1974 the town was a county borough in Cheshire but lost that status (and gained in area) when it became a metropolitan district with the title of Borough in Greater Manchester county.

Apart from brief operations by the Manchester Suburban Tramway Co in 1880, horse trams of two companies ran in Stockport: those of Manchester Carriage & Tramways from 1881-1901 and Stockport & Hazel Grove C&T from 1890 to 1905. The Corporation opened six electrified routes based partly on the ex-company lines, the first in 1901. Eventually 85 trams were owned, all double-deckers.

Routes joint with Manchester CTD and SHMD Joint Board were operated and in fact the former ran four miles beyond the town centre to Hazel Grove. Stockport cars ventured to within yards of the Salford boundary with Manchester, which at that point is the River Irwell, another Mersey tributary.

Unlike most towns, the Stockport tram system escaped piece-meal dismembering, remaining largely intact until 1950. The final car ran in 1951, the area's last.

Three trolleybuses were bought in 1913 but withdrawn in 1919. The operating system, Lloyd-Kohler, involved a single pair of vertically-aligned wires. Vehicles exchanged power pickup carriages and cables when they met, which was not conducive to efficiency.

They were replaced by Stockport's first buses, AECs. Subsequently, until 1934, only Crossley, Leyland and Vulcan single-deckers were operated. The first double-deckers were Leyland Titan TD3cs and Crossley later supplied two Mancunians. Wartime deliveries, MoS Guy Arab utilities, arrived and ran painted overall grey. Some gave over 20 years' service.

After 1946, influenced by the location of Crossley Motors' works in the town, many of that make were purchased but when the chassis marque became unobtainable, loyalty reverted to Leyland. However, some Titans had Crossley bodies as late as 1958. Saloon acquisitions were Tiger Cubs and Leopards.

Stockport tram and bus livery was always red and cream, though some prewar Leyland Tigers received a brown streamlined flash, possibly influenced by curvaceous developments on Manchester and SHMD vehicles.

Buses received DB and JA (and serial) registration marks from Stockport CB Licensing Office but the indices were familiar over a wider area on vehicles belonging to the first North Western Road Car Co, whose head office was in the town until 1972.

When Selnec PTE was formed from 11 municipalities in 1969, Stockport and SHMD constituted the NE Cheshire contingent, the former contributing 149 buses to the new fleet, the latter 87 (some NWRCC vehicles later joined them). Stockport's four Leyland Leopards were then only a year old but of more interest were 12 Titan PD3/14s, six of which were rear- and six front-loaders. These were only months old and one was the last rear-entrance bus built for service in the UK.

A large number of the ex-Stockport vehicles passed to Greater Manchester PTE when it replaced Selnec in 1974 and although some gave service until 1982, their relatively early demise was determined by their unsuitability for one-person operation, then newly legalised.

The orange-based liveries of Selnec and GMPTE were obvious antecedents of the similar colours used after 1986 by GM Buses Ltd. A complete break came in 1996 when Stagecoach bought GM Buses South Ltd from the PTE and corporate stripes began to take over in Stockport, which is in fact the new 'Stagecoach Manchester's' headquarters.

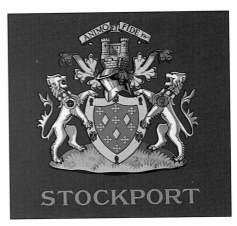

Above:
Coat of arms photo date: 19 April 1969.

Left:
It is difficult in 1996 when multicoloured liveries are the fashion, to understand why Stockport persisted with red and cream when larger operators Manchester and North Western, both seen in the town in large numbers, used similar colours. Many towns would have turned to a contrasting livery to assert independence but Stockport had a very conservative outlook – for instance it took delivery of front-engined, open-radiator buses as late as 1969, only months before becoming part of the Southern division of Selnec. No 334 (NDB 367) was new in 1958 and carried one of the last Crossley bodies built, although by then the marque was a subsidiary of Associated Commercial Vehicles. Configuration was H33/28R, carried on a Leyland Titan PD2/30 chassis with 'Midland Red' style front. As Selnec No 5934 it served for only one year before withdrawal. Here it is portrayed at the old Chorlton Street stands in Manchester on 4 October 1959.

Stockton Corporation Transport

Famous for its association with the 1825 Stockton & Darlington Railway, possessing a High Street reputed to be the broadest in the country, and home of the man who invented the friction match, the current prosperity of Stockton-on-Tees depends largely upon chemical manufacturing in its major suburb, Billingham.

Its road transport history really started in 1881 when the Stockton & Darlington Steam Tramways Co, using cars in chocolate and white livery, opened a route to South Stockton (later called Thornaby). This became Stockton-on-Tees and District Tramways in 1893 (same livery) and was bought by the Imperial Tramways Co in 1896. The group had interests in other parts of the British Isles. It ran the steam trams unchanged during electrification and opened the modernised system in 1898, trading as Middlesbrough, Stockton & Thornaby Electric Tramways. A link between the first-named towns became a fact. This had been long forecast in the name of the Middlesbrough & Stockton Tramway, a company purchased by Imperial in 1878. It had opened in 1874 but never extended to Stockton.

The electric cars were painted red and cream and ran unchanged until 1921 when the undertaking was purchased jointly by the corporations of Stockton, Middlesbrough and Thornaby. Stockton's share of the fleet was 20 open-top trams and 17 buses. Thornaby received nine open-top cars. The 29 trams were operated until 1930 as Stockton & Thornaby Joint

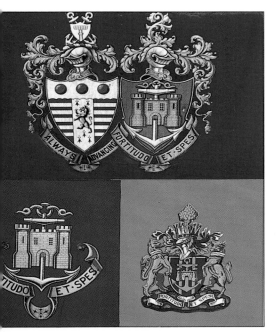

Corporation Tramways, still using red and cream livery but with a dual crest. The former was in County Durham, the latter in the North Riding.

Thornaby sold its interests to Stockton, which ran the trams alone until 31 December 1931 when buses replaced them.

Green and cream was adopted as livery and by 1935 70 vehicles were operated, half being double-deckers. Most were Leylands and AECs. Between 1937 and 1943 Daimlers were bought and from 1948 Leylands predominated.

Teesside Municipal Transport, formed in 1968 from the Middlesbrough, Stockton and Tees-side Railless undertakings, reflected the formation of a new Teesside county borough which absorbed Middlesbrough county borough.

Stockton's and the others' buses were repainted into turquoise and cream (still with their own insignia until 1 April 1968) from late 1966.

Further local government reorganisation on 1 April 1974 saw Teesside CB abolished and four districts, of which Stockton was one, formed to comprise Cleveland county. Stockton and Hartlepool came from County Durham, Middlesbrough and Langbaurgh from the old North Riding. Cleveland Transit took over the bus undertaking, its full title being Langbaurgh, Middlesbrough and Stockton Joint Committee. A true green and darker cream was chosen as livery, with orange and cream on Cleveland Coaches.

Above:
Stockton was one of those fleets – Middlesbrough was another – which once displayed a coat of arms on both the upper and lower panels of double-deckers. By 1 April 1967, the date of this photograph, standard practice for civic pride on the High Street was confined to the top deck. The vehicle is No 111 (4711 UP), a H36/28F Weymann-bodied Leyland Titan PD2/37 dating from 1963.

Left:
Coats of arms: top – as used by Stockton & Thornaby JCT 1921-1930; lower left — Stockton arms used until at least 1947; lower right — Stockton arms used postwar and as shown, on the final 1966-68 (pre-TMT) livery. *Courtesy Cleveland Transit Ltd*

In 1986 the undertaking, still joint committee-owned, became Cleveland Transit Ltd, marked by adding yellow to the livery. Yet another change occurred in 1994 when the company was sold to Stagecoach Holdings. The ubiquitous striped livery appeared in 1995 and the name became Stagecoach Transit in 1996.

On 1 April that year Cleveland county was dissolved and Stockton-on-Tees became a unitary authority, a new-style county borough but opting to use the title of Borough.

Sunderland Corporation Transport Department

The Venerable Bede made his home in Sunderland for a while and in AD674 built a church, parts of which still survive. It was the 18th century before the town grew, with four strands to its industrial life. First was coal, then the port from which to transport it, shipbuilding on the River Wear and lastly glass making. Only the latter still thrives, although other industries, particularly automotive, have moved in nearby.

Horse tramways run by the Sunderland Tramways Co opened in 1879. Other lines were constructed by the Corporation and leased to that company. An experiment with steam trams in 1880-81 was not pursued.

Sunderland Corporation took the necessary legal steps to purchase the undertaking, assuming control on 1 January 1900. Electrification quickly progressed, the first tram running eight months later. Eventually, at the southern boundary, cars of the semi-rural Sunderland District Electric Tramways Co met the corporation system and there was through working to the town centre from 1921 until SDET closed in 1925. The company cars were originally blue and white, although some had been repainted magenta and white in the through running years.

Sunderland Corporation livery was maroon and cream until 1935, then red and cream until 1952 when, in anticipation of a new tram replacement bus fleet, green and cream was adopted to impart a new image.

Buses had commenced operating in 1928, initially hired from Northern General. The Corporation took delivery of a fleet of Leyland PLSC Lions the following year. Its tramway system was not run down, in fact the last extension was built as late as 1949. Many trams were modern, the last, bought new in 1940, being centre-entrance and streamlined. Other relatively modern cars were bought from London, Manchester, Huddersfield and South Shields.

In the 1930s, Dennis and Daimler buses were followed by two Crossleys. Two Leylands and many Guy utilities arrived during World War 2.

Closure of the tramways became a long-term policy in 1946 but it was 1950 before any route closed. Full abandonment came in 1954.

The many Daimler, Guy and Crossley buses bought as tram replacements were orthodox rear-loaders but Sunderland was an early customer for rear-engined Daimler Fleetlines, the first arriving in 1962. At that time the fleet totalled 179. Later in the 1960s a fleet of dual-door single-deckers was purchased and used in flat-fare operations. The bodywork of these (mainly Leyland Panthers) was unusual in having forward-leaning window pillars, creating a modern American-influenced style. Revenue from the services failed to meet expectations, however, and the undertaking

Above:
Daimler CVG5 No 158 (DBR 658) awaits departure on 20 July 1963. It has a Roe H35/28R body and was built in 1954 as a tram replacement, thus being among the first Sunderland buses to carry green and cream livery. 'Shop at Binns' was an exhortation carried on the front of a substantial proportion of double-deckers of all northeast England operators not so long ago.

Inset:
Coat of arms photo date: 3 April 1971.

suffered a setback. Truly an idea before its time.

The department merged with Tyneside PTE on 1 April 1973, one year before Sunderland lost its county borough status and became a metropolitan district (borough) of Tyne and Wear county. In later years it became one of Britain's newest cities.

The PTE's name changed to Tyne & Wear on 1 April 1974 but livery for both phases of bus ownership was yellow and cream. A green area was incorporated on vehicles working in Sunderland when the undertaking became Busways Travel Services Ltd in 1986.

That company was sold by its employees to Stagecoach Holdings in 1994 and buses began to appear in corporate white with red, mustard and blue stripes late in 1995.

Pre-1974, Sunderland registration marks were BR and GR and all corporation buses carried those or their serials.

Swindon Corporation Passenger Transport Department

To many transport enthusiasts the name Swindon means the Great Western Railway and its museum. Today its centre consists mainly of office blocks and service industries. In the early 1800s it was a village in agricultural Wiltshire but within 50 years had become an important railway junction with a locomotive works employing 12,000 at its peak. Now the original GWR is a memory and the works closed. The town's 1974-97 name of Thamesdown seems curiously distant from the traditions of the place.

In contrast to Swindon's extensive rail history, its road transport story is less complex than most other towns. Corporation electric tramways opened in 1904, three short routes starting near the railway station. Eventually 13 four-wheeled, open-top cars were operated, seven being delivered for the opening, No 13 as late as 1921.

Motorbuses were first acquired in 1927, more arriving to permit tramway abandonment in 1929. By the late 1930s Swindon was buying Leyland and Daimler double-deckers but in 1942 had the 'honour' of receiving almost the first Guy Arab utility double-decker, built to a Ministry of Supply specification.

Early deliveries of this type were very Spartan with wooden slatted seats and few opening windows. More Guys, then Daimlers, followed. Only the latter make was bought between 1947 and 1961, the first being centre-entrance saloons, unusual anywhere. Six years later Daimler Freelines, also centre-entrance, arrived.

A 1961 batch of 10 7ft 6in wide, full height, 'tin-fronted' Daimler double-deckers, with Roe bodies featuring shallow upper windows, was an obvious candidate for a 'most ungainly bus award'. Leyland PD2s and AEC Reliances were more attractive purchases later in the 1960s.

Tram livery had been maroon and cream but bus colours were deep blue and deep cream until around 1969, when a change to brighter peacock blue accompanied a delivery of Daimler Fleetlines. These colours were retained with cream predominating after 1974, when the department became Thamesdown District Council Transport Undertaking with a fleet of 70. The town subsequently readopted the title of Borough.

Thereafter orders included Fleetline, Atlantean and Dennis Dominator double-deckers, together with Bristol RE and Dennis Dominator saloons.

After 1986, the year the operator became Thamesdown Transport Ltd, two shades of blue on a cream base was adopted as livery. In mid-1997 the company remained in local authority ownership, but is forecast to retain the Thamesdown name even though the town reverted to Swindon Borough upon being made a unitary authority on 1 April 1997.

Prior to 1974 Wiltshire County Council's five marks were used to register Swindon's buses. Since then only four have been allotted to Swindon LVLO, WV having been reassigned to Brighton.

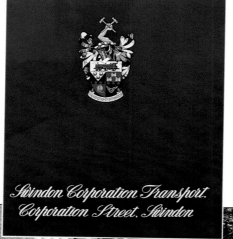

Below:
Centre-entrance municipal single-deckers have never been common but Swindon bought batches in two decades. The first, totalling 15, is represented by 1947 Daimler CVD6SD No 56 (EMW 892) seen on 24 August 1963. Nos 56-61 had Daimler 6-cylinder engines, Nos 62-70 Gardner 5LWs. All carried Park Royal 35-seat bodies. The second batch were 1954 Daimler Freelines.

Left:
Coat of arms photo date: 3 August 1975.

Teesside Municipal Transport

This short-lived motorbus and trolleybus operator was formed on 1 April 1968 when the borough of Stockton-on-Tees (formerly in County Durham), the county borough of Middlesbrough and the urban district of Eston (both in the North Riding of Yorkshire) were merged. (The new county borough of Teesside was deemed to be in the North Riding.) Stockton Corporation and Middlesbrough Corporation buses and the trolleybuses and buses of the Tees-side Railless Traction Board (a joint Eston and Middlesbrough undertaking) were transferred to the new Teesside Municipal Transport fleet on that date.

A livery of turquoise and cream had been gradually introduced by the three operators, using their own insignia, from late 1966. After the merger the Teesside CB coat of arms and fleetname was applied. (See the pages for the three former operators for more details.) Even the trolleybuses appeared in the new identity, though their last full day of operation came only three years later, on 3 April 1971.

In 1973 a bus service run jointly with Hartlepool crossed the Middlesbrough Transporter Bridge over the River Tees. The

bridge, one of only two in Britain still in public service, was and still is managed by the current municipality. Passengers remained on the bus during the crossing – the original 'air-bus'?

From 1974 vehicle repaints appeared in the green and darker cream livery to be used by Cleveland Transit, the successor undertaking. Its full title was Langbaurgh, Middlesbrough and Stockton-on-Tees Joint Committee. These were three of the four new districts, the other being Hartlepool, which comprised the county of Cleveland. 'Transit' was adopted as the logo.

In the early 1980s Cleveland Coaches, in an orange and cream livery, developed from a private hire operation using similar colours.

The next change in status occurred in

1986 when the department became a local authority-owned company and yellow was added to the bus livery. A remarkable development in December 1993 saw Cleveland Transit purchase a major shareholding in Kingston upon Hull City Transport. November 1994 saw the end of local control of public transport on Teesside when the company and its subsidiaries were acquired by Stagecoach Holdings. Adoption of Stagecoach corporate livery eventually followed.

It may be of interest that Teesside CB took over the registration marks DC and XG previously assigned to Middlesbrough. In 1974 XG was withdrawn from further issue but the new Middlesbrough LVLO received DC plus AJ, PY and VN from North Yorkshire, EF from Hartlepool and HN from Darlington.

Above left:
Coat of arms photo date: 3 April 1971.

Below:
This short-lived municipal undertaking inherited the majority of its rolling stock from the three merged predecessors. Teesside No L509 (VXG 509J) was an exception, being new in 1971. It is a Daimler Fleetline CRL6-30 with a Northern Counties H43/27D body, portrayed near South Bank trolleybus depot on 3 April of that year, the day the 'silent service' celebrated its last full day of operation.

Tees-side Railless Traction Board

This operator's territory was decidedly not scenic. The western terminus was in the Middlesbrough suburb of North Ormesby, the middle section passed one of the largest steelworks in Britain and the eastern termini served housing estates. However, its vehicles were always smart.

Never a tramway operator, the Board, in the North Riding, introduced trolleybuses in 1919. The original intention had been for the steelworks company Bolckow Vaughan to operate the service and four miles of overhead was erected in 1915/6. Local authorities Eston Urban District Council and Middlesbrough County Borough Council adopted the scheme and formed a joint board, the former owning two thirds. Until 1955, however, the traction current was drawn from the steelworks.

Single-deckers came first, then a curious petrol-electric hybrid which could work beyond the end of the overhead. Double-deckers became the norm, usually about 15, and all were Sunbeams after World War 2. Several built for Reading in 1961 were bought when that system closed in 1968.

Route extensions were made, especially after 1951, and a circular service through Eston was created. The final extension in 1967/8 was the last on public roads in Britain. The trolleybus system closed in 1971, three years after ownership had passed to Teesside Municipal Transport.

Buses were introduced in 1924, eventually becoming more numerous than the

trolleybuses. They were basically Leylands and mostly double-deckers, although a few Daimler utilities were acquired. Trolleybus replacements were all Leylands.

Livery for both modes was dark green and cream, although there was a lighter green around the windows of a few prewar saloons. In 1966 repaints appeared in turquoise and cream with 'Teesside Transport' in white lettering above the lower windows replacing the 'TRTB' logo. This was in preparation for 1 April 1968 when the board merged with Middlesbrough and Stockton municipal undertakings to form Teesside Municipal Transport, a title which subsequently appeared at waist level in small gilt letters on both buses and trolleybuses. The new livery was also prematurely adopted by the other constituents.

The structural change was caused by the merging of Middlesbrough and Stockton with Eston to form Teesside county borough. The new authority was partly in County Durham, partly in the North Riding, but when further local government changes occurred nationwide in 1974 the county

borough, with Hartlepool CB, formed the basis for the new county of Cleveland.

The Teesside municipal undertaking became Cleveland Transit, full title Langbaurgh, Middlesbrough and Stockton Joint Committee. A true green and cream livery was chosen, and 'Transit' adopted as fleet logo. In 1986 the undertaking became Cleveland Transit Ltd, a change marked by adding yellow to the livery.

The latest development occurred in 1994 when the company was bought by Stagecoach Holdings. Corporate livery appeared on buses before the end of 1995.

Above:
This location, nostalgic for many, is the Tees-side Railless Traction Board depot at South Bank where No 17 overtakes No 18 (CPY 288/9) on 22 October 1962. Both were Sunbeam Ws built in 1944 and originally fitted with Weymann utility bodies. The replacements, in 1960, were Roe H61Rs.

Below:
Tees-side Railless Traction Board logo.
Courtesy Robert Kell

Left:
Todmorden's tiny bus station was adjacent to a viaduct carrying the Halifax-Rochdale railway. Depicted there is No 32 (GWW 43), all-Leyland Titan PD2/1, rear-entrance, lowbridge height, seating 27/26. When this photograph was taken on 25 April 1968 the Joint Omnibus Committee's entire fleet was similar. The red attaché-case is typical of the type used by conductors in that era to carry tickets and paraphernalia. Livery variations in the JOC fleet were infrequent. In the 1950s a white roof was standard and by the late 1960s, cream on double-deckers was confined to window surrounds on both decks and the cantrail, whilst new saloons were all-cream with green window surrounds (see Calderdale).

Below:
Coat of arms: prior to nationalisation of the railways in 1948 Todmorden JOC buses carried both the town and LMS Railway insignia. The latter was eventually changed to British Railways' (later British Rail's) logo but as late as 1962 some buses still bore the LMSR badge. For a short while, around 1969-71, buses carried only the Todmorden arms.

Todmorden Joint Omnibus Committee (Corporation & British Railways)

In the heart of the Pennines at the junction of three valleys lies the Yorkshire town of Todmorden. The valley to the east is that of the River Calder. It provides the only low-level pass from Lancashire to central West Yorkshire. Until 1888 the county boundary cut the town in two, passing through the town hall. Industry based on cotton and wool relied on plentiful water from the surrounding hills and moors.

Horse buses of the Todmorden & District Carriage Co ran in the last decade of the 19th century and into the 20th. Todmorden Corporation investigated tramway operation (which would possibly have enabled a determined passenger to travel from Leeds to Liverpool by tram) but concluded that equipment costs would be too high to ensure financial success. Instead, they bought one single-deck and three double-deck buses and commenced operating three services on 1 January 1907. Eventually there were several local routes and some quite long ones to Burnley, Halifax, Keighley and Rochdale. Todmorden was therefore one of only 15 UK municipal bus operators never to have had trams.

After World War 1 it was decided to buy only Leylands and this policy never wavered; indeed even during World War 2 the JOC received four 'unfrozen' Leyland Titan TD7s.

The livery of green and cream lasted throughout the undertaking's life. Only in the final years did a variation occur – one or two saloons received cream with just green window surrounds.

The railways had their own buses and services in several areas of Britain in the 1920s, but by 1929 were seeking to buy established companies and enter into joint arrangements with municipalities. Such co-operation was realised in four Yorkshire towns, the smallest being Todmorden. Its Joint Omnibus Committee met for the first time in January 1931. Todmorden Corporation and the London, Midland & Scottish Railway each owned half of the fleet, although all buses carried both the municipal and LMS crests.

After 1947 individual buses were nominally owned by one or the other partners. Nevertheless, the attractive double insignia continued to be displayed on all, though from Railway nationalisation in 1948 British Railways' name and logo gradually replaced the LMS's.

Todmorden bought the first production Leyland Titan PD2/1 in 1948 and altogether took 38 PD1s and PD2s. Some were still in service in 1971 when the fleet, by then reduced to 12, was absorbed into Calderdale JOC. This undertaking was created following the 1969 formation of the National Bus Company and allowed BR to combine its Halifax JOC and Todmorden JOC bus interests under the supervision of

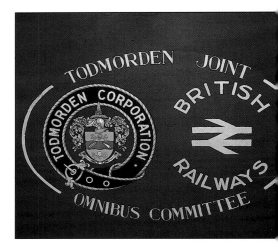

Associated Passenger Transport, a non-operational NBC holding company. The 'Joint' referred only to Todmorden and APT, as Halifax continued to operate its purely municipal fleet until 1 April 1974. Then Halifax and Calderdale became part of the West Yorkshire PTE.

During its three-year life CJOC buses originating from Halifax remained in orange, green and cream livery but without insignia. Some Todmorden vehicles were also painted into it. Those remaining in green and cream carried only the Todmorden crest, still accompanied by the TJOC lettering. Subsequently a few ex-Todmorden buses operated in service for the Calderdale unit of Metro (WYPTE).

Todmorden is currently part of the Metropolitan District (Borough) of Calderdale, in the county of West Yorkshire, and served by buses of the Calderline division of Yorkshire Rider.

Wallasey Corporation Motor Buses

The northeast tip of the Wirral peninsula is occupied by the town of Wallasey, now part of the Metropolitan District (Borough) of Wirral, Merseyside. Before 1974 it was in Cheshire, and may possibly return to it. The name is believed to mean 'Isle of the Welsh', from its inhabitants in pre-Anglo-Saxon times. With a splendid seafront, part Irish Sea part Mersey estuary, the town is attractively restoring its resort suburb New Brighton. There is minimal industry, many people commuting to Birkenhead or Liverpool, hence municipal ownership of ferries until Merseyside PTE took over.

A private horse bus service started in 1861 and others followed. Loadings, especially to and from the ferries, were such that the Wallasey Tramways Co (livery red and cream) was formed to build and operate a horse-drawn line which opened in 1879. A new company, Wallasey United Tramways & Omnibuses (livery maroon and cream) took over WTC and several horse bus operators in 1891.

The town's population was growing fast and local government changes reflected it. From local board to urban district in 1894, to borough in 1910, and county borough in 1913, the rise was phenomenal. One consequence was the allocation of HF in 1913 as the registration index of the new CBC.

In 1901 the Council had bought the company tramway etc and proceeded to electrify the routes. Meanwhile several horse trams continued to run, supplemented by horse buses provided by the Seacombe & New Brighton Omnibus Co. There were no plans for tram lines to cross the Great Float (docks) to connect with Birkenhead's system but a Birkenhead & Seacombe Omnibus Co joined the towns in 1903. This service, originally horse then motor then horse again, lasted until 1919. From 1907 to 1910, with council encouragement, Seacombe, Poulton & Wallasey Omnibuses foreshadowed a tram route extension.

Electric tram service started in 1902. Eventually, with a maximum fleet of 78 cars, track costs forced gradual abandonment and the last tram ran in 1933.

AEC buses were bought in 1920-22 and joint operation with Birkenhead Corporation started in 1921. The AECs were replaced by Leylands and Karriers in 1927/8, but it was open-staired Leyland Titan TD1s that were chosen for tram replacement.

Two AEC Q double-deckers were bought in 1934, but otherwise acquisitions were orthodox – Leylands, AECs, a few Daimlers and some single-deckers.

Wallasey hired buses to other operators, notably Crosville, during World War 2 and did not need to buy utility models. All 130 postwar double-deckers were Leylands, the tiny number of single-deckers consisting of two Titan-chassised coaches, four Albions, plus one Trojan and one Bedford minibus. On 8 December 1958 Wallasey was probably the first municipal operator to put a Leyland Atlantean into service and that was followed by 29 more.

Original tram livery was officially sea green (a light shade) and cream. This faded and apple green replaced it until 1924, when primrose green was adopted. This also appeared on the bus fleet.

Trams were originally lettered 'Wallasey Council Tramways', the middle word being changed after 1910 to 'Corporation'. Buses, including the first six Atlanteans, showed 'Wallasey Corporation Motors' in large gilt characters – a charming anachronism swept away by a new manager in 1960. Henceforth only the crest was carried.

The undertaking contributed 75 buses to Merseyside PTE, formed on 1 December 1969. Because Wallasey and Birkenhead were then in Cheshire, for political reasons

the PTE Wirral fleet became blue and cream. After Merseyside county was formed in 1974, light green and cream, later with brown, was used in all areas. Merseyside Transport Ltd, formed in 1986, briefly tried two greens in 1987, but adopted maroon and cream the following year. The company was sold to a consortium of employees and financial backers in 1992 and adopted the title MTL Trust Holdings. A corporate livery of cream and crimson was introduced in 1994, accompanied in Wirral by the fleetname 'Wirral Peninsula Buses'.

Above:
Wallasey's first buses, 1920 AECs, bore the title 'Wallasey Corporation Motor Buses' in large serifed letters in a straight line. The shortened title illustrated came into use in 1926 when Leyland used it on a batch of LSC 1 Lions. Wallasey preferred the style and it lasted over 30 years. Leyland Atlantean PDR1/1 No 3 (FHF 453) was delivered in September 1959, nearly a year after No 1, which is now preserved and famous. The batch of six had MCCW H44/33F bodies painted in the old livery complete with 'Wallasey Corporation Motors'. Subsequent batches had a modified livery and only the coat of arms. Because of duplication No 3 was renumbered 203 by Merseyside PTE in 1970. It later gained Wirral Division blue and cream. The illustration dates from 6 October 1959 and the location is Seacombe Ferry terminus. No 3 was withdrawn in 1978.

Left:
Coat of arms photo date: 15 June 1970.

Walsall Corporation Transport Department

Currently a metropolitan district (borough) of the West Midlands county, Walsall was a part of Staffordshire until 1974, and known as 'the town of 100 trades'. It is on the fringe of the Black Country and, typically for that area, has metal-based industries.

The Birmingham & South Staffordshire Steam Tramways Co, which started serving the town and district in 1884, became the South Staffordshire Tramways Co in 1889. This concern was a very early convert to electric traction, starting in 1893. It was one of a BET-owned group known collectively as the Black Country Tramways system. Walsall Corporation purchased the company in 1901 and ran it as a lessee for three years before becoming the direct operator in 1904. Tramway replacement by buses began in 1925, continued with trolleybuses in 1931 and was complete in 1933.

Within the county borough over this period of nearly 50 years, all tramway operators used liveries of brown and cream or maroon and cream.

Buses were first acquired in 1915 and by 1918 the fleet consisted of 17 Tilling-Stevens petrol-electrics. With the arrival of the first trolleybuses in 1931 the pneumatic fleet quickly grew, attaining a total of 275 by 1962, 20% being electric.

Although Walsall favoured the neigh-bouring firm of Guy for many post-World War 2 buses, other makes were purchased, both double- and single-deckers. AEC, Bedford, Daimler, Dennis (Lolines) and Leyland buses featured in the fleet along-side BUT, Crossley, Karrier and Sunbeam trolleybuses. Some of the latter were second-hand and originally with Cleethorpes, Hastings Tramways Co and Pontypridd.

The town was a pioneer in operating two-axle, 30ft vehicles, acquiring some in 1955 and running them with special consent until that length became legal in 1956.

A joint service with Wolverhampton Corporation saw the green and primrose trolleybuses of that operator in Walsall town centre until 1967.

Walsall bus and trolleybus livery was originally light blue and cream. Two shades of blue replaced that in the early 1940s and all-grey and blue and grey were also used during the war. Later, overall blue with yellow mouldings became standard.

The undertaking was notable for several double-deck vehicle design experiments initiated by one of its general managers. Among them were very short Daimler Fleetlines and one 36ft long.

On 1 October 1969 the Walsall fleet merged with those of Birmingham, West Bromwich and Wolverhampton to form that of the West Midlands PTE and painting into a darker blue and cream began. The trol-leybuses, unique in a PTE fleet, continued for a year but closed in October 1970, having been the penultimate British system.

The undertaking became West Midlands Travel Ltd in 1986 and was sold to its employees in 1991, having by then adopted a blue, silver and red livery. A merger with National Express came in 1995.

The county borough registration mark was DH from 1903 until transferred to Dudley Licensing Office in 1974. Since that LVLO closed in 1993, DH-based serials are issued only if requested.

Above:
To complement new purchases, Walsall picked up several second-hand trolleybus bargains from defunct systems. No 875 (GFU 693) was one of a batch of four acquired from Grimsby-Cleethorpes in 1960. They were BUT/MV 9611T with Northern Coachbuilders H54R bodies, built in 1950. Walsall was the first undertaking to operate trolleybuses 30ft long on two axles. By the time No 875 was seen here in the town's bus station on 5 August 1967 it had been length-ened and rebuilt with a front entrance. The Walsall trolleybus system operated in West Midlands PTE ownership for a year before closing.

Left:
Coat of arms photo date: 11 October 1969.

Warrington Corporation Transport Department

Traditionally Lancastrian but since 1974 part of Cheshire, Warrington's main industries were soap and wire making. To a great extent these have been replaced by detergents, engineering, brewing and vodka. Its southern suburbs straddle the Manchester Ship Canal and 12,500-ton ships regularly passed through – rare nowadays. The town is on the main West Coast railway line and close to the M6, M56 and M62, connections which have encouraged growth.

Private horse-drawn buses were active in Warrington towards the end of the 19th century. It was the 1902 opening of electric tramways, with an initial fleet of 21 cars, which brought the town into the municipal transport era. An extension along Wilderspool Causeway and over a Ship Canal swing bridge in 1905 was called the Stockton Heath Light Railway.

Three petrol-electric Tilling-Stevens buses were purchased in 1913 but tramway expansion was not finished, six further cars arriving in 1919. It was 1928 before Leyland Leviathans opened the next bus route. In the early 1930s, however, the tram system was reduced and it closed in 1935. At that time a change in title from Warrington Corporation Tramways to that in the heading reflected the new situation.

The year 1938 saw a local competitor, the Suburban Motor Services Co, purchased and absorbed, seven buses passing into the corporation fleet.

Only three semi-utility buses, all Guys, were bought and those not until 1946. Later postwar acquisitions were Bristols, Fodens, Guys and Leylands. Later still came Daimler Fleetlines and Leyland Atlanteans.

Over the years, buses of St Helens, Salford and Leigh could be seen terminating in the town, which was also a meeting place for Crosville, LUT and Ribble.

In 1974 Warrington lost county borough status (registration mark ED), the town became a district council with the title of Borough and the undertaking took the name Warrington Borough Council Transport Department. The coat of arms on buses was replaced by a 'W' logo, but reinstated in 1984.

Municipal livery changed several times over the years but not drastically. The trams were originally crimson and light yellow, altered to dark maroon and primrose yellow in 1933. Maroon and ivory was tried in 1945, but two years later red and cream became standard and lasted until 1974. White and red then followed, the red darkening in 1984.

Conversion to a municipal company in 1986 resulted in another name change to Warrington Borough Transport Ltd and advantage was taken of the new competitiveness. A Coachlines subsidiary was formed, using the same blue and yellow livery as the new Minilines minibuses. Mid-Cheshire Bus Lines ran double-deckers to Northwich in ivory and blue, name and colours 'borrowed' from a 1920s operator. Midilines later used Dennis Darts, painted in two shades of blue with yellow.

In mid-1997 the undertaking was still local authority owned and the specialised subsidiaries have tended to revert to corporate red and cream. It is forecast that Warrington will be made a unitary authority on 1 April 1998.

Left:
Coat of arms photo date: 19 January 1974.

Below:
The postwar Warrington fleet needed few single-decker buses, so Nos 95-97 (FED 17/583/584) were adequate for many years. They were Guy Arab IIIs with Gardner 6LW engines and had Guy B33F bodies, new in 1948/9. No 97, seen here in the depot yard on 9 June 1964, was not withdrawn until 1968. It was the last survivor of the trio, by then 5LW and one-person operated.

West Bridgford Urban District Council Passenger Transport Department

Some cities have suburbs, often separated from them by a river or other natural feature, which are independently administered. Such was the case with West Bridgford, Nottinghamshire, lying as it does south of the River Trent yet barely a mile from the centre of Nottingham. The crest of the UDC, seemingly never used on its buses, depicted horses pulling a cart of sacks against a background of a bridge, rising sun and castle. This perhaps signified the past agricultural relationship between the district and city.

The number of urban district council transport operators was never large. About 10 operated tramcars prior to 1933, although many more owned tracks. Ten have operated buses since World War 2, the complete list comprising Aberdare, Bedwas & Machen, Bedwellty & Mynyddislwyn (West Mon), Caerphilly, Eston (joint with Middlesbrough CB in Tees-side RTB), Gelligaer, Llandudno, Pontypridd, Ramsbottom and West

Bridgford. All except Eston, Ramsbottom and West Bridgford are in Wales.

West Bridgford was never a tramway operator but was, in 1914, the first UDC to start a bus service. This was short-lived as the vehicles were requisitioned by the army. As soon as new buses could be obtained the operation restarted, within the boundary at first, but by 1930 crossing Trent Bridge into Nottingham. Joint services followed and in the 1960s lowbridge types came into the fleet. A small number were converted from normal height for use on a route to Clifton overspill housing estate.

West Bridgford's fleet rarely if ever rose above 30, and pre-World War 2 all were AECs. In 1930 it included two Regent Is with Ransomes, Sims & Jeffries bodies, the set-back upper deck of which gave an appearance almost identical to a London General ST. These were sold to Nottingham in 1945.

The first non-Regent was a 1945 Daimler CWA6 with a Brush 'relaxed' utility body. Two 10-year-old Duple-bodied versions

were bought from Huddersfield in 1955. Postwar new purchases were again all AECs, some being lowbridge Renowns.

West Bridgford buses invariably looked immaculate in a livery of dark maroon (almost brown) and deep cream. In the 1930s the title 'West Bridgford Urban District Council' appeared in full in large gilt letters along the entire length of the lower panels. After 1945 there was a contraction to the initials, enclosed by the words 'Passenger Transport Dept'.

In 1968 the Council sold the undertaking to Nottingham Transport.

Local government reorganisation in 1974 resulted not in the town being merged with Nottingham, but in becoming a part of the district of Rushcliffe.

Left:
Logo. *Courtesy Roy Marshall/Photobus*

Below:
Possibly because it was felt that buses going into Nottingham should not be open to criticism by its operational 'big brother', the West Bridgford fleet was maintained to a high standard of appearance. Here No 34 (334 GNN) heads for Trent Bridge and the big city on 8 August 1964. It is an AEC Regent V built in 1960, and carries an East Lancashire L35/28R body. In later years several highbridge buses in the fleet were rebuilt to low height to cope with a bridge on a new route to Clifton.

West Bromwich (County Borough of) Transport Department

The name means broom village, not the housekeeping tool but the bush which covered the heathland on which the town was built in the 18th century. Formerly a coal-mining area, it now lives by engineering. Historically in the far south of Staffordshire, in 1974 it became part of the Metropolitan District (Borough) of Sandwell, West Midlands.

Horse bus services ran to neighbouring towns as early as 1834 and the Birmingham & District Tramways Co opened a horse-drawn line in 1872. This failed, however, and not until 1883 did locomotives and cars of the South Staffordshire & Birmingham District Steam Tramways Co appear. The line was an early section of what became known as the Black Country system. The 1872 company had used crimson and cream livery, its successor brown and cream.

Birmingham & Midland Steam Tramways also had a branch into the town.

A BET subsidiary, South Staffordshire Tramways (Lessee) Ltd eventually bought all the tracks and sold them to West Bromwich Corporation in 1902, but the town never operated tramcars. The system was converted to electric traction and leased to the two existing operators. When the lease expired in 1924 Birmingham City Transport took it over and operated trams into West Bromwich until 1939.

Bus operation started in 1914 when the Corporation acquired Albions, the chassis of which were commandeered by the army a month later. Putting the bodies onto Edison accumulator-powered chassis enabled the service to restart in 1915. After 15 years the fleet consisted of 37 single-deckers. Twenty double-deckers had been added by 1938 and 31 Daimler double-deckers were bought to replace the Birmingham trams. Birmingham, Walsall and Wolverhampton ran buses to West Bromwich on joint services.

Postwar purchases were predominantly Daimlers, a smaller number of single-deckers being Leylands.

Livery was dark blue lower and light blue upper panels with cream elsewhere. Single-deckers had light blue window surrounds and roofs.

In 1967 Daimler Fleetlines, the first rear-engined buses for the fleet, introduced a new livery of cream with two light blue bands. This modernised the image and it also served to mark the buses as 13ft 6in high, suitable for a low bridge route previously run by saloons.

The West Bromwich fleet was naturally registered with EA, or later, xEA marks allocated to the county borough until 1974.

On 1 October 1969 West Bromwich bus fleet was merged with those of Birmingham, Walsall and Wolverhampton, to form that of the West Midlands PTE. This adopted a dark blue and cream livery not unlike that of the largest contributor. In the early 1980s a lighter blue came into use, but before the entire fleet received it, the undertaking became West Midlands Travel Ltd in 1986. The company eventually standardised on blue, silver and red.

In 1991 it was sold to its management and employees. It later took the trading name of West Midlands Buses and subsequently became associated with National Express.

Left:
Coat of arms photo date: 12 October 1969. The neat fleetname style depicted replaced a somewhat larger version which can still be seen on preserved Dennis single-decker No 32.

Above:
With arguably the nicest livery in the Midlands, West Bromwich, on its half-cabs, set it off with lining-out right up to the day it was absorbed by West Midlands PTE. No 264 (CEA 264C), built in 1965, here heads north on 30 May 1968. The chassis is Daimler CVG6, the body Metro-Cammell Orion H63R.

West Hartlepool Corporation Transport (pre-1967 County Borough)

Hartlepool has the most important harbour between the Tees and the Tyne and was in County Durham until 1974. Until then it consisted of two authorities known collectively as The Hartlepools. The northeastern peninsula called the Headland was Hartlepool Borough and possesses a pleasant historical centre. West Hartlepool, a borough in 1887 and county borough from 1902, was on the south side of Hartlepool Bay and controlled the major docks. They merged on 1 April 1967 to become Hartlepool County Borough. Underused port facilities are currently being developed as a marina and maritime museum.

The Hartlepools Steam Tramways Co commenced operating between the towns in 1884. After seven years it failed and the tracks lay unused for five years until the General Electric Tramways Co electrified and reopened the route in 1896.

The Hartlepool Electric Tramways Co (part of the BET group) opened two new routes in 1900 and took over operation of the original line, although GET retained ownership of facilities and some track. HET livery was orange-yellow and white.

In 1911 West Hartlepool Corporation bought two lines and seven trams from HET but leased them back. The following year it re-acquired them, bought the remaining lines within its boundary and the last 14 trams. HET was wound up but GET continued to own track in Hartlepool, which it leased to West Hartlepool.

Hartlepool never became a tramcar operator, although in 1925 it bought the GET track and continued the lease. West Hartlepool took several years to repaint the ex-HET cars into its preferred red and cream livery.

Trolleybus operation in West Hartlepool commenced in 1924 and from 1927 (when the last tram route closed) there was a joint management committee with Hartlepool. Each authority owned the overhead equipment within its own boundary. Twelve single-deckers were owned jointly and displayed dual emblems, others were owned by West Hartlepool alone and all were in the latter's red and cream. Early vehicles were built by Garrett, Railless and Straker-Clough. Double-deck Daimlers and

Leylands bought in 1938/9 ran until the system closed in 1953. Replacement buses were separately owned, Hartlepool becoming an operator (qv).

West Hartlepool had run buses since 1920, AECs and Bristols initially but Daimlers in the 1930s. Some had polished aluminium panels. Five Guy Arab utilities arrived in overall grey-green during World War 2. Postwar purchases were Leylands and Daimlers, a batch of 15 of the latter replacing the trolleybuses.

On 1 April 1967 the four Hartlepool AEC double-deckers, at least one already repainted from blue and cream to red and cream, joined the West Hartlepool vehicles in a new Hartlepool County Borough fleet. A Hartlepool seal, similar to that previously displayed on the four AECs but differently coloured, replaced West Hartlepool's coat of arms.

Single-deck buses ordered by both previous operators were delivered after merging. Subsequent purchases were also saloons and included Bristol RE, Leyland National and Dennis Dominator/Falcon models.

Until 1974 vehicles were always registered with the county borough marks EF or xEF. In that year the undertaking became Hartlepool Borough Transport Department, reflecting municipal changes, including transfer to the new Cleveland county.

Company status in 1986 confirmed a livery with more cream and less red, introduced in the late 1970s. The operating area expanded, one route extending as far as Newcastle, but the fleet changed little. The 68-vehicle operation was purchased by its employees in June 1993 and sold on to Stagecoach Holdings in December 1994. Buses appeared in striped corporate livery during 1995.

When Cleveland was dismantled on 1 April 1996 Hartlepool became a unitary authority, one of the new-style county boroughs, but, initially at least, chose to be known as a borough.

Above left:
Coat of arms: pre-1967. (See also Hartlepool CB.) *Courtesy Robert Kell*

Left:
When this photograph was taken near the Royal Hotel on 31 March 1967 it was the last day of existence of the West Hartlepool undertaking and there were very few buses left in the fleet with two-letter registrations. No 60 (EF 8997) was one, part of a batch of nine purchased in 1949. The Roe H31/25R body sits on a Daimler CVG6 chassis. West Hartlepool positioned the route number box to the offside on its later buses (and Hartlepool's four were rebuilt that way after the merger in 1974). A nearside position would surely have provided intending passengers with a clearer view, but maybe it was the driver who was being considered.

West Monmouthshire Omnibus Board (Bedwellty UDC & Mynyddislwyn UDC)

Bedwellty and Mynyddislwyn and other places in the mining district of the Sirhowy Valley were in Monmouthshire (technically England) until the countrywide administrative earthquake of 1974 transferred them to the new county of Gwent, firmly Welsh. Previously the terminology used had been 'Wales & Monmouthshire'. The largest urban area served by West Mon was Blackwood but the UDC owners took their names from hill villages.

Municipal transport in the Sirhowy Valley of South Wales was conceived when Bedwellty made an unsuccessful attempt to start bus services in the early 1920s. Established private operators thwarted that bid but were unable to stop similar action initiated by Mynyddislwyn which resulted in a joint venture in 1926. The undertaking was named West Monmouthshire Omnibus Board.

Several routes were acquired from the Griffin Motor Co, Valleys Motor Bus Service, and Western Valleys Services/Sirhowy Valley Motor Transport. One of them included the famous 1:4¼ (24%), gravel-surfaced gradient in Aberbargoed. To cope, one of the first

buses bought in 1927 was a Swiss-built Saurer, normal control, with special engine brakes. In 1930 the replacement was a Leyland Bull TQ2, a goods chassis modified to carry a 32-seat body and fitted with a four-wheel handbrake and sprag gear to prevent runaways. Another bought in 1935 was a TSC9 Bull.

The fleet contained two other buses especially worthy of mention, both built for Southern Africa but diverted to West Mon due to shipping difficulties in 1940. One of them, a Daimler COG6 intended for Johannesburg, was the undertaking's first double-decker – the other was an 8ft-wide, 30ft-long COG5 saloon (maximum legal width at that time was 7ft 6in, so special route approval was necessary).

After World War 2 Fodens replaced the Bulls, followed in 1959 by a Leyland Titan with a single-deck body. One of the Bulls received a utility Burlingham body in 1944 and survived until 1957.

The prewar fleet had been Leyland. Double-decked utility Daimlers and Guys arrived towards the end of hostilities and AEC ensured Leyland did not have a clear field postwar. Peak fleet size was in the low 30s.

Livery was maroon and cream until 1970 when light blue and cream was introduced

and the 'West Mon' fleetname (with coat of arms) on the vehicles changed to 'West Monmouthshire Omnibus Board'.

The undertaking became Islwyn Borough Council Transport department on 1 April 1974 when the local authorities merged. Blue livery was retained and the fleetname 'Islwyn Borough Transport' adopted. In 1986 came the change to a limited company, 'Ltd' became part of the title and of the fleetname and to the livery was added a second shade of blue and an 'IBT' logo. In mid-1997 the company remained local authority owned. Further Welsh local government reorganisation effective on 1 April 1996 resulted in Islwyn becoming a part of the unitary authority Caerphilly County Borough and that council taking over ownership of the company. However, there is currently no intention of changing the company name to reflect the ownership.

Left:
Coat of arms photo date: 30 May 1970.

Above:
The depot yard at Blackwood contains a fine variety of interesting buses when seen on 30 May 1970 shortly after the change to blue and cream livery came into effect. No 24 (XWO 473), a lowbridge Longwell Green-bodied Leyland Titan PD2/40 with 27/28 capacity and platform doors, was a likely candidate for blue as it was then only 10 years old. The only other bus bought in 1960 was a Willowbrook/Leyland Tiger Cub PSUC1/1, six years younger than the ex-Trent example (FCH 9) seen in the background.

Widnes Corporation Motor Omnibus Department

Situated at a fordable spot where the River Mersey narrows to the Runcorn Gap, Widnes grew from a village to be the chemical capital of Lancashire because a canal, a railway and a dock enabled salt, the raw material, to meet coal, the source of energy. When high-level rail and road (transporter) bridges were built, connections with Cheshire became easier. The transporter was replaced by a fixed road bridge in 1961. Trams were never operated nor a tramway owned.

Widnes Corporation held trials with buses in 1907 but it was 1909 when four Commer double-deckers started services. These were probably the first in the world with covered tops and were 16ft 6in high (current normal height is 14ft 6in). By 1921 the borough fleet included 12 Tilling-Stevens single-deckers and a joint service with St Helens had begun. Purchases in the 1930s again included double-deckers – Crossleys and Leylands. Twelve utility Daimlers arrived between 1943-45, some of which were later rebodied, extending the life of the chassis to over 20 years.

In 1942, part of the bus depot was demolished, and a double-decker overturned, by a whirlwind.

Second-hand buses were not unknown. In the mid-1920s small batches were acquired from Blackpool and Southport coach operators and after World War 2 double-deckers came from Ashton, London and Wigan, while Chester later provided one saloon.

Postwar deliveries of new buses started in 1946 with Leyland Titan PD1s. In batches of two or three a year, 37 Leyland double-deckers and two single-deckers were bought by 1966. Policy changed and only saloons were bought from 1967. These were Leyland Leopards and Bristol REs initially, then a Leyland National, one of the first, in 1972.

On 1 April 1974 a large area of south-west Lancashire was transferred to Cheshire and the district (borough) of Halton was formed from Widnes and Runcorn, now both in the same county. The name was taken from a castle near Runcorn.

The first purchase by Halton was two Leyland coaches in 1975. These were rebodied as buses in 1983. Cross-bridge bus services increased and Halton Corporation Motor Bus Department (one of only five municipal operators to retain the word 'Corporation' in their title) continued to buy only saloons. Bristol REs were first, then only Nationals until 1985. The final National was the last to be delivered anywhere in Britain. A solitary Leyland Lynx arrived in October 1986, the same month that the undertaking became Halton Borough Transport Ltd.

Under the new competitive regime routes were started to Liverpool and Warrington. Many second-hand Nationals were acquired while new purchases centred on Lynxes. When these became unavailable in 1993 the Dennis Dart was favoured.

Livery over the years has been at the red end of the spectrum, apart from the first Commers which were cream overall. Later buses were maroon and light yellow, sometimes with a white roof. In 1930 the colours changed to red and yellow, changing again to red and cream after World War 2 and to a lighter red in 1959. Wartime Daimlers went into service painted grey or buff, as delivered.

The influx of single-deckers after 1967 bore cream lower panels and window surrounds with a red waist and roof. Nationals and Lynxes received a red skirt and roof.

In mid-1997 the undertaking remains in the ownership of what is forecast to be, from 1 April 1998, the unitary authority of Halton.

Above left:
Coat of arms photo date: 4 February 1973.

Below:
Fleet No 36 (6981 TJ), first of a batch of two built in 1963, was a Leyland Titan PD2/40 and had an East Lancs H37/28R body. The camera has captured it speeding round a traffic island near Widnes Town Hall on 6 April 1968. In the mid-1960s Widnes livery was modified from one cream band above the lower windows with the fleet name on the lower panels, to that depicted. The result, a reversion to pre-1956 style, was, as seen here, considerably brighter and the fleetname more prominent. No further change was made to double-deck livery and the layout was continued by Halton after 1974.

Wigan is an ancient place

Wigan is an ancient place, the site of a Roman fort, and was a medieval market town with a charter dated AD1246. Coal mining and weaving were the chief industries and in the 19th century it expanded greatly, becoming a county borough. This century, although older industries have been active, it has become known to transport people for its bus body builders, the erstwhile Massey Bros and Northern Counties, the latter currently enjoying a bus fleet replacement boom.

The Wigan Tramways Co (& District Co from 1893) ran horse-drawn services from 1880-5 and steam trams from 1882. Passenger vehicles were painted dark red and cream, locomotives brown and cream.

Wigan Corporation Tramways opened an electric line in 1901 and took over the company system in 1902. The 3ft 6in gauge steam lines were electrified by 1904 and, except for one route converted to trolleybus operation in 1925, were all widened to standard gauge to suit Pemberton UDC which owned some of the track.

Buses, which replaced the trams and the four Straker-Squire trolleybuses in 1931, first arrived in 1919 when two locally-built Pagefields and an AEC were delivered. Other makes gave way to Leyland in 1927 and, apart from World War 2 utility Bristols and Guys, the town purchased that make exclusively until 1974.

'Piano-fronted' bodies were popular with Wigan. The first arrived in 1929 and incredibly the last, a Leyland Titan TD5, not until 1938, well after some other undertakings were running streamliners. The department patronised Northern Counties and Massey

Wigan Corporation Transport Department

frequently, the firms sharing the 1938 order though both had modern styles available. Due to many low railway bridges, all double-deckers were low configuration until 1947.

The first postwar buses, Leyland Titan PD1s, arrived in 1946 and regular deliveries of PD2s continued until 1958. Then for three years PD3s with front entrances were favoured. In 1962 there was a reversion to PD2s, still with front entrances, and some were delivered as late as 1968, almost the last half-cabs built. Over the years there were always a few single-deckers in the fleet, half-cabs until 1957 but latterly Leyland Panthers.

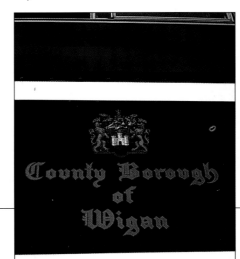

Intake of dual-doored Leyland Atlanteans started in 1968 and continued until the undertaking's fleet of 130 was merged with Selnec's into Greater Manchester Transport in 1974. The town, absorbing Leigh, became a metropolitan district (borough) of Greater Manchester also on 1 April 1974. An outstanding order for six Bristol LHL6s with ECW bodies was delivered to GMT.

No Wigan bus survived into GM Buses ownership in 1986, though one of the last batch of Atlanteans missed it by only 11 months.

Wigan livery from 1901 to 1974 was consistent, crimson and cream until 1913, then crimson and white. Buses were registered with the town's marks EK or JP (or their serials). JP was in use until 1952 and the WCT intake that year were among the last municipal buses to receive two-letter registrations.

Wigan's fleet was usually immaculate, with coat of arms (on a double-decker) on the centre upper panels, showing those who used their buses as hoardings how it should be done. Needless to say, after 1974 they were painted orange and cream and plastered with advertisements very quickly.

Little change in livery followed the formation of GM Buses Ltd in 1986 but overall orange (or 99% anyway) was an eventual consequence of the division of GMB in 1993 and the sale of the North half to FirstBus in 1996. The fleetname now used is 'Greater Manchester', somehow more inappropriate in Wigan than other towns in the conurbation.

Above left:
Wigan's idiosyncratic gap-filling numbering system did not greatly affect seven of the Leyland PD2/12s registered AEK 501-512 as a block was available for them. They were allocated Nos 93-99 (the earlier five received Nos 8, 15-17, 63). The all-Leyland H33/28R vehicles were built in 1953 and, together with four Royal Tigers, were the first Wigan CTD buses to receive three-letter registrations from the local licensing office. No 98 was withdrawn before Greater Manchester PTE took over in 1974. On 11 June 1967 it awaits return to town from a terminus near Ashton-in-Makerfield.

Left:
Coat of arms photo date: 30 June 1973. No 98 illustrates the earlier style of fleetname which survived on some buses until the PTE era. Newer vehicles and recent repaints by then carried, on the upper panels of double-deckers, the style shown in close-up. There was also a transitional style which appeared with the first rear-engined Wigan buses in 1969. This took the form 'Wigan Corporation' in two lines on the upper panels and the coat of arms on white above (nearside) or level with (offside) the lower windows.

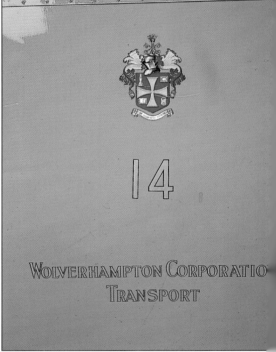

Wolverhampton Corporation Transport Department

Wolverhampton is called the capital of The Black Country, 80 square miles of one of the greatest industrial conurbations in Europe and originally based on local deposits of ironstone and coal. 'Black' describes local soil colour. The first part of the name is derived from Wulfruna, a Mercian princess. Guy Motors, once a bus builder in the town, adapted the name for its Wulfrunian model. Sunbeam trolleybuses were also manufactured in Wolverhampton.

As a county borough, corporation vehicles were always registered with the local marks DA, UK, JW or serials. When it lost that status in 1974, the town, which had historically been in Staffordshire, became a metropolitan district (borough) in the county of West Midlands.

The Wolverhampton Tramways Co opened a horse-drawn service in the town in 1878 and another was started in 1883 by the Dudley, Sedgley & Wolverhampton Tramways Co. The former used maroon (or brown) and white, the latter maroon and yellow. The Corporation eventually purchased parts of both systems, electri-

fying with Loran surface contacts in 1902 but changing to overhead wires and trolleypoles in 1921. There were links with the BET-owned Black Country tram network. Its local subsidiary operating to the south and southeast of the town was Wolverhampton & District Electric Tramways, successor to the rump of WTC in 1900.

Between 1925 and 1928 the corporation bought the remaining W&D undertaking in four stages, running WCT trams on the routes until 1929, 13 months after the original municipal system closed. W&D had successive liveries of yellow and cream, crimson and cream in 1902, then green and cream until the end.

Trolleybuses of the antique design then fashionable started work in 1923 and were used as tram replacements. In 1926, however, the Corporation introduced vehicles of more modern appearance, the first in Britain. From 1931 there was a joint service with Walsall trolleybuses. In 1961 a decision was taken to abandon the trolley system and the last one ran in 1967.

Corporation motor buses operated initially from 1905 but only until 1909. Services restarted with more reliable machines in 1911, after which they ran until 1969.

Naturally Guy buses and Sunbeam trolleybuses featured frequently in Wolverhampton's purchases until 1969 when production ceased. Only two of the ill-fated Wulfrunians were bought. Other makes acquired were Daimlers and AECs.

Wolverhampton Corporation livery was dark green and primrose from 1902-28 and apple green and primrose thereafter. Before World War 2 the relief was arranged in three bands, but later extended from the upper windows to waist level. The final version was only one primrose band.

When West Midlands PTE was formed on 1 October 1969, Wolverhampton contributed nearly 300 buses. The liveries of the other constituents, Birmingham, Walsall and West Bromwich, were blue-based so it was natural that the combined fleet donned dark blue and cream. This lasted, latterly with a lighter blue, until 1986 when the undertaking became West Midlands Travel, and blue, silver and red was adopted. In 1991 WMT was sold to its employees, later becoming part of the National Express group.

Above left:
No 1 (SUK 1) seen here on 11 October 1969 was far from being a lemon. The Guy Arab IV was a reliable workhorse and could still have been Wolverhampton's principal choice of motorbus in the 1950s even if it had not been built in the town. They bought 53. A batch of 18 (SUK 1-18) purchased in 1957 had Metro-Cammell H60R bodies. Nos 1-6 and 13-18 were engined by Meadows, the others having Gardner 6LWs. Livery of green with a single primrose band replaced a more pleasing version with primrose from beneath the upper windows to beneath the lower windows starting in 1958. One Guy, SUK 11 (by then numbered 11N), survived in the livery depicted until at least October 1975, six years into West Midlands PTE ownership.

Above:
Coat of arms photo date: 11 October 1969.

Bristol Joint Services Committee

Horse trams came to this city in 1875 when the Bristol Tramways Co started a service on track owned by the Corporation. Then briefly in 1880 there was steam traction on one route. Electrification commenced in 1895 and was completed in 1900.

The city warrants inclusion in this book because in 1935 its Corporation exercised the option, available every seven years, to buy the local tramways from the Bristol Tramways & Carriage Co. They thereby became joint owners of the city transport system, although the blue and cream trams carrying the municipal coat of arms, were actually still operated by BTCC personnel.

The change took effect in 1937, with BTCC remaining the owner and operator of the blue and cream bus fleet, which also traditionally carried the arms. The system was called Bristol Joint Services and was administered by a committee of city and company representatives.

Tramway services, run entirely with open-top cars of 1900s design, ended in 1941 when Bristol was severely bombed and the system put out of action.

Although the Corporation subsequently owned no vehicles, what had become Bristol City Services was a bus undertaking controlled jointly by the city and BTCC (and later by its successor the Bristol Omnibus Co). Postwar livery became green

and cream (as a Tilling company the basic choice was that or red and cream), although at first retaining a full-sized Bristol coat of arms. Later a smaller transfer of the arms was used above 'Bristol' in script, but subsequently the insignia was omitted entirely.

The joint arrangement continued with the British Transport Commission after 1948, and with its successor the Transport Holding Company, but was dissolved in 1978 by agreement with what had by then become the National Bus Company.

Having been known as the City and County of Bristol prior to 1974 when it became a district council (with the title of city) in the county of Avon, Bristol, on 1 April 1996 when Avon was dissolved, became a unitary authority with powers similar to those it once possessed as a county borough.

Gloucester – As an aside and to satisfy the curiosity of those who remember buses carrying Gloucester's name and coat of

arms during the years covered by this book, some explanation is warranted.

In 1936 Bristol TCC leased the Gloucester Corporation undertaking of 38 buses for 21 years and it was overseen by a joint committee until 1957. Later, although by then entirely company owned, green and cream buses on Gloucester city services around 1970 carried the name 'Gloucester' and the city arms. During the late 1970s/early 1980s an NBC vinyl logo was added. When, around 1985, the local livery became dark blue and white, the fleetname 'City of Gloucester' gained currency, still accompanied by the coat of arms and NBC logo, though both were vinyl. This lasted only a year or two.

Cheltenham – Although never a municipal undertaking, buses in this town had some resemblance to one, as they carried the coat of arms between the words 'Cheltenham District'. Later, in the NBC era, local livery reverted to the former dark red and cream, now accompanied by the coat of arms and corporate logo, both vinyls.

Below:
Seen here on 1 September 1959 is Bristol KSW No 8175 (SHW 345) built in 1954 and fitted with the highbridge, rear-entrance style of ECW body suitable for service on City of Bristol Joint Committee routes. Judging by the indicator display it must have also strayed onto country routes.

Above left:
Coat of arms photo date: 21 May 1978.

Keighley–West Yorkshire Services

The reason for including the Keighley Corporation/West Yorkshire joint under-taking in this book is that the arrangement lasted until 1973, therefore coming within its scope.

Keighley lies at the junction of Airedale and the Worth Valley, eight miles north-west of Bradford and until 1974 was in the West Riding.

The Keighley Tramways Co opened a horse-drawn service in 1889. The borough bought that loss-making concern in 1901 and operated the horse cars until electrifi-cation permitted eight new trams to start work in 1904. Keighley Corporation Tramways was initially profitable but outlying areas needed serving and buses were thought suitable. Those bought in 1909 proved to be unreliable.

Trackless vehicles (trolleybuses) oper-ating a Cedes-Stoll system started work in

Above:
West Yorkshire Road Car controlled the choice of vehicles purchased for the joint operator and prefixed the fleet numbers with 'K'. These tended to be registered in runs distinct from buses used solely by WY. One of eight with consecutive marks is (GWX 123) No KDB 28, illustrated in Keighley on 21 May 1960. It is a Bristol K6B with ECW L27/28R body. In 1964 the Keighley fleet totalled 52 Bristols, six of which were LL5G saloons, the 46 double-deckers comprising 13 K6B lowbridge and 33 Lodekkas (11 LD6B, 22 FS6B).

1913 following a trial. They were also unre-liable by 1921 and Leyland single-decker buses were acquired to supplement them. Trackless vehicles using trolleypoles on overhead lines came into service in 1924, replacing all the trams. This was the first complete municipal tramway system in Britain to be abandoned.

Double-deck, open-staired Leyland Titans bought in 1928 carried the title 'KCT

Omnibus Services', as previously used on the saloons.

Trolleybuses ran for the last time on 31 August 1932 and motorbuses on 30 September. So ended 31 years of direct municipal operation.

Keighley's trams, trolleybuses and buses were always crimson and white.

From 1 October 1932 services were provided by a 50/50-owned joint company: Keighley-West Yorkshire Services Ltd. Three of the seven directors were town councillors, the others represented the West Yorkshire Road Car Co.

The joint company buses were in red and cream similar to West Yorkshire's livery, but fleet numbers had a 'K' prefix and the fleetname was 'Keighley-West Yorkshire'.

On 1 October 1973 the operating agree-ment was terminated and WYRC assumed complete control. This outcome was influ-enced by imminent local government changes which resulted in Keighley becoming a part of the metropolitan district of Bradford (with city title) in the county of West Yorkshire on 1 April 1974.

York–West Yorkshire Joint Committee

This undertaking is included because the committee existed until 1983, therefore coming within the scope of the book.

Twenty miles northeast of Leeds lies the City of York, before 1974 a county borough, independent of the three Ridings of Yorkshire. In that year it became a district council with the title of city. It was redesignated a unitary authority taking the title City of York Council in 1996.

The York Tramways Co operated horse cars in the city from 1880 to 1886, when it was bought by the City of York Tramways Co (owned by the Imperial Tramways group). Both operators used brown and white livery. In 1909 York Corporation took the system over, operating the horse cars for a few months until electrification permitted new trams to enter service in January 1910.

The city twice operated trolleybuses, firstly from 1920 to 1929, and with more modern vehicles from 1931. The first fleet were Rail-less, the second Karriers, all single-deckers. Only one route was served.

Motorbuses were also operated from the 1920s, some of them Daimler double-deckers.

The blue and white livery introduced with the York CTD electric trams was also carried by trolleybuses and buses.

On 1 April 1934 the York–West Yorkshire Joint Committee assumed responsibility for public transport services within the city and for 18 months continued to run the trolleybuses and trams until both systems closed in 1935. Unlike the arrangement in Keighley, York–West Yorkshire was not a joint company, though in similar fashion the West Yorkshire Road Car Co provided all the buses.

Livery was red and cream but fleet numbers had a 'Y' prefix and the fleetname used was 'York–West Yorkshire'. After 1974 buses appeared in NBC poppy red and white accompanied by a 'double N' logo. From about 1980 the fleetname 'York' appeared between the City arms and the logo.

The joint committee was disbanded in March 1986 when York City Council sold its interest to the NBC (WYRCC). This action was evidently influenced by bus service deregulation, which became effective on 26 October 1986.

WYRCC buses lettered 'York City & District' soon appeared, still in red and cream, but a few years later the livery was replaced by the green and cream of Rider York, a subsidiary of Leeds-based Yorkshire Rider.

Although York CBC issued registrations until 1974 (DN, VY and their serials), all new joint committee buses were registered with West Riding CC marks by WYRCC. The original York CTD buses carried VY marks and remained in service for a little while with the joint committee.

Below:
Fortuitously, the registration of York–West Yorkshire YDB 73 (GWX 120) was in the same run as that of the Keighley bus also illustrated, so not surprisingly they were both new around the same time in 1949. However, the York example was highbridge. In 1964 the York (Y-prefixed) fleet totalled 60, all double-decked Bristols, and consisted of 21 K5G highbridges, 23 K6Bs (four of them lowbridge) and 26 Lodekkas (three LD6Bs, 23 FS6Bs). The bus depicted (YDB 73), stands near to a section of the city walls. It carries a 56-seat highbridge ECW body.

Municipal fleet sizes in 1961

As reported in *Passenger Transport Yearbook 1962* and other sources.
Figures for coaches may be under-reported due to undertakings having varying perceptions of what constitutes a dual-purpose vehicle.

FLEET	TOTAL	BUSES		COACHES	TROLLEYBUSES	TRAMS	BRITISH ISLES RANKING	
		DD	SD				Municipal (97)	All (160)
Aberdare	35	18	17		+		85	142
Aberdeen	237	230	5		2		22	61
Accrington	58	46	12				71	124
Ashton-under-Lyne	70	52	1		17dd		60	112
Barrow-in-Furness	63	60	3				66	119
Bedwas & Machen	7	5		2			95	156
Belfast	553	333	13		207dd		8	28
Birkenhead	228	224	4				24	65
Birmingham	1,714*	1,679*	35*		+		1	2
Blackburn	109	99	10				42	90
Blackpool	327	154	8			165	13	47
Bolton	274	263	6	1	(4dd) ¢		17	54
Bournemouth	171	65		16	90dd		30	75
Bradford	380*	188*	2		190dd*		11	42
Brighton	73	64			+	9 (Volk's)	65	118
Burnley C & N	147	107	40				36	83
Burton upon Trent	46	44	2				78	133
Bury	98	88	10				49	99
Caerphilly	31	21	10				87	146
Cardiff	258	170	9		73dd/6sd		19	57
Chester	49	45	4				75	129
Chesterfield	131	108	21	2	+		39	86
Colchester	39	39					82	138
Colwyn Bay	5			5			96	159
Coventry	343	324	16		3		12	46
Darlington	63	38	25		+		67	120
Darwen	35	30	5				86	143
Derby	165	92			73dd		33	78
Doncaster	108	73	7		28dd		43	91
Douglas	74	31	12			31 (horse)	57	109
Dundee	245	226	19		+		20	58
Eastbourne	56	54	2				72	125
Edinburgh	706	566	118	22			6	19
Exeter	67	61	6				63	116
Gelligaer	29	5		24			89	148
Glasgow	1,735*	1,222	70		172dd/21sd	200$	2	3
Great Yarmouth	68	57	11				62	115
Grimsby-Cleethorpes	102	78	24		+		45	95
Halifax	168	140	28		+		32	77
Hartlepool (Borough)	4	4					97	160

Above:
Shown wearing the light blue and cream livery which was Bradford's standard in postwar years is trolleybus No 845 (JWW 375). The date, 26 March 1972, was the final operational day of Britain's last trolleybus system. New as Mexborough & Swinton Traction Co single-decker No 37 in August 1950, this Sunbeam F4 was one of six bought by Bradford when the smaller operator, also in Yorkshire, ceased operating electrically on 26 March 1961. Its Brush centre-entrance body was scrapped and replaced by a 66-seat double-decked East Lancs one.

FLEET	TOTAL	BUSES		COACHES	TROLLEYBUSES	TRAMS	BRITISH ISLES RANKING	
		DD	SD				Municipal (97)	All (160)
Haslingden	18	14	4				91	151
Huddersfield	212	70	26		116dd		25	66
Ipswich	66	36	8		22dd		64	117
Kingston-upon-Hull	238	155	20		63dd		21	60
Lancaster	39	26	13				83	139
Leeds	638	626	12		+		7	24
Leicester	208	198	10				26	67
Leigh	61	59	2				68	121
Lincoln	61	54	7				69	122
Liverpool	1,224	1,214	6		4 (w/d 1961)		4	8
Llandudno	13			13			94	155
Lowestoft	17	17					92	152
Luton	73	73					58	110
Lytham St Annes	40	34		6			80	136
Maidstone	53	29			24dd		73	126
Manchester	1,457	1,296	45		116dd		3	4
Merthyr Tydfil	76	66	10				56	108
Middlesbrough	95	93	2				50	100
Morecambe & Heysham	49	49					76	130

FLEET	TOTAL	BUSES		COACHES	TROLLEYBUSES	TRAMS	BRITISH ISLES RANKING	
		DD	SD				Municipal (97)	All (160)
Newcastle on Tyne	434	246	3		185dd		9	35
Newport	121	106	15				40	87
Northampton	91	91					52	102
Nottingham	425	283	4		138dd		10	36
Oldham	233	219	14		+		23	62
Plymouth	266	266					18	55
Pontypridd	50	37	13		+		74	128
Portsmouth	206	144	19		43dd		27	69
Preston	100	98	2				47	97
Ramsbottom	14	8	6		+		93	153
Rawtenstall	47	40	7				77	132
Reading	104	37	23		44dd		44	93
Rochdale	151	140	11				35	81
Rotherham	144	98	20		20dd/6sd		37	84
St Helens	140	134	6		+		38	85
Salford	312	302	9	1			15	49
Sheffield	861	798	63				5	17
South Shields	100	48			52dd		48	98
Southampton	190	175	15				28	72
Southend-on-Sea	87	81	6		+		53	104
Southport	69	63	6				61	113
SHMD	79	66	13				54	105
Stockport	170	148	22		+		31	76
Stockton-on-Tees	102	101	1				46	96
Sunderland	178	167	11				29	74
Swindon	72	56	16				59	111
Tees-side RTB	41	24		2	15dd		79	135
Todmorden	38	38					84	140
Wallasey	96	90	4	2			51	101
Walsall	275	204	16		55dd		16	53
Warrington	81	78	3				55	107
West Bridgford	28	28					90	149
West Bromwich	120	107	13				41	88
West Hartlepool	61	61			+		70	123
West Monmouthshire	30	17	13				88	147
Widnes	40	38	2				81	137
Wigan	154	143	11		+		34	80
Wolverhampton	316	153	10		153dd		14	48
OVERALL TOTAL	**19,735**	**16,145**	**1,134**	**68**	**1,900/33 dd/sd**	**455**		

* approximately

¢ four dd trolleybuses owned but operated by South Lancashire Transport Co in SLT livery.

$ plus 50 Underground motor-cars and trailers. Trams ceased operating 4.9.62.

+ previously operated trolleybuses (as did Keighley CT and York CT before 1936).

Note: Hartlepool County Borough, Rossendale Joint and Teesside County Borough undertakings were not created until after 1961.

Name	Period	Main Livery
Ayr Corporation Tramways	1901-31	maroon and primrose
Barking Town UDC Light Railways	1903-06	crimson and cream
ditto	1907-29	green and cream
Batley Corporation Tramways	1903-25	green and cream
ditto	1925-34	maroon and primrose
Bexley Tramways & Dartford Light Railways JC	1917-33	chocolate and cream
Bexley UDC Tramways	1903-17	maroon and cream
Burnley Corporation Tramways	1901-33	maroon and cream
Cleethorpes UDC Tramways	1936-37	green and cream
Cleethorpes Corporation Tramways/Transport	1937-57	grey and blue
Colne Corporation Light Railways	1914-22	dark blue and cream
ditto	1922-33	maroon and cream
Croydon Corporation Tramways	1902-27	chocolate and cream
ditto	1927-28	red and cream
ditto	1928-33	red and grey
Dartford UDC Light Railways	1906-17	maroon and cream
Dearne District Light Railways Joint Committee	1924-33	red and cream
Dover Corporation Tramways	1897-1927	green and cream
ditto	1927-36	dark red and cream
East Ham Corporation Tramways	1901-33	brown and cream
Erith UDC Tramways	1905-17	green and primrose
ditto	1917-33	dark red and cream
Farnworth UDC Tramways	1902-06	chocolate and yellow
Gloucester Corporation Light Railways	1903-15	crimson and cream
ditto	1915-33	grey
Grimsby Corporation Tramways	1925-37	maroon and cream
Grimsby Corporation Transport	1937-57	deep maroon and cream
Heywood Corporation Tramways	1904-05	brown and cream
Ilford Corporation Tramways	1913-18	crimson and cream
ditto	1918-33	green and cream
Ilkeston Corporation Tramways	1903-16	maroon and cream
Keighley Corporation Tramways	1901-24	crimson and cream
Kilmarnock Corporation Tramways/Transport	1904-32	green and cream
Kirkcaldy Corporation Tramways	1913-31	dark green and cream
Leith Corporation Tramways	1904-05	blue and cream
ditto	1905-20	maroon and cream
Leyton UDC Tramways	1906-31	dark green and primrose
ditto	1931-33	red and cream
London County Council Tramways	1896-1931	purple and primrose
ditto	1926-33	crimson and cream
Matlock UDC Tramways	1898-1927	blue and cream
Morecambe Corporation Tramways	1909-26	green and white
Neath Corporation Tramways	1916-20	brown and cream

Name	Period	Main Livery
Nelson Corporation Tramways	1902-33	biscuit and cream
Perth Corporation Tramways	1903-05	dark red and yellow
Perth Corporation Tramways*	1905-29	dark green and cream
Perth Corporation Transport (buses)	1929-34	red and cream
Pwllheli Corporation Tramways	1899-1920	green
St Annes UDC Tramways	1920-22	light blue and cream
Stockton & Thornaby Joint Corporation Tramways	1921-31	red and white
Walthamstow UDC Light Railways	1905-33	red and yellow
West Ham Corporation Tramways	1904-33	maroon and cream
York Corporation Tramways	1909-34	blue and ivory

* Operated first Scottish municipal motor bus in 1911.

By 1924 a total of 181 municipalities had owned or did own tramways. Of these only 112 actually operated tramcars themselves. Devonport, Worcester and Scarborough had fleeting involvement in tramways but never operated themselves, bringing the overall figure to 184. All are either listed here, or, as survivors after 1960, and usually bus operators, are covered in the body of this book.

Bristol Corporation was involved financially in the Bristol City operations of Bristol Tramways & Carriage Company from 1937 to 1978.

Keighley Corporation continued operating after its tramway closed in 1924 and from 1932 to 1973 participated in a local joint company with West Yorkshire Road Car Company.

York Corporation ceased operating on its own in 1934 and participated in a York-West Yorkshire Joint Committee with WYRCC until 1986.

Below:
Birmingham Corporation buses rarely saw later service with other municipalities but four registered FOP became Southend on Sea open-toppers in 1955 after Eastern National converted, used and then sold them. New in 1945 as BCT No 1462 (FOP 462), this Daimler CWA6 carried a Park Royal body (O33/26R), originally a covered semi-utility. As Southend 242 it bore a reversed livery and is seen here on the seafront service on 28 May 1967.

The former municipal operators of 1945 who no longer existed in 1986

Operator	Absorbed into/*Became*	Year	Notes
Aberdare	*Cynon Valley*	1974	
Aberdeen	*Grampian*	1975	*
Accrington	*Hyndburn*	1974	
Ashton-under-Lyne	Selnec PTE	1969	(1)
Bedwas & Machen	Rhymney Valley	1974	
Belfast	NITHC (*Citybus*)	1973	(2)*
Birkenhead	Merseyside PTE	1969	*
Birmingham	West Midlands PTE	1969	*
Bolton	Selnec PTE	1969	*
Bradford	West Yorkshire PTE	1974	*
Burnley Colne & Nelson	*Burnley & Pendle*	1974	Burnley*
Burton upon Trent	*East Staffs*	1974	*
Bury	Selnec PTE	1969	*
Caerphilly	Rhymney Valley	1974	
Cleethorpes	Grimsby-Cleethorpes	1957	
Colwyn Bay	ceased operating	1986	
Coventry	West Midlands PTE	1974	*
Darwen	Blackburn	1974	
Doncaster	South Yorkshire PTE	1974	*
Douglas	Isle of Man National Transport	1976	
Dundee	*Tayside*	1975	*
Edinburgh	*Lothian*	1975	*
Exeter	National Bus Co (Devon General)	1970	*
Gelligaer	Rhymney Valley	1974	
Glasgow	Greater Glasgow PTE	1973	(3)*
Grimsby	Grimsby-Cleethorpes	1957	*
Halifax	West Yorkshire PTE	1974	(4)*
Hartlepool (Borough)	*Hartlepool (County Borough)*	1967	
Haslingden	Rossendale	1968	
Huddersfield	West Yorkshire PTE	1974	*
Leeds	West Yorkshire PTE	1974	*
Leigh	Selnec PTE	1969	
Liverpool	Merseyside PTE	1969	*
Llandudno	*Aberconwy*	1974	
Lowestoft	*Waveney*	1974	(5)
Luton	National Bus Co (United Counties)	1970	*
Lytham St Annes	*Fylde*	1974	
Manchester	Selnec PTE	1969	*
Middlesbrough	Teesside County Borough	1968	(6)*
Morecambe & Heysham	Lancaster	1974	
Newcastle upon Tyne	Tyneside PTE	1970	(7)*
Oldham	Selnec PTE	1969	*
Pontypridd	*Taff Ely*	1974	
Ramsbottom	Selnec PTE	1969	
Rawtenstall	Rossendale	1968	
Rochdale	Selnec PTE	1969	*

Operator	Absorbed into/*Became*	Year	Notes
Rotherham	South Yorkshire PTE	1974	*
St Helens	Merseyside PTE	1974	*
Salford	Selnec PTE	1969	*
Sheffield	South Yorkshire PTE	1974	*
South Shields	Tyneside PTE	1970	(7)*
Southport	Merseyside PTE	1974	*
SHMD	Selnec PTE	1969	(8)
Stockport	Selnec PTE	1969	*
Stockton-on-Tees	Teesside County Borough	1968	(6)
Sunderland	Tyne & Wear PTE	1974	*
Swindon	*Thamesdown*	1974	
Tees-side RTB	Teesside County Borough	1968	(6,9)
Todmorden	West Yorkshire PTE	1974	(4)
Wallasey	Merseyside PTE	1969	*
Walsall	West Midlands PTE	1969	*
West Bridgford	Nottingham	1968	
West Bromwich	West Midlands PTE	1969	*
West Hartlepool	*Hartlepool (County Borough)*	1967	*
West Monmouthshire	*Islwyn*	1974	(10)
Widnes	*Halton*	1974	
Wigan	Greater Manchester PTE	1974	*
Wolverhampton	West Midlands PTE	1969	*

Notes

(1)   Selnec (South East Lancashire North East Cheshire PTE) became Greater Manchester PTE in 1974.

(2)   NITHC – Northern Ireland Transport Holding Company.

(3)   Greater Glasgow PTE became Strathclyde PTE in 1980. In the early 1980s the fleetname 'Transclyde' was used, later replaced by 'Strathclyde Transport'. After 1986 the fleetname 'Strathclyde's Buses' came into use.

(4)   Halifax JOC merged with Todmorden JOC to become Calderdale JOC in 1971. Calderdale was absorbed into West Yorkshire PTE in 1974.

(5)   Waveney was taken over by the National Bus Co (Eastern Counties) in 1977.

(6)   Teesside (CB) became Cleveland Transit in 1974.

(7)   Tyneside PTE became Tyne & Wear PTE in 1974.

(8)   SHMD was the Stalybridge, Hyde, Mossley and Dukinfield Transport & Electricity Board.

(9)   Tees-side Railless Traction Board was Middlesbrough CB and Eston UDC jointly.

(10)   West Monmouthshire Omnibus Board was Bedwellty UDC and Mynyddislwyn UDC jointly.

PTE is a Passenger Transport Executive, the operational arm of a joint local government Passenger Transport Authority.

JOC was a Joint Omnibus Committee where Railway-owned buses operated alongside municipally-owned buses with shared arrangements.

* Until 31.3.1974 was a County Borough (or Burgh with population above 50,000).

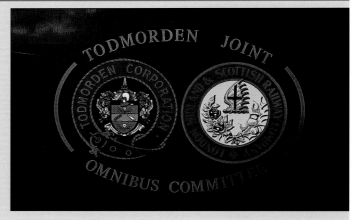

Above:
From 1931 to 1948 Todmorden JOC applied both arms of the town and London Midland & Scottish Railway Co to its buses. As shown on page 104 British Railways then adopted a logo which replaced the LMS badge.

Below:
Halifax Joint Omnibus Committee used, before 1948, a badge combining the civic crest with those of the LMS and LNE Railways.

UNDERTAKING	CURRENT OWNER (YEAR)/STATUS	ORIGINAL SALE etc
Barrow	No longer trading	Partly to Stagecoach, 1989
Blackburn	Local authority	
Blackpool	Local authority	
Bournemouth	Local authority	
Brighton	Go-Ahead (1997)	ESOP (1993)
Burnley & Pendle	Stagecoach (1996)	B & P bought separately
Cardiff	Local authority	
Chester	Local authority	
Chesterfield	Stagecoach (1995)	MBO 1990
Cleveland Transit	Stagecoach (1994)	MBO 1991
Colchester	Cowie (1996)	Bought by British Bus 1993
Cynon Valley	No longer trading	Bought by Red & White 1992
Darlington	No longer trading	Ceased trading 1994
Derby	Cowie (1996)	MBO 1989, Luton & D, B. Bus
East Staffordshire	No longer trading	Stevensons control, 1985
Eastbourne	Local authority	
Fylde	Blackpool (1994)	
Grampian	FirstBus (1995)	Bought by GRT 1989
Great Yarmouth	FirstBus (1996)	
Grimsby-Cleethorpes	Stagecoach (1993)	
Halton	Local authority	
Hartlepool	Stagecoach (1994)	ESOP 1993
Hyndburn	Stagecoach (1996)	
Rhymney Valley (IVL)	No longer trading	Bought by Nat Welsh 1989
Ipswich	Local authority	
Islwyn	Local authority (Caerphilly CBC 1996)	
Kingston upon Hull	Stagecoach (1994)	Bought by Cleveland T1993
Lancaster	No longer trading	Ribble (Stagecoach) 1993
Leicester	FirstBus (1995)	Bought by GRT 1993
Lincoln	Yorkshire Traction (1993)	MEBO/Derby CT 1991
Lothian	Local authorities	
Maidstone	No longer trading	Ceased trading 1992
Merthyr Tydfil	No longer trading	Ceased trading 1989
Newport	Local authority	
Northampton	FirstBus (1995)	Bought by GRT 1993
Nottingham	Local authority	
Plymouth	Local authority	
Portsmouth	FirstBus (1996)	See main text for history
Preston	MEBO (1993)	
Reading	Local authority	
Rossendale	Local authority	
Southampton	FirstBus (1997)	Employees (1993)
Southend	Cowie (1996)	Bought by British Bus 1993
Taff-Ely	No longer trading	Bought by Nat Welsh 1988
Tayside	National Express (1997)	Employees 1991
Thamesdown	Local authority	
Warrington	Local authority	

Total number remaining in local authority ownership - 17. Total in 1985 = 47.
ESOP = Employee share ownership plan.
MBO = Management buyout
MEBO = Management and employee buyout.

Operator's municipal status on 1 January 1974

Registration Marks Issued to Municipalities for New Buses, Trolleybuses and Coaches Pre-1.10.74

Operator	Local Licensing Authority (until 1 October 1974)	In order of original issue (Three-letter marks have a serial prefix letter)							
Aberdare UDC	Glamorganshire CC	L	NY	TX	TG				
Aberdeen CTD	Aberdeen BC		RS	RG					
Accrington CTD	Lancashire CC	B	TB	TC	TD	TE	TF	TJ	
Ashton-under-Lyne CPT	Lancashire CC	B	TB	TC	TD	TE	TF	TJ	
Barrow-in-Furness CT	Barrow-in-Furness CBC		EO						
Bedwas & Machen UDCOD	Monmouthshire CC		AX	WO					
Belfast CTD	Belfast CBC		OI	XI	AZ	CZ	EZ	FZ	GZ	MZ
			OZ	PZ	TZ	UZ	WZ		
Birkenhead MT	Birkenhead CBC		CM	BG					
Birmingham CT*	Birmingham CBC	O	OA	OB	OE	OH	OK	OL	OM	ON
			OP	OX	VP	OF	OG	OV	OJ	OC
Blackburn CTD	Blackburn CBC		CB	BV					
Blackpool CT	Blackpool CBC		FR	FV					
Bolton CBTD	Bolton CBC		BN	WH					
Bournemouth CT	Bournemouth CBC		EL	RU	LJ				
Bradford CT*	Bradford CBC		AK	KU	KW	KY			
Brighton CT	Brighton CBC		CD	UF					
Burnley, Colne & Nelson JTC	Burnley CBC		CW	HG					
Burton upon Trent CTD	Burton on Trent CBC		FA						
Bury CT	Bury CBC		EN						
Caerphilly UDCTD	Glamorganshire CC	L	NY	TX	TG				
Cardiff CTD	Cardiff CBC		BO	UH	KG				
Chester CT	Chester CBC		FM						
Chesterfield CTD	Derbyshire CC	R	NU	RA	RB				
Cleethorpes CT(-1956)	Lindsey CC		BE	FU	FW				
Colchester CTD	Essex CC	F	HK	NO	PU	TW	VW	VX	EV
Colwyn Bay BC	Denbighshire CC.		CA	UN					
Coventry CT	Coventry CBC		DU	HP	RW	WK	VC	KV	
Darlington CTD	Darlington CBC		HN						
Darwen CTD	Lancashire CC	B	TB	TC	TD	TE	TF	TJ	
Derby COD	Derby CBC		CH	RC					
Doncaster CTD	Doncaster CBC		DT						
Douglas CTD	Isle of Man Govt		MN MAN (M in MAN not serial)						
Dundee CTD	Dundee BC		TS	YJ					
Eastbourne CTD	Eastbourne CBC		HC	JK					
Edinburgh CT	Edinburgh BC	S	SG	SF	SC	FS	WS		
Exeter CT	Exeter CBC		FJ						
Gelligaer UDCOD	Glamorganshire CC	L	NY	TX	TG				
Glasgow CT	Glasgow BC	G	GA	GB	GD	GE	GG	US	YS
Great Yarmouth CTD	Great Yarmouth CBC		EX						
Grimsby CT (-1956)	Grimsby CBC		EE	JV					
Grimsby & Cleethorpes TJC (1957-)	Grimsby CBC		EE	JV					
Halifax PTD	Halifax CBC		CP	JX					

Operator's Municipal Status on 1 January 1974	Registration Marks Issued to Municipalities for New Buses, Trolleybuses and Coaches Pre-1.10.74	
Operator	**Local Licensing Authority (until 1 October 1974)**	**In order of original issue (Three-letter marks have a serial prefix letter)**
Hartlepool (BC) CT (-30.3.1967)	Durham CC	J PT UP
Hartlepool (CBC) BTD (1.4.1967-)	Hartlepool CBC	EF
Haslingden CTD	Lancashire CC	B TB TC TD TE TF TJ
Huddersfield CTD	Huddersfield CBC	CX VH
Ipswich CTD	Ipswich CBC	DX PV
Kingston upon Hull CT	Kingston u Hull CBC	AT KH RH
Lancaster CT*	Lancashire CC	B TB TC TD TE TF TJ
Leeds CTD*	Leeds CBC	U NW UM UA UB UG
Leicester* CT	Leicester CBC	BC RY JF
Leigh CT	Lancashire CC	B TB TC TD TE TF TJ
Lincoln CTD	Lincoln CBC	FE VL
Liverpool CPT	Liverpool CBC	K KB KC KA KD KF LV
Llandudno UDC	Caernarvonshire CC	CC JC
Lowestoft CTD	East Suffolk CC	BJ RT
Luton CT (-30.3.1964)	Bedfordshire CC	BH PP XX
Luton CT (1.4.1964-)	Luton CBC	XD XE
Lytham St Annes CTD	Lancashire CC	B TB TC TD TE TF TJ
Maidstone CTD	Kent CC	D KT KN KE KK KL KM KO KP KR KJ
Manchester CTD	Manchester CBC	N NA NB NC ND NE NF VM VR VU XJ
Merthyr Tydfil CPTD	Merthyr Tydfil CBC	HB
Middlesbrough CTD (- 30.3.68)	Middlesbrough CBC	DC XG
Morecambe & Heysham CTD	Lancashire CC	B TB TC TD TE TF TJ
Newcastle upon Tyne CT & EU	Newcastle u Tyne CBC	BB TN VK
Newport CT	Newport CBC	DW
Northampton CT	Northampton CBC	NH VV
Nottingham CT*	Nottingham CBC	AU TO TV
Oldham CPTD	Oldham CBC	BU
Plymouth CT*	Plymouth CBC	CO DR JY
Pontypridd UDCTD	Glamorganshire CC	L NY TX TG
Portsmouth CPTD*	Portsmouth CBC	BK TP RV
Preston CTD	Preston CBC	CK RN
Ramsbottom UDCTD	Lancashire CC	B TB TC TD TE TF TJ
Rawtenstall CM	Lancashire CC	B TB TC TD TE TF TJ
Reading CT	Reading CBC	DP RD
Rochdale CTD	Rochdale CBC	DK
Rossendale JTC	Lancashire CC	B TB TC TD TE TF TJ
Rotherham CTD	Rotherham CBC	ET
St Helens CT	St Helens CBC	DJ
Salford CT*	Salford CBC	BA RJ
Sheffield TD	Sheffield CBC	W WA WB WE WJ
South Shields CTD	South Shields CBC	CU
Southampton CT	Southampton CBC	CR TR OW
Southend-on-Sea CT	Southend-on-Sea CBC	HJ JN
Southport CTD	Southport CBC	FY WM
SHMD T&EB	Cheshire CC	M MA MB TU LG
Stockport CTD	Stockport CBC	DB JA
Stockton CT (-30.3.68)	Durham CC	J PT UP

Operator's Municipal Status on 1 January 1974		Registration Marks Issued to Municipalities for New Buses, Trolleybuses and Coaches Pre-1.10.74						
Operator	**Local Licensing Authority (until 1 October 1974)**	**In order of original issue (Three-letter marks have a serial prefix letter)**						
Sunderland CTD	Sunderland CBC		BR	GR				
Swindon CPTD	Wiltshire CC		AM	HR	MR	MW	WV	
Tees-side RTB (-30.3.68)	N. R. Yorkshire CC		AJ	PY	VN			
Teesside MT (1.4.68-)	Teesside CBC		DC	XG				
Todmorden JOC	W. R. Yorkshire CC	C	WR	WY	WT	WU	WW	WX	YG
Wallasey CMB	Wallasey CBC		HF					
Walsall CTD	Walsall CBC		DH					
Warrington CTD	Warrington CBC		ED					
West Bridgford UDCPTD	Nottinghamshire CC		AL	NN	RR	VO		
West Bromwich CBTD	West Bromwich CBC		EA					
West Hartlepool CT (-30.3.67)	West Hartlepool CBC		EF					
West Monmouthshire OB	Monmouthshire CC		AX	WO				
Widnes CMOD	Lancashire CC	B	TB	TC	TD	TE	TF	TJ
Wigan CTD	Wigan CBC		EK	JP				
Wolverhampton CTD	Wolverhampton CBC		DA	UK	JW			

KEY – Column 1

* City in title

BC	Borough Council	CTD	Corporation Transport Dept
BTD	Borough Transport Dept	JOC	Joint Omnibus Committee
CBTD	County Borough Transport Dept	JTC	Joint Transport Committee
CM	Corporation Motors	MT	Municipal Transport
CMB	Corporation Motor Buses	OB	Omnibus Board
CMOD	Corporation Motor Omnibus Dept	PTD	Passenger Transport Dept
COD	Corporation Omnibus Dept	T&EB	Transport & Electricity Board
CPT	Corporation Passenger Transport	TB	Traction Board
CPTD	Corporation Passenger Transport Dept	TD	Transport Department
CT	Corporation Transport (* City)	TJC	Transport Joint Committee
CT & EU	Corporation Transport & Electricity Undertaking	UDC	Urban District Council

KEY – Column 2

BC	Burgh Council (Scotland)
CC	County Council
CBC	County Borough Council

Left:
A brown streamline was used by Stockport only once, on its prewar Leyland Tiger TS7s, some of which served until the mid-1960s. Their English Electric centre-entrance bodies were unusual for a municipality. Waiting in the depot yard and available for service on 27 May 1962 is No 191 (JA 7591).